Kenneth Hudson

THE ARCHAEOLOGY OF THE CONSUMER SOCIETY

The Second Industrial Revolution in Britain

Kenneth Hudson

THE ARCHAEOLOGY OF THE CONSUMER SOCIETY

The Second Industrial Revolution in Britain

HEINEMANN · LONDON

Heinemann Educational Books Ltd
22 Bedford Square, London WC1B 3HH
LONDON EDINBURGH MELBOURNE AUCKLAND
HONG KONG SINGAPORE KUALA LUMPUR NEW DELHI
IBADAN NAIROBI JOHANNESBURG
EXETER (NH) KINGSTON PORT OF SPAIN

© Kenneth Hudson 1983
First published 1983

Hudson, Kenneth
  The archaeology of the consumer society.
  1. Industrial archaeology — Great Britain
  I. Title
  609'.41 T26.G7

ISBN 0-435-32959-6

Typeset in Hong Kong by Graphicraft Typesetters
Printed in Hong Kong by
Wing King Tong Co., Ltd.

Frontispiece The administration block, Hoover Ltd,
Western Avenue, London, 1980.

Contents

Acknowledgements

Acknowledgements are made to the following for their kind permission to use photographic material:
Ann Nicholls (3-6, 8-10, 12, 24, 27, 33, 38, 39, 45, 54-65, 68-73, 83, 97, 99-102, 104, 110, 115, 117, 118, 122-4, 127, 129, 130, 134-7, 143-6, 152-5, 158); Russell Adams (7); Aer Lingus (120); Aerpix Press (53); Bollom Ltd. (103); Boots Co. Ltd. (42, 43); Bowyers Ltd. (23, 25, 26, 44); British Airways Corporation (119, 128); British Aluminium Co. Ltd. (66, 67); British Broadcasting Corporation (147-50); British Leyland (108, 109); *The Building News* (98); Carreras Rothman Ltd. (11); Central Electricity Generating Board (81); Chloride Industrial Batteries (116); Courtaulds Ltd. (89-91, 94); Dunlop Ltd. (106); EMI Ltd. (139-42); East Midlands Gas Board (85-7); Ferranti Ltd. (75, 76, 80); Ford Motor Co. (111, 112); Gascoigne, Gush and Dent (40, 41); Gestetner Ltd. (156, 157); Gillette Industries Ltd. (84); *Good Housekeeping* (105); Heinz Ltd. (20-22); IBM UK Ltd. (14-16); ICI Fibres (95); ICI Ltd. (92, 93, 96); *The Illustrated London News* (138); *The Isle of Thanet News* (49); The John Doran Museum (88); Leedex Ltd. (52); Lufthansa (121); Mac Fisheries Ltd. (46, 47); Bill Mackenzie (13); *Motor Cars* (107); Nabisco Ltd. (29); National Film Archive (131-3); Pedigree Petfoods Ltd. (34-6); Proctor and Gamble Ltd. (82); Sainsbury (48); The Science Museum (77); Selfridges (50, 51); Joe Smith (frontispiece, 1); Smiths Food Group (31, 32); South Western Electricity Board (78, 79); Ray Sutcliffe (2); Suttons Seeds Ltd. (37); Switchgear Testing Ltd. (17-19); *The Times* (74, 151); The University of Southampton (159, 160); Weetabix Ltd. (28, 30); Westland Aircraft Ltd. (113, 114, 125, 126).

I should also like to express my particular gratitude to the following for the time they so generously devoted to providing me with information and to suggesting ideas and approaches which would not otherwise have occurred to me:
W.J. Arnold (The Wrigley Co. Ltd.); Frank Atkinson (Beamish: North of England Open-Air Museum); D.J. Bridges (British Cellophane Ltd.); Harold Brooks; A.R. Bulfield (Dunlop Ltd.); Stanley Burton (The Burton Group); Neil Cossons and Stuart Smith (Ironbridge Gorge Museum Trust); Ernest Craven (Sketchley Cleaners); George Crook; Ernest Davis (Formica Ltd.); Margaret Davis (University of Southampton); J. Dorlay (Roneo Ltd.); R.A. Fenwick, Harry Hill and Rosie Weatherley (Smiths Food Group); E.H. Gray (Suttons Seeds Ltd.); Norman Hearson (IBM UK Ltd.); David Gwynne Jones and Michael Warner (Gwynne Hart and Associates); D.S. Miller (The Fyffes Group); Dora Newbold; Valerie Noon (Lec Refrigertion Ltd.); Sue Pealing (EMI Ltd); H. Pilkington (The Braby Group); A.P. Ridley-Thompson (The Boots Co. Ltd.); R. Roberts; Arthur Roome; Barry Scott (The British Aluminium Co. Ltd.); C. Webster (East Midlands Gas Board); John Weinthal (Society of Motor Manufacturers and Traders); Peter West (British Broadcasting Corporation); Gerald Whiting (John Lewis Partnership); W.E. Williams; R. Winsby (Trafford Park Estates).

List of Colour Photographs

List of Black and White Illustrations

1 Shoreham Airport, Sussex: the oldest surviving airport in the world still operating scheduled services.

Introduction

Until now industrial archaeologists have been obsessed — the word is not too strong — with the eighteenth and nineteenth centuries, with the age of iron, steam and railways. Indeed, some of them have gone so far as to say that industrial archaeology, almost by definition, is the archaeology of the First Industrial Revolution. As a result, after 20 years of great effort on behalf of old steam engines, waterwheels, cotton mills and railway stations, many people find it difficult to think of industrial archaeology in any other terms.

There seem to be two fundamental reasons for this over-concentration on the earlier period of industrialisation. The first is that the eighteenth and most of the nineteenth century was the period of British industrial supremacy, the period when Britain taught the world, exported to the world and grew fat on the proceeds. In Britain's present state of industrial decline it is perhaps only natural to want to look back and to draw patriotic comfort and encouragement from the days when things were different. The second reason is that until the twentieth century, industry was on a conveniently compact and simple scale. Machinery was limited in size; it was relatively easy to understand, even by people with no technical training; and enthusiastic conservationists in the first wave of the industrial archaeology movement could lead campaigns to save this or that memento of our industrial past with some hope of success. The older factories were solidly built and were not infrequently blessed with a romantic appearance and location, especially in the rural areas. The monuments of twentieth-century industry, by contrast, were felt to be utilitarian, hardly old enough to be interesting and, worst of all, too large to make preservation a practical proposition in many instances. Technology, too, was growing more complicated each year and the economic, social and architectural historians who still form most of the 'professional' backbone of industrial archaeology felt unacceptably perplexed and humiliated when faced with the hardware and the theory of the Second Industrial Revolution, that is, with the industry of the twentieth century.

These, however, are problems to be faced and overcome. They do not justify postulating a limit to industrial archaeology as a subject at 1900, 1914 or at some other arbitrary point. The present book is an attempt to show how the industrial archaeology of this century can be researched and written. It aims to show that the industrial history of our century is just as interesting and significant as that of the 150 years which preceded it, and that its archaeology is possibly even richer and more rewarding.

To provide a definition of the Second Industrial Revolution is not an easy matter. In effect, it is to ask for a definition and characterisation of contemporary industrial society, for very few areas of human endeavour have remained untouched by the immense developments in technology, and their application to production, over the last century. It is not just that very few aspects of life now remain immune from mechanisation or an industrial process somewhere along the line, but that the inter-relatedness of different features of modern industrial life is so marked. As we shall see, it is almost impossible to isolate certain industries from one another if we are to understand their individual natures and the cumulative effect of their development. Consideration of aircraft manufacture, for example, cannot be seen in isolation from aluminium production, which itself can only occur with the harnessing of large quantities of electricity, a process which requires consideration of the electricity supply industry and the various technological developments which made all of this possible. This is not to say that this sort of interdependence did not exist during the First Industrial Revolution, but the scale and nature of these relationships were then very different, and much still remained beyond the scope of industrialisation altogether.

Iron, coal, steam engines and railways have typically been seen as the foundations on which the industries of the First Industrial Revolution were built. The Second Industrial Revolution, on the other hand, is to a large extent characterised by the gradual loosening of their dominance as new materials, processes and technology have been grafted on to the former industrial base. Coal is still, of course, a major fuel and raw material, but it has been toppled from its previous position as a result of the development of alternative sources of energy, particularly oil and electricity. Iron, too, is no longer *the* metal. It has been complemented by the introduction of new metals such as aluminium and platinum, while the position of railways and canals has suffered through the growth of air travel and a revitalised system of road transport. A prerequisite of these changes has been the development and application of new techniques, a more sophisticated technology, and this itself should be regarded as a major distinguishing characteristic of the Second Industrial Revolution.

As new industries have arisen, based on these new technical possibilities, so industrial location has changed. Whole new areas have become industrialised, where before only cows and sheep were the inhabitants, although, as we shall see, many former First Industrial Revolution sites are still in occupation, but by modern industrial tenants. Nor should we forget the very different organisational circumstances in which these industries operate. Increasingly, local, regional and national authorities have dropped their *laissez-faire* approach and taken a direct interest, financial and otherwise, in most aspects of industrial development. The appearance of industrial estates, with all the financial and planning problems involved, perhaps symbolises this changed outlook more than anything else.

The range of industries with a claim to inclusion in this book is huge, and for practical reasons a fairly drastic selection has been inevitable. Broadly, two kinds of industry will involve us: 1. those, like nylon, computers and aircraft, which did not exist at all before this century; and 2. those which had their beginnings in the nineteenth century but which became important only in this one — aluminium and moving pictures are good examples.

Industrial archaeology is not concerned merely with machines, factories and processes. The condition of the men and women who worked in these industries is no less important — indeed, perhaps more so. And just as the industrial base has changed, so too have the lifestyles, conditions of work and aspirations of the labour force at all levels. It would be pointless even to try to list the changes here; they extend to every kind of human activity. As this book is about people as much as things, and concerned with the consumer society as well as the industrial base in which that society is rooted, it was decided to cast the net fairly wide and to include material on industries which cater for basic human needs such as food, clothing and housing. All of these, of course, are now major employers and users of capital resources. Since 1900 far-reaching changes in technology and organisation have occurred in these fields and it seemed time to draw attention to them, and to outline the kind of research which industrial archaeologists might now usefully carry out in connection with them. Consequently, many important industries with a claim upon our attention have been only lightly touched on or omitted altogether. These include road building and construction, chemicals and petro-chemicals, electricity generation and supply, and shipping. This is regrettable, but adequate coverage of them would have involved a book ten times the size, with little cohesion or readability.

The method followed in this book has been to present the Second Industrial Revolution in two ways. First, there is what might be described the running text, which tells the story industry by industry. The outlines given in this way are filled in by photographs and detailed captions, many of which deal more particularly with the archaeology, the physical remains, itself. A list of key inventions and discoveries, provided as the Appendix, will help the reader to check his historical bearings.

Some readers may feel that the book unduly favours the South. This is inevitable for the Second Industrial Revolution, unlike the First, has been largely made in the South. There are important exceptions to this generalisation, but for the most part the new industries with which we are concerned were born and nursed through their infant days no further north than Derby and Nottingham.

It should be noted that very few twentieth-century industrial and commercial buildings are so far protected by being officially listed by the Department of the Environment as of historical or architectural importance. The destruction, in October 1980, of the former Firestone Tyre factory at Brentford makes the point very forcefully. Built in 1928 in the Art Deco style, with a façade that was notable for its decorative tile work, the factory had been described, with justice, as 'a rare and valued example of the best in 1920s industrial architecture'. When tyre production ceased early in 1980, the building was bought by an investment company, which lost no time in vandalising it.

Of the architecturally distinguished industrial buildings in the London outskirts, only the Hoover, Roche and Gillette factories have so far been listed. The unlisted and therefore vulnerable include the Pyrene, Yardley and Coty buildings and the Martini tower. Among the many power stations built during the twenties and thirties, only Battersea has so far been protected. Denham Film Studios were not listed and were demolished early in 1981, unrecorded in any way by the property company which had bought the site. On this occasion the majority of buildings on the site were partially destroyed at once so that the main demolition could then be undertaken at leisure — an increasingly popular technique. Among other significant buildings of the interwar period which have suffered as a result of the Department of the Environment's conservative and unimaginative policy are the Strand Palace Hotel, which has been stripped of its distinctive illuminated entrance, and the Cumberland Hotel, which has been shorn of many of its period fittings.

A careful check reveals that at the moment of writing, August 1981, only about a hundred twentieth-century buildings of all types are listed, a pathetically small number. Most of them are in London. They include three cinemas, the Dorchester and Savoy Hotels, Broadcasting House, Barkers, Derry and Toms, and the headquarters of Morgan Grenfell, the merchant bankers. Nabisco (Shredded Wheat) at Welwyn is also protected.

One of the purposes of the present book is to indicate the wide range of twentiety-century industrial and commerical buildings which can be considered historically important and candidates for listing and protection. At the present time, only architectural merit or interest appears to qualify a building for listing, a prejudice which has fortunately been abandoned in the case of eighteenth and nineteenth-century survivals, although the battle with both the Government Department concerned and its advisers was long drawn out and fiercely fought. The more difficult struggle on behalf of twentieth-century buildings is evidently only just beginning. As matters stand at present, the more distinguished a building's architect, the better its chances of receiving the (admittedly limited) protection of an official listing.

2 The author outside Kensal House flats, London, during filming of *The Electric Revolution* for BBC Television, February 1981.

Chapter 1

The Nature of the Second Industrial Revolution and its Archaeology

Range and Scope

In the Introduction some note was made of the distinguishing characteristics of the Second Industrial Revolution. The industries in question, those which mark off the twentieth from the nineteenth century, are all connected in one way or another with either electricity or petroleum, and not infrequently with both. A good way of illustrating their range and type is to take a look at the place which has as rightful a claim as any other to be considered the cradle of the Second Industrial Revolution, as the Coalbrookdale area is of the First. This is the Trafford Park Industrial Estate on the outskirts of Manchester, which was registered as a public company in 1896 and is now possibly the site of greatest concentration of industrial archaeology in Britain. Such a survey will also serve to highlight some of the broader themes and problems to be discussed in this book.

Strategically placed between the Bridgewater Canal and the Manchester Ship Canal and served from the beginning by a network of railways and tramways, Trafford Park was planned and laid out as an industrial estate in an age when the concept was very new. The Estate depended heavily on electricity from the beginning, and it was a pioneer in this respect as well. The Trafford Power and Light Supply Co. Ltd., formed in 1902, built a power station on Trafford Park to supply firms there with electric power; and as soon as power was available, the Estates Company built a tramway system along the main routes through the Park to take

workers to and from Manchester. The last tram ran in 1946, the services by then having been completely replaced by buses.

Many industries and many well-known companies have been associated with Trafford Park at some point in its history. The first major tenant, for example, was the British Westinghouse Electrical and Manufacturing Co. Ltd., an offshoot of the Westinghouse Co. of the USA. It took a large site and built a huge factory for the production of all kinds of heavy electrical equipment. Within a short time the company passed into British control, and in 1919 changed its name to Metropolitan Vickers Electrical Co. Ltd. As a result of mergers and takeovers it has lost its independence and is currently part of General Electric, but the old name can still be read across the gable of the main assembly hall.

In 1902, Mr Royce, who built the first Rolls Royce car at Hulme, took a site in Trafford Park for the manufacture of Royce cranes. In 1904 the American Car and Foundry Co. took premises in which it constructed carriages for the London underground railways. The Ford Motor Co. set up in Trafford Park in 1911 to assemble parts made in America and to supply the British market with Ford cars. Twenty years later they moved to their new factory in Dagenham, Essex, and their original premises are now occupied by the Carborundum Co.

The chemical industry was first represented by Thomas Hedley and Co. of Newcastle, which built a soap factory on the Estate in the 1930s. Their name has changed and so has the product, for Proctor and Gamble

now make detergents rather than soap, but additional continuity is represented in the site, although Proctor and Gamble have greatly extended the original premises of Hedleys'.

Between 1939 and 1945 Trafford Park became an arsenal. Existing factories were converted to the production of war materials and supplies of all kinds, and two large new factories were built — one by Fords to make Merlin aero-engines, and the other by Metropolitan Vickers for Lancaster bombers. These specific industries have since gone but others have taken their place. Now, in effect, the archaeologist is faced with a vast industrial palimpsest, in which the past has to be recreated by stripping one layer off another. Two wars and great changes in technology have produced considerable modifications, facelifts and decay, both in individual buildings and the Estate as a whole, apart from the great number of changes in tenancies of sites and premises.

The cumulative result is that there is no comparable place in Britain where an informed stroll can produce such an awareness of what the Second Industrial Revolution has involved in economic, technical and human terms. Yet it is an extraordinary fact that this great industrial venture has attracted so little attention from historians. The development of one of the most important enterprises in the North-West has apparently presented no attractions for any kind of scholar. The photographic record is very poor, oral history is almost non-existent and no serious attempt has been made to document the rise and fall of particular companies on the Estate. There is a major research task to be undertaken

3 Morell Mills factory, Trafford Park.

4 Metropolitan-Vickers factory, Trafford Park; training school.

5 Workers' housing, Trafford Park.

6 Part of Slough Trading Estate.

7 Gloucester Trading Estate, Hucclecote. The First World War aircraft hangars, now incorporated in the Estate, are clearly visible, right centre.

Nineteenth-century factories were built more or less where the owners wanted them to be. Because canal and railway access were important for the transport of coal, raw materials and finished goods, there was considerable concentration of factories in those parts of a city where these services were most easily provided. Since, in the days of steam-power and factory chimneys, these areas were the dirtiest and, from a living point of view, the most unpleasant and most undesirable, a certain rough and ready division of the major industrial centres into industrial sections and dwelling sections became noticeable.

The notion of setting aside a large area of land specifically for factory

here and one can only hope that it will start at the eleventh hour, not the thirteenth.

What are the reasons for this strange neglect of our own century? It is at this point that we run headlong into entrenched attitudes and professional prejudice. There are those who identify industrial archaeology so completely with the eighteenth and nineteenth centuries, and with the industries which existed at that time, that they find it hard to admit that the industrial archaeology of the twentieth century can also exist. The attitude is a curious one. If the archaeological approach is valid for the nineteenth century, why should it not be equally useful for the twentieth? How can a Victorian factory or factory-worker's house possess some intrinsic quality which makes it more important to study than a factory or house built in the 1930s? Moreover, the archaeology of twentieth-century industry has much to contribute to our understanding of the social and economic history of the immediate past, as this study will attempt to demonstrate. A rapid survey of the rise and development of one industry — rubber tyres — will suggest the role and significance of industrial archaeology in our understanding of the earlier twentieth century.

In order to get our bearings we must first note the beginnings of the industry in the last century. In 1846 Robert Thomson took out a patent for his Aerial Wheel. The prototype, a rubbered-canvas inner-tube and a leather outer-casting, worked reasonably well, but no manufacturer at that time considered it worthwhile to develop so it disappeared from the scene.[1] Then, in 1885, J.S. Stanley invented the Rover safety cycle with its diamond-shaped frame and rear-wheel drive. The need for adequate tyres was both obvious and urgent, and three years later came John Boyd Dunlop's re-invention and patenting of the pneumatic tyre. Although it was a clumsy affair, being built up in position on the wire-spoked cycle wheel,[2] using layer upon layer of rubbered sailcloth, commercial development began in 1889 by a small company in Belfast. This was the Pneumatic Tyre and Booth's Cycle Agency which functioned in makeshift premises. These are no longer in existence, so this stage of the development of the pneumatic tyre and its industry has no archaeological record. All that remains of the factory is an address, a photograph and one or two catalogues.

Improvement and change from then on was rapid: Welch's wired-on tyre in 1890; Bartlett's beaded-edge tyre in 1891 (the Pneumatic Tyre Co. bought the rights to both); and Charles Wood's 1891 patent for the first satisfactory valve, which was sold to the Pneumatic Tyre Co. for £1000 and has remained substantially the same ever since.

The early cycle tyres were smooth, giving no sideways grip on the kind of roads which existed at the time: loose-surfaced or polished granite setts. Moulded treads were available for the first time in the mid-1890s. This was first achieved satisfactorily on the Doughty press, an American invention for which the British rights were bought by the Rubber Tyre Manufacturing Co., taken over by the Pneumatic Tyre Co. in 1901. This combination became the Dunlop Rubber Co. in 1901 and at that point manufacture was concentrated in Birmingham, with factories at Aston Cross and Manor Mills. Production was still mostly concerned with cycle tyres, for pneumatic tyres for carriages caught on to only limited extent, and then mainly as a status symbol.

Our information on the history of the pneumatic tyre to c.1900 is derived 85 per cent from printed and manuscript sources, 10 per cent from museum objects and, at a generous estimate, 5 per cent from archaeology. The nature of the archaeology is worth analysing. It consists of the much-modified remnants of two factories in the Midlands and, equally important if we are to appreciate the nature of these early machines, stretches of road which still have much the same kind of

---

[1] Partial specimens of these tyres are preserved in the Royal Scottish Museum, Edinburgh.
[2] There is a decrepit example at the Science Museum, London, together with plenty of bicycles of the period.

---

building, laying out roads and installing water, gas, sewage and electricity, and then persuading firms to establish themselves there is a twentieth-century phenomenon, and few towns are now without their industrial estate. In their modern form, these estates are based on electric power and motor transport, but the earliest beginnings, at Manchester, were made when industry depended on steam and railways. Trafford Park was created in the years following 1896 on 1,200 acres beside the Manchester Ship Canal, service roads and railway sidings being installed by the estate authorities. Slough set a new pattern. It was set up by the Government in 1929, as a measure to create local employment during the Depression. The site, a former First World War stores depot, already had roads, and factories of a standard size and design were erected for letting to tenants whose business was suited to the kind of accommodation offered. The result was reasonably efficient, but drab and unexciting, and the name Slough came to symbolise this kind of industrial development, commemorated by John Betjeman during the 1939-45 War in the famous couplet:

Come, friendly bombs and fall on Slough
It isn't fit for humans now

Since 1945 many of the original factories have been rebuilt or given a welcome face-lift. The Treforest and Team Valley Estates, both established in 1936, were somewhat improved pre-Second World War versions of the Slough model.

The 420-acre Gloucester Trading Estate was formed in 1964 to take over the complex of aircraft hangars and manufacturing facilities belonging to the Hawker Siddeley Group. The Estate is a private venture and provides factories and warehouses for more than 40 companies. It differs from other industrial estates in its system of central services — heating, compressed air, security, canteens, maintenance and medical attention — which are offered to the tenants more cheaply than they themselves could organise individually.

6

surface as they did in the 1890s — non-macadamised lanes and farm roads, and sections of city street which have preserved their stone setts. One cannot arrive at a proper understanding of the cycling and motoring problems which the Victorians and Edwardians had to face, especially the skids and never-ending punctures, without very literally trying to come to grips with their roads. Nor can we understand the design features, limitations, and the urge towards improvement of the machines themselves.[3]

The early cars handled badly on the rough roads of the time. On their solid tyres, they could travel at no more than about 12 m.p.h. without producing such vibration that the vehicles rapidly shook themselves to pieces. The Michelin brothers, André and Edouard, already well-known for their cycle tyres, had pneumatic tyres on a car of their own construction in the Paris-Bordeaux race in 1895. Even so, it is curious that the lessons already learned in making cycle tyres — the need for a tread pattern and for a cord, not woven fabric, casing — were ignored in the early development of car tyres. Because of patent restrictions British manufacturers had to content themselves for many years with very inferior types of tyre-to-rim attachment. For this reason mending punctures was a daunting undertaking and, since solid rubber tyres lasted twice as long anyway, pneumatics were deservedly unpopular and took a lot of selling.

Only when one has looked at the roads and the museum specimens with the imagination they deserve is one in a position to appreciate certain features of the social history of motoring, such as the fact that early cars were expected to skid-swing when they braked. In 1905 Rolls Royce advised their drivers, 'Always remember that when a car is being braked it occupies twice as much road as when travelling normally'. More bluntly, only the rear wheels were braked. They locked and, on the road surfaces

of the time, swung the car at an angle of 45° to its direction of travel. In 1902 Dr Fred Lanchester of the Lanchester Bros. firm which produced Birmingham's first well-engineered cars, wrote a driving manual issued to Lanchester purchasers, which included advice on how to side-slip and to make use of the 'swing-around stop':

The speed should be 9-11 m.p.h. The car is braked and at the same time steered. The tail comes round and the car describes a U-turn, ready to return on the other side of the road. It should on no account be attempted in the presence of other traffic, as it is a performance thoroughly disconcerting to other users of the road. Remember that, whatever the state of the road, it is bad driving to navigate the car sideways.

In order that drivers should not be obliged to 'navigate the car sideways', and to improve tyre wear, the studded leather over-jacket was introduced. It lasted until nearly up to the First World War.

The first attempts to give the tyre itself a grip were made, not by the tyre-manufacturers, but by the re-treaders. As early as 1903 remoulded tyres appeared with an inlaid leather tread, complete with steel studs embedded in the original moulding of a new tyre. This type of tyre was generally available by 1905. Many people are now unaware that London taxis had to be equipped with these tyres until well into the 1920s.

The main effect of the First World War on the tyre industry was the stepping-up of the production of solid tyres for lorries which forced manufacturers to operate on an altogether different scale and involved large capital investment. The most notable example was the great new tyre-making 'castle' Fort Dunlop, built by the Dunlop Co. in 1916 on a 300-acre site four miles out in the fields from the original factory at Aston Cross. This massive, multi-storey brick building on its railside site is evidence that the manufacture of motor-tyres was now an important industry in its own right, economically sound and promising enough to justify a major investment in buildings and plant. What is nearly always overlooked, however, is that Fort Dunlop was established as the great national temple of the solid, not the pneumatic tyre, which in the

immediate post-war years was still a very imperfect article, not at all in favour with motorists. Thereafter, however, progress was rapid. At the first post-war Motor Show in 1920 all the cars still had beaded-edge tyres. At the 1922 Show, however, Dunlop exhibited a wired-type tyre on a detachable flange rim; by 1924 this was standard. This soon led to the one-piece well-base rim, giving the car-designers a very simple tyre and wheel unit, such as the cycle world had had for a long time. The Morris Cowley and Austin 7 cars of the 1920s, the basis of popular motoring in Britain, were constructed with this type of tyre and rim and indeed would not have been possible without it.

Another development of the 1920s was the replacement of canvas by cord as a casing reinforcement. This increased the life of the tyre by a factor of three to five. For the first time the casing could be relied upon to outlast the tread, but shock absorbers had to be improved because, with cord, the cushioning effect of the crossed threads had gone. At the same time the introduction of carbon-black into the rubber mix greatly improved the wearing quality of the tread. Until then the sulphur-rubber mix contained fillers, such as china-clay, and other ingredients — zinc oxide, litharge, magnesia — to speed up the vulcanisation process and make the colour acceptable. Because large quantities of zinc oxide were normally used, the tyres manufactured before the mid-1920s were white or cream in colour. The usefulness of the very fine soot known as carbon-black was discovered in 1910 by a London firm, the Silvertown Rubber Co. The Americans were the first to make carbon-black on a large scale, burning natural gas, of which they had a plentiful supply, in order to obtain it. Other countries soon came to depend on American exports of carbon-black and by 1930, after a transitional stage during which tyres had a black tread and white sidewalls — to allow motorists to accustom themselves gradually to the change — the black tyre had become universal. By a pleasant stroke of irony the old-style tyres, with white sidewalls, have always had a fashion appeal in the USA.

Subsequent developments can be briefly indicated: scientific tyre research from the mid-1920s; the

[3]It is a remarkable fact that horse-drawn carriages and early motorcars are nearly always displayed in museums on a smooth, flat floor. This makes it difficult to comprehend why the construction of these vehicles was so solid and massive and, in particular, why they had such large, strong springs. Present them on a rutted, stony road surface and the point immediately becomes clear.

introduction of rayon cord from the late 1930s; the appearance of nylon in Second World War aircraft tyres; the extensive use of synthetic rubber during the Second World War and the greatly improved rubber polymers afterwards. They are all fully documented and each improvement can be followed and studied in museum collections. The point to be emphasised here is the extent to which archaeological evidence can be of help in correcting or filling out the record. It may be suggested that since super-annuated tyre-makers' machinery is only to be found, where it exists at all, in museums, survivals of the buildings in which they were located are important for an understanding of the history of the industry for three reasons: first, to indicate the kind of premises (new or converted, impressive, mean or ramshackle), in which tyres and the materials needed for tyres have been made; second, to show the geographical distribution of the industry; and third, to provide collaborative evidence of the road surfaces on which tyres have, at different periods, been required to perform. Furthermore, the plan and construction of the buildings themselves can reveal a great deal about the social history of the industry and about the conditions in which the workforce toiled.

We have selected the history of tyres in order to discuss and establish certain general principles. We could equally well have picked radio, synthetic fibres, computers or any other of the new industries which have given the twentieth century its special character.

Methodology and Problems

In going about his work the archaeologist is often faced with obstacles and difficulties. First, there is the major problem of the survival of buildings in the form in which they were originally used by a particular concern. We have already seen from the example of Trafford Park that mergers and take-overs commonly lead to the modification of buildings for purposes altogether different from those for which they were originally built. This, of course, assumes that the buildings in question still stand. The

This group of pictures illustrates a familiar process in Britain, whereby Second Industrial Revolution concerns have taken over and adapted buildings originally constructed to meet the needs of the First Industrial Revolution. Frome was an important centre of the woollen industry during the eighteenth and nineteenth centuries. The industry has fallen away during the twentieth century, however, and after the Second World War the surviving mills, solidly built of stone, were either demolished or bought for use in other types of manufacturing. The railway ceased to have any industrial importance and today's factories in Frome depend entirely on road transport. The milk depots and maltings, strategically placed by railway sidings, were no longer located where they could be most useful and profitable and consequently they were nearly all closed during the 1950s and 1960s. Fine-quality West Country woollen fabrics gave way to carpets for motor-cars and for the homes of the newly affluent working-class.

factories of the First Industrial Revolution were almost invariably solidly constructed of brick or stone but the Second Industrial Revolution has inclined towards light-weight skins fixed to a steel or concrete skeleton. Nowadays, it is fully expected that an industrial building will be either demolished or replaced within 50 years at most, or remodelled internally out of all recognition. Very frequently the factory is a semi-sham, with a solidly-built office block along the road front and a range of the usual twentieth-century type of worksheds behind it; perfectly efficient but with little aesthetic appeal and unlikely to survive as an industrial monument.

The archaeologist confronts the problem of impermanency in another form as well for modern companies and corporations are often no more permanent than their buildings. When one dies or become absorbed into a larger group, little mercy is likely to be shown to its records, its buildings or its equipment, no matter what their historical importance may be. It is unlikely for a group to show the same degree of interest in the history of its component companies as the people

8 Reeves Building Supplies, Frome; formerly a depot for milk transported to London by rail.

9 Venture Carpets, Frome; a former woollen mill with later extensions.

10 Part of the Marglass factory, Sherborne; a former silk factory (1753), now used for weaving glass-fibre fabrics.

11 Carreras factory, Mornington Crescent, London: in its cigarette-manufacturing days.

The factory known as the Arcadia Works was opened in 1928 to meet the increasing demand for 'Black Cat' and 'Craven A' cigarettes. Designed by the M.E. and O.H. Collins partnership, it was reckoned to be the largest and best-equipped cigarette factory in the world. It had a 550 feet frontage and the reinforced concrete structure was dressed up with enormous 'Egyptian' columns and a great central, temple-like entrance doorway, flanked by two huge black cats as symbols of the cigarettes made there. There was also Egyptianised lettering running down the boilerhouse chimney.

After the Second World War, production was moved to a new factory near Southend and, stripped of its ornamentation, the factory became a conventional office block. The Arcadia Works remains, however, as a symbol of an environmental crime which helped more than any other event to bring the age of buccaneering free-for-all to an end and to stimulate a proper concern for town-planning in London. The site was a small, early nineteenth-century park, with a curved terrace of late Georgian houses running along its edge; and the new factory, a vast, undistinguished building in the wrong place, covered the entire area of the Park. It was, even so, a very large employer of local labour and its closure caused considerable social problems in the district.

12 Carreras factory: now shorn of its Egyptian ornamentation

who worked for those companies prior to the merger or take-over, but where the company has remained one unit the chances of finding good records are far greater.

Let us consider one major group, Imperial, with this thought in mind. The Imperial, formerly the Imperial Tobacco, Group, contains 112 separate operating companies, arranged in four divisions: Tobacco; Paper; Board, Packaging and Plastics; Food, and Brewing. The Tobacco Division, from which the whole enterprise originally sprang, has a common interest and therefore, one supposes, a certain cohesion. In the other divisions, however, it is not easy to see close commercial links between book-printing and fibre-board drums, waste-paper and expanded polystyrene, broiler chickens and potato crisps, shrimps and pickles, turkeys and roses. Every effort is no doubt made to foster both a divisional and a group spirit, but it is difficult to believe that the employees of John Smith's Tadcaster Brewery would fight very hard for the protection of the records and historic premises of Ross Poultry Ltd. or Ashton Saw Mills (Western) Ltd.

Apart from the effects of changes in industrial structure much depends upon attitudes. Some firms — Mullard and Roneo are two examples — have recently decided to create archives at the thirteenth hour, using materials preserved outside the company and in the hands of long-serving members of staff. Others, such as Kodak, Marks and Spencer, and Pilkington, have looked after their records in a systematic way for 50 years or more. Generally, however, it is likely that a twentieth-century industrial or commercial concern will display these characteristics:

1. it will not be in its original buildings;
2. it will have either very poor records or, especially for its earlier history, none at all;
3. it will have no written company history, apart from a few sketchy and often inaccurate notes.

There are, of course, refreshing exceptions to this generalisation, but for most of the time the researcher into the history of the Second Industrial Revolution will be faced with these handicaps.

Most firms are willing to be co-operative with the industrial archaeologist. They will produce what they have in the way of records — often with an apology that it is so little —, enlist the help of former employees, make available facilities for research purposes, and be generous with food, drink and managerial time. One can reciprocate only by presenting them with a copy of the old-timers' reminiscences with a request that they will check and amplify them. This allows the company to participate in the investigation in a constructive way and at the same time gives them an opportunity to put on their files historical material of which they would otherwise be ignorant.

The archaeologist who decides to busy himself with twentieth-century material has one enormous advantage over those whose interests lie in earlier centuries; he can talk to people who themselves helped to make the archaeology. These are the old men and women who can tell the archaeologist about the early days of the industry in which they spent their working lives. To meet these veterans and to collect their reminiscences provides the researcher with an opportunity to avoid the limitations and pitfalls which bedevil those who can work only with written materials and the survivals of buildings and machines. One may have taken great pains to locate and survey old industrial premises and to discover through records as much as one can about them, but the perspective changes and the interest grows when it is possible to hear the workers' own memories of events and things. Better still, a chance remark often suggests a line of enquiry that would never have occurred to even the most imaginative and knowledgeable specialist.

By following up every lead that the industrial veteran provides, the archaeologist is able to construct a more satisfactory picture of the particular building or premises in its working days, or at a specific point in its history. He finds out about such things as its fire precautions, first-aid equipment, methods of dealing with accidents, canteen facilities, and the heating and ventilation. This is precisely the kind of information ignored by most company and industrial historians, whose interests tend to be very selective and who, with rare exceptions, concentrate their attention on economic and technical developments rather than on working conditions. The great weakness of most industrial history, in this sense, is that it has been written from the management point of view — being, in fact, 'boardroom history' — without the realisation that all industries look quite different when viewed through the eyes of the people who take orders rather than give them. The proportions of the story and the significant details are different. In practice, one needs to blend and compare the view from the top with the view from the bottom, and the latter is to be obtained almost entirely by making a direct approach to people who have been directly involved in the processes the technical historians describe so impersonally.

Sometimes it is useful to approach the public direct, by means of a letter in the local paper or an appeal over local radio. The information which results can often be of considerable importance to the archaeologist. For example, a letter in the *Oxford Mail*, aimed at discovering people who had worked at Morris Motors during the 1920s and 1930s, produced a good crop of replies. One of them came from Mr Bob Roberts who started working at the Cowley factory in 1925 as a skilled sheet-metal worker.[4]

'The wooden body frames,' he remembers. 'were made at a factory in the North of England. I'm certain it was in Manchester, as the manager there at that time was Mr Priestley, who a few years later came to the Cowley Works as manager.' The hours at the Body Shop were from 8 am to 5 pm, but the timetable was likely to be altered if the frames had failed to arrive from Manchester. The men could be told to go away and to come back after lunch. On those occasions the foreman

would come dashing out to us and said they were nearly here. This was between 2 and 2.30. When they arrived at the Body Shop, we all just dashed out to the lorries. Then we all started shaping and panelling them. We didn't clock in until the frame arrived and then we carried on work on them until 1 am, sometimes 2.30 a.m, so that the paint shop could have the panelled bodies

[4]Reply of 10 June 1977.

at 8 am when they started the following morning. But we were only paid our hourly rate of 2/-. There was no overtime money. We were just paid for the work we did.

There was no canteen, 'so seeing I was a leading hand, they allowed me to go to the fish and chip shop in Towns Road, and, when the owner saw the fish and chip list I handed him at about 9 pm, he said "You'll have to get a wheel truck to carry all those packs." I've wondered on several occasions if they'd work like that today. I doubt it.' But he enjoyed the job and the owner of the business was a real person to him, someone he knew and respected. 'My pal and partner Vic, and I', he remembers, 'were allowed to panel the first aluminium-metalled long-wheelbase car model to go to South Africa. When we'd finished it, Vic and I had to go in on a Saturday morning, as Mr William Morris — I only knew him as Billie — was coming in to see it, with all his head staff, directors and managers. When Mr Morris started to look around it, he suddenly turned round to his top staff and shouted, "Who designed this stuff?" One of the directors shouted back, "I did". Back from Billie Morris came, "It's like a funeral hearse. Throw it on the scrap heap." '

A letter of thanks and a questionnaire went back to Mr Roberts. The questions, and Mr Roberts' answers were:

1. *Where were you working before you went to Morris at Cowley?*
   Apprentice at J.H. Grant, Ironmongers and Constructional Engineering. The full history is attached. Then joined the Army and finished as Sergeant in the Royal Tank Corps.
2. *What did your work on the bull-nosed Morrises actually consist of? Did you operate a press, cut, beat and drill panels by hand, or what?*
   No press work. It was cut, beat and drill panels by hand, planish them on sandbags to have them to the shape of the wood body frames, finish them off by filing and sandpapering. The steel panels, cold-tooled and close-annealed metal which would never go rusty, were shaped by floor-pressure at the Camden Engineering

Co., London.
3. *How were the body panels fixed to the wooden frames? Were these frames made of ash?*
   By screws and bolts. The frames were ash. We drilled the holes and sunk the holes to have the screws and bolts level with the panels, and then put special soldering around the heads.
4. *How were the body frames transported from Manchester to Cowley?*
   In sections, side frames, bulkhead frames, trunk frames and door frames. These were assembled by the carpenters in the body shop, supervised by a charge hand from the Experimental Department.
5. *Did William Morris have the reputation of being a tough man, or a bad-tempered man?*
   Mr William Morris was a real Gentleman, but he was to the highest degree a tough man, who dealt direct with the top Departmental manager. If there was a failure in Car Assembly or Production, he hit them for six. The work had to be absolutely top-class all the time.

Armed with this kind of first-hand information, one is in a position to make better sense of the biographies of Morris and the printed histories of the British motor industry. Plans of the old works begin to come to life and the early buildings are no longer entirely dead shells. Equally important, one can be led into areas of research which one had previously never thought of. A chance remark by an old lady who worked as a rayon-spinner during the 1920s that 'we used to have to line up every hour to have our eyes bathed', suggests a number of useful questions about working conditions in the industry and about the Factory Acts. The statement that, 'A lot of the men weren't money-minded', causes one to think about incentive payments in a different way. 'The recruitment of unskilled labour' takes on another, more human meaning when one hears stories like the following: 'My father came from Oxfordshire. He was a groom. This lady — I forget her name — used to keep racehorses. She moved to Burton Lazers and Dad came with her. He came to work with the horses, and when the lady died all the horses

were sold. Then Dad went to work with the Midland Woodworking Company. He was there 43 years and then he retired.'

It is quite wrong to suppose that the Second Industrial Revolution has been a dull, prosaic affair compared with the First, or that its archaeology has none of the magic and poetry of the days of steam. In Clerkenwell Road, London, there is a building, Nos. 102-108, which is now occupied by the Bell Telephone Co. When Robert Dockerill went to work there in 1920, as an office boy straight from school, it was the headquarters of the Columbia Gramophone Co. The recording studios were on the top floor, with the offices below. The reason for this, Mr Dockerill remembers, was that if the studios had been nearer to street level, the rumbling and vibration of the trams would have interfered with recording. Consequently, visiting singers and musicians had to take a trip upstairs. 'We always knew when a celebrity such as Dame Clara Butt was coming', he recalls, 'because they always had the red carpet put down for them from the very meagre entrance to the lift. They went in the lift up to the fourth floor and then they had to walk up two small flights of stairs to the fifth floor. Once they got there, they had the red carpet right into the oak-panelled recording room'.[5] With this knowledge it is impossible to stand outside Nos. 102–108 and look upwards without thinking of those impressive royal progresses from the taxi to the fifth floor. The young Robert Dockerill was understandably impressed. The building, however, has not yet been scheduled as the historic monument it certainly is, for it illustrates the modest beginnings of this large and prosperous twentieth-century industry in a way that no written record can do. To compare the size of the Clerkenwell Road premises with that of the buildings occupied by Columbia's heirs today, EMI, is to have the progress of the industry forced on one's attention.

One of the purposes of this book is to draw attention to such places as Nos. 102-108 Clerkenwell Road, partly as a matter of justice — the First

[5] Conversation and correspondence with the author, November — December 1976.

13 Stage 1: Wigmore Street, London, now occupied by Ardente.

14 Stage 2: A new building on the other side of the road in Wigmore Street. In 1981 IBM gave up this building and moved into larger premises next door.

Four stages of IBM's administration in the UK illustrated by its buildings.

15 Stage 3: Gunnersbury, still occupied by IBM, but long outgrown as a headquarters building.

The differences in size, amenities and also location of these buildings provide an excellent example of how industrial development is catered for as standards change through time, and of how a company sheds its earlier skins as it grows and develops. At present, Cosham is as near as one can get to a symbol of the advanced Second Industrial Revolution in Britain, but it is only the latest link in the IBM chain. Further buildings will doubtless be added to the chain in the future.

16 Stage 4: Cosham, Portsmouth, opened in 1976 and now extended further.

12

Industrial Revolution should not be allowed all the limelight, all the commemorative plaques and all the entries in the tourist guides and lists of historic monuments — and partly to encourage readers to search out similar places for themselves. In the pages that follow it has been necessary to be selective. The number of possible sites is very large and one can do no more than indicate certain particularly fruitful fields for investigation. What has had to be omitted is, in many cases, as interesting and as important as what has been included. Bananas, cosmetics and sports goods, for example, are all well worth the industrial archaeologist's attention.. All have been unreasonably neglected so far. Taken together, however, the chapters which follow give a fair impression of the totality, scale and scope of the Second Industrial Revolution, and suggest how one may usefully and pleasantly explore its history.

Two points should be made, however, before passing to a consideration of particular industries. The first is that the great majority of the Second Industrial Revolution's key inventions were made and first developed outside Britain.[6] For the First Industrial Revolution precisely the opposite is true. The second observation is that the First Industrial Revolution was the period of bankruptcies whereas the Second has been typified more by mergers and takeovers. Certain important consequences follow from these two facts. The history of industry and commerce becomes increasingly complicated after c.1870 as licensing agreements, cartels, international groups, import controls, and government direction and intervention have increasingly to be taken into account. All combine to produce a situation which makes the world of Watt, Brunel and their contemporaries

[6]The Appendix makes this clear.

seem very small and simple. Equally tiresome for the archaeologist is the need to follow the archaeology of an industry from one country and one continent to another. If one is concerned with the history of iron-making between c.1700 and c.1850, all the essential developments can be documented by studying British sites. If, however, the field is cornflakes, tractors or telephones then the early shrines are to be found in North America. The same is true regarding most electrical appliances, safety razors, escalators, passenger lifts, linotype and monotype printing, roll-film cameras, aeroplanes, cinemas, petroleum extraction and refining, incandescent lamps, typewriters and refrigerators. The Americans got there first and Europe came in one or two rungs up the ladder. The significance of these observations for the study of the archaeology of the Second Industrial Revolution in Britain will become more evident in the pages which follow.

17 Westinghouse works, Trafford Park: coil-winding in G Aisle, 1902.

The history and archaeology of the British electrical industry is complicated. Since 1968 the field has been dominated by GEC, which absorbed first AEI and then English Electric. During the previous 50 years, however, all three of these concerns had themselves been involved in mergers and regroupings, with the result that factories have changed their names in a bewildering and unsettling fashion. The outline of the story, which begins in America, is as follows.

In 1879 and 1880, Edison in the USA and Swan in Britain independently invented the incandescent electric lamp. To exploit this, the Edison and Swan Electric Light Co. (Ediswan) was formed in Britain. The American interests were looked after by Edison's own company, which became General Electric of America in 1892. This acquired a virtual monopoly of the highly profitable lamp business, through its patents for the carbon filament lamp. Until 1893, when the patents ran out, Ediswan monopolised the British lamp market, each lamp selling for 3s. 9d., compared with 1/ after 1893.

In 1905 the Germans developed the vastly more efficient tungsten filament lamp, which led to the creation of a new industrial structure in Europe. The General Electric Co. had been formed in Britain in 1889, completely independently of the American GEC. In 1901-2, it built a plant at Witton, Birmingham, primarily to make dynamos, motors and switchgear, and in 1905, in association with a German company, it set up the Osram lamp works at Hammersmith. Like all electrical companies, GEC did very well out of the War, and in 1920 it moved into a new and prestigious headquarters building — Magnet House, Kingsway, London. This has since been demolished.

In 1894 British Thompson Houston (BTH) was formed, as a subsidiary of GEC, to make lamps. It entered heavy electrical manufacturing in 1902, building a large factory at Rugby for the purpose, and in 1911 it acquired the American patents for drawn-wire filaments, together with the trade-name, Mazda. During the 1920s, BTH greatly expanded, with new factories or extensions at Rugby, Willesden, Coventry, Birmingham, Chesterfield and Lutterworth. In 1929 it merged with Metropolitan-Vickers (Metrovick) to form AEI.

British Westinghouse was established in 1899 and in 1901-2 built a very large factory at Trafford Park, Manchester, mainly for the manufacture of generating sets. In 1918 it merged with the electrical interests of Vickers and the Metropolitan and Carriage Works to become Metropolitan-Vickers and its subsequent history is that of AEI.

English Electric was created in 1919 from a hotchpotch of companies making light electrical goods. It immediately bought the Siemens dynamo works at Stafford, which had been taken over by the Government as enemy property during the War. In 1938 it went into aircraft manufacturing, with its main factory at Preston.

The post-war changes are easier to follow. English Electric bought Marconi in 1947, which gave them the Marconi site at Aldwych, where in time they built a new headquarters, currently the offices of Citibank. In 1967 they achieved their last acquisition with the takeover of Elliott Automation. AEI, too, was moving into its last phase as an independent company with the purchase of Aldermaston as a research centre in 1947 and Siemens' British interests in 1955. The future turned out to be with GEC. In 1961 GEC bought the Sobell and Weinstock company, Radio and Allied, which brought Arnold Weinstock first onto the GEC Board and then, within a very short time, into control of the Company. AEI fell to Weinstock in 1967.

18 Westinghouse works, Trafford Park: mechanical-plant manufacture in B Aisle, 1911.

19 Westinghouse works, Trafford Park: D Aisle in 1977.

Chapter 2

Food Production and Processing

Between 1800 and 1900 the number of people living in urban areas in England and Wales rose from under 2.5 million to over 25 million. As these town dwellers were food consumers and not food producers, the demands upon the traditional systems of food production and supply were intense. One major consequence was the increasing reliance upon imports from abroad — at first from North West Europe and North America, and later from Australia and New Zealand. This development, of course, has continued into the twentieth century for Britain, like most industrialised countries, cannot possibly be fully self-sufficient in food. (The details of this particular development will not concern us here, however.)

Food Production

The effects on British agriculture of this unprecedented demand for foodstuffs were dramatic. The change from self-sufficiency to a degree of dependence on overseas supplies was far from painless. Many farmers failed to adapt to the new conditions and went bankrupt. Those who survived did so by becoming more efficient, an achievement owing much to increased production and improved quality. In 1851, 18 per cent of the occupied population of Britain earned a living from agriculture; in 1871 the figure had fallen to 11 per cent, and the trend continued thereafter. Farmers were employing considerably fewer people by 1900 than in 1850, although the total population rose considerably over the same period. At the same time they were producing a great deal more food

following the application of new techniques. Investment in steam engines, threshing machines, reaping machines and other equipment proceeded apace. More attention was paid to the condition of livestock, and the scientific management of farms slowly became standard practice. These changes can be studied by the archaeologist.

Fertilisers

One of the most important developments in food production since c.1850 has been the increased use of fertilisers, pesticides and herbicides, and thus of an industry geared to meeting the demand. The history of the Fisons Group is an excellent illustration of this. It began in 1847 as a family business in East Anglia but today it is an international pharmaceutical and chemical organisation controlling 63 companies and employing more than 10,000 people. It is an industrialist's dream and an industrial archaeologist's nightmare, for its growth has obliterated a large number of previously independent concerns. This, together with a continuous programme of modernisation and rationalisation, makes the archaeology of Fisons difficult to establish.

The original Group was formed in 1929 with the amalgamation of three well-known fertiliser firms in East Anglia — Packards, James Fison and Prentice Bros. — with factories in Boston and Ipswich. In 1930 two other companies were acquired — Doughty Richardson Fertilisers of Lincoln, and W.G. Hammond of Boston. At this stage the Group was still based solidly in East Anglia, but the next decade saw expansion into more distant

regions with the acquisition of companies as far afield as Newcastle, York, Liverpool, Widnes and Plymouth. In 1944 the Group expanded into Wales and Scotland.

From the point of view of the historian and archaeologist this catalogue of mergers and acquisitions represents the extinction of the majority of independent fertiliser firms in Britain. Their names have disappeared; their records have ended up in obscurity or even destruction; and their former premises have become merely a part of the Group pool, to be treated in a purely strategic manner. As with other major industrial groups, the full story of the buildings and plant which Fisons inherited in the course of its growth would make a most valuable and interesting record.

Food Marketing and Processing

With some justification the term 'the Agricultural Revolution' has commonly been used to describe the developments which occurred in farming in the nineteenth and twentieth centuries. More accurately, however, it should be termed 'the Food Revolution' since it is meaningless and unhelpful to separate the new techniques of food production from those involved in supplying farm produce to the consumer. The two are complementary and mutually reinforcing; one could not have occurred without the other.

Modern food marketing has its origins in the last century, and in Britain the major stimulus to innovation came — yet again — as a result of foreign competition. The Danes, Dutch, Germans and others quickly realised the importance of quality control and reliability. They took great pains to ensure that they met their customers' requirements, and that the quality of successive consignments of butter, cheese, meat, vegetables and other produce was consistent. This was in marked contrast to the perennial complaints on the part of wholesalers and others in Britain that British farmers were failing to meet market needs. Under competitive pressure British producers slowly and painfully learned the lesson.

Milk

One consequence of this new drive towards quality was the establishment of larger processing units. The milk suppliers showed the way. The first large-scale depots to be set up in Britain were in Wiltshire, the pioneer being established by the Maggs family — later to become the dominant force in United Dairies — at Semley, Wiltshire, in 1871. These Victorian depots were always built by the side of a railway so that the milk could be easily and quickly shipped to London, Manchester and other major cities. Indeed, without the expanding trade in what was called 'railway milk', dairy farming would have been ruined. Since 1950 the pattern has completely changed as railways have been closed and dairy products, especially liquid milk, have come to be moved by road, not rail. The network of small collection and distribution points has become completely unnecessary, and most of the depots have been closed down and the buildings sold. There are dozens of former milk depots scattered over the dairy farming areas of Britain, now functioning as factories, warehouses, garages and builders' merchants' premises.

The archaeology of the first phase of the attempt to industrialise the dairy industry is abundant and worth studying in a comprehensive way, if only to show how very small were these units until comparatively recently. They were strategically located so that the milk could be brought in each day by horse and cart, and were closest together where there are, and have been for generations, most cows to the acre. As soon as the milk was transported by lorry, instead of by horse-drawn transport, most of them became redundant, although in many cases they survived, for reasons of tradition and conservation, much longer than could be economically justified.

The case of United Dairies illustrates the trends. In 1902, after absorbing a number of smaller firms, the founder of the business, the enterprising Charles Maggs, found it necessary to create specialised centres, butter-making being concentrated at Devizes and condensed milk at Melksham. Other large concerns such as Nestlé and the Express Dairy developed in the same way. During the First World War three of the large wholesale dairies mainly concerned with the London market found it impossible to continue in competition. Their horses had been requisitioned and their men had been conscripted into the Forces and the war industries. These three, the Dairy Supply Co., Metropolitan and Great Western Dairies and Wilts United Dairies, merged to form United Dairies.

Soon after the end of the War, United Dairies decided to pasteurise all except tuberculin-tested milk. They built new centres for the purpose but had to go to America for the equipment which British manufacturers were unable to design or supply at that time. The decision to pasteurise involved a great deal of redistribution of United Dairies' plants even before the changes of the 1950s and 1960s. Lorry collections from farms were begun in the 1920s and in 1937 a further step forward was taken with the introduction of the first glass-lined rail tanks. In 1928 United Dairies took possession of their new bottling plant in Vauxhall, London and opened their first Central Laboratory at Wood Lane in 1934.

As a result of all the technical and organisational changes of the past 50 years or so, United Dairies displays what might be termed 'three-layer archaeology'. There are, first, the superannuated collecting and processing centres. Then come the factories, such as Melksham, which are still fulfilling much the same function as they were 50 years ago, but with greatly improved equipment. Third, there are the sites, such as St. Erth and Chard, which still preserve a core of original buildings but which have been enlarged and modernised out of all recognition. Chard is a particularly good example of this. Once a modest-sized factory for making butter and cheese, it is now the largest butter-producing plant in the world with a capacity of more than 100 tons per day.

The far-reaching developments in milk processing, as in the food industries as a whole, can be studied only in terms of buildings, printed material and personal reminiscences, for, with very few exceptions, the old equipment has entirely gone; nobody thought of preserving it at the time. A single example will illustrate the kind of gaps which exist. Until the 1930s many town-dairymen's shops had an appliance on their door which allowed milk to be sold when the shop itself was closed. It consisted of a brass plate fixed to the outside of the door, containing a spout and a slot into which customers inserted their pennies. On the inside of the door, and connected to the spout, was a churn of milk. A penny in the slot delivered milk into a jug or can held under the spout. It was a simple system but an unhygienic one, since not only was the apparatus difficult to clean, but dogs and cats enjoyed licking the spout. In its day it formed a much-appreciated and useful part of the system of distributing liquid milk but, although many people remember it, it appears to be completely undocumented. Diligent enquiry has unearthed no photograph and no surviving museum example.

On the marketing side of the food business, it is essential to bear in mind social developments such as the rise in working-class spending-power, the great increase in the number of working-wives, the existence of domestic refrigerators and freezers, and the growing unwillingness of people to devote more than a minimum of time to shopping and cooking. In marketing, as on the farms, the twin demands of low price and reliable quality have given nearly all the advantages to the big unit. This became apparent in America before it did in Europe. The international Heinz concern illustrates this very well.

Heinz

H.J. Heinz established his food-processing business in 1876, and by 1919 it had 6,500 employees. In a country where the Pure Food Campaign was gaining ground very fast, partly as a result of a number of major

20 Heinz factory, Harlesden (1925), in 1929.

21 Heinz factory, Harlesden (1925), in c. 1930: interior.

22 (below)
Heinz factory, Kitt Green, Wirral, (1959): the second generation of factories.

When American food companies such as Heinz set up their first factories in Britain, mostly during the 1920s, they knew what they wanted. The pioneering years had been in America, not Britain, and the overseas factories were set up to put experience and proven techniques and machinery into action. British companies like Bowyers, on the other hand, built as they developed, so their plants usually have a decidedly irregular and piecemeal appearance. Their infancy, adolescence and maturity are generally all found together on the same site. With rare exceptions, brand new, integrated food and drink factories in Britain have been built for one of two reasons: either to manufacture a completely new product, or to establish the firm or the industry in an area in which it did not previously exist.

Bowyers is a microcosm of the developing British food industry. Until 1924 it was a small family concern. After steady growth over the next half-century it merged with Scot of Bletchley in 1972, and in the same year this concern became the meat division of Unigate. It is now the second largest manufacturer of meat products in the UK.

Bowyers' nationwide growth would have been impossible without motor transport and an efficient road system; as long as it had to depend on the railway and horse-drawn vehicles business remained confined to a 50-mile radius. In Trowbridge itself it has progressively bought and converted disused woollen mills, an interesting example of new industry taking over a town's old redundant buildings.

23 (above)
Display of products in the Market Place, Trowbridge, by Bowyers, c. 1880. This faded photograph provides an interesting commentary on Victorian concepts of food hygiene.

24 (right)
Bowyers factory, Trowbridge. This section of the plant was formerly a woollen mill.

25 (below)
Bowyers factory, Trowbridge: part of the butchery section, a labour intensive department in the 1960s.

26 (below)
Bowyers factory, Trowbridge: a fully mechanised department — sausage meat production.

18

and well-publicised scandals, keen attention to hygiene and attractive working conditions was seen to be desirable. The firm's public image was of the utmost importance. The girls who worked at the Heinz factories were given private lockers for their personal belongings, snow-white uniforms, weekly manicures, free medical attention, homemaking classes, a swimming pool, a gymnasium and a 500-seat dining room — with an Orphenion, imported from Germany, to provide music at lunch time. Guided tours were provided for visitors, who went away with free samples of the firm's products and green pickle-pins to wear in their lapels or on their bosoms.

This was very exceptional in Victorian America. Heinz had the foresight and the good sense to see that in the food business cleanliness and welfare were of immense benefit to sales. In other types of industry the advantages were less obvious and only very rarely was an employer likely to spend money on such frills. It was natural when Heinz eventually set up factories abroad that these should follow the American precedent. The factory at Harlesden, North West London, built just after the First World War, was 'a little America', a cultural transfer, although by that time many other firms in the food business were operating in a similar way. The Heinz regime was not wholly popular, however. The author, who worked at the Harlesden factory for a time during the 1930s, remembers the rule which kept employees confined to the factory grounds — very pleasant grounds — for the statutory eight hours a day. The reason given was that it was too expensive and time-consuming to frisk the staff more than once a day as they went out through the gates, in case they should happen to have tins of baked beans or, more probably, sardines, concealed about their persons. The Harlesden factory, considerably extended since the 1930s, is a monument to autocratic paternalism as well as to hygiene and efficiency.

It is also the centre of an agricultural spider's web. Every food-processing plant controls the lives and methods of the farmers and growers who supply it with its raw materials. It draws up contracts, fixes prices, determines varieties, specifies harvesting dates and keeps a keen eye on quality. The Italian who sends his tomatoes to Harlesden, or the Lancashire market-gardener who grows peas and carrots for the other Heinz factory in the Wirral, might in many ways be on the Heinz staff, for he is his own master in only a very restricted sense of the term. To a modern food company, quality is defined against the demands of its manufacturing and marketing techniques. There is nothing inferior about a potato four inches in diameter except that crisp manufacturers demand something smaller. There is nothing dangerous or unattractive about a six-inch carrot except that it is too big to suit the company's carrot-buyer. Whether the commodity is milk, beans, strawberries or potatoes, the twentieth-century food-processor must have a standardised, reliable product. The fact that it has little or no taste is immaterial. The chemists can look after its taste. At a Coca-Cola plant, for instance, the most important task is to remove every scrap of taste from the local water used for manufacturing purposes. This ensures that, no matter where in the world the factory may be, the water can be depended on to be exactly the same. All one has to do is to add the correct amount of vital essence, received in sealed drums from America, and the Coca-Cola supplied to the customer in Naples and the customer in Hawaii must be identical.

Breakfast Foods

The history of prepared breakfast foods is built around a few key innovations mostly made by nineteenth-century food faddists of whom, for some reason, the USA appears to have had more than its fair share. Graham Crackers (1829), the brain-child of Sylvester Graham, a temperance lecturer who promised to save souls through the stomach, began the series. Then, after the Civil War, came Granula, the forerunner of Grape Nuts (1863), Shredded Wheat (1893) and Puffed Wheat (1902). The key date, however, is 1866, when the Seventh Day Adventists set up the Western Health Reform Institute, later to become the Battle Creek Sanitarium (sic), at Battle Creek, Michigan, a town which, under the leadership of Dr John Harvey Kellogg, earned the title of 'Cereal Capital of the World'. Kellogg was appointed Director of the Institute in 1876, and one of his patients was Charles W. Post. During his stay at Battle Creek he had plenty of time for original thinking and quiet reflection and became aware, not without encouragement, of the commercial possibilities of health foods. In 1897, Post established the Postum Cereal Co., which produced and promoted Postum and Grape Nuts. (The Postum Cereal Co. was the mother firm from which the world-conquering General Foods Corporation eventually sprang).

The Kellogg empire was founded later, in 1906, after William K. Kellogg, who had been helping his brother to run the sanitarium, left in order to branch out on his own with the Battle Creek Toasted Corn Flake Co. The fashion caught on and within a few years many different brands of cornflakes had appeared on the market. The subsequent history of what is now an enormous international industry has been characterised by remarkable processing developments for flaking, rolling, shredding, puffing, baking, grinding and re-vitaminising the simple, nutritious grain to yield vastly more expensive products of varying flavour, form and texture. Breakfast foods are the perfect example of a twentieth-century consumer industry, with the demand almost wholly created and sustained by advertising and with the retail price bearing no relation whatever to the intrinsic value of the goods.

All the major American breakfast cereals are manufactured in Britain, and some of the factories, such as that of Nabisco (formerly Shredded Wheat) are of interest to the historians of industrial architecture. They have undergone few external changes of any consequence since they were built in the 1920s and 1930s. Weetabix, the only British-owned cereal of any consequence, is another story, however. Production of Weetabix started in 1932 in a disused mill at Burton Latimer, near Kettering, Northamptonshire. Weetabix is still manufactured solely in Burton Latimer, but the company has grown to the point that it now exports to more than 60 countries, and has a 20 per cent share of the breakfast cereal market in the United Kingdom. A fully automated plant was built in 1967 but the old mill is still in use, and if any building is entitled to be called a British example of breakfast cereal archaeology, this is it.

27 Kelloggs, Trafford Park.

Kelloggs began manufacturing in Britain in the 1920s. They selected a site on the Trafford Park Industrial Estate, which allowed the raw material, maize, to be brought directly from America via the Manchester Ship Canal. The establishment of this factory is evidence that by this time enough British people had been converted to the breakfast cereal fashion to make production here worthwhile and also that the habit of shipping packets across the Atlantic had at last been discovered to be uneconomic. Kelloggs at Trafford Park, greatly expanded since the 1920s, but still preserving most of the original buildings, is one of the most noteworthy symbols of the spread of American food habits to Britain.

28 Weetabix, Burton Latimer: the late nineteenth-century flour mill in which production of Weetabix began in 1932.

30 (below)
Weetabix, Burton Latimer: an aerial view of the plant showing the original mill building in the centre of the picture. Although the nineteenth-century owners of the mill chose the site largely because of its easy access to the railway, Weetabix has no need for railway services, so the siding has consequently been built over.

29 Nabisco, Welwyn Garden City, c. 1926.

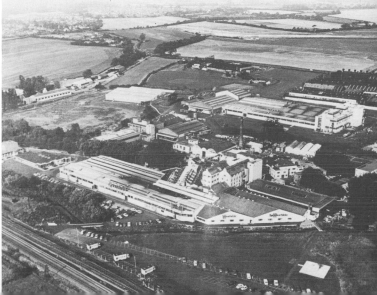

Potato Crisps

Potato crisps are a younger industry than breakfast cereals, but they are a British development, if not a British invention. The growth of the industry in this century has been remarkable. It is estimated that every man, woman and child in Britain now eats one packet of crisps a week, which represents an annual consumption of about 2.5 lb per capita, and a total national expenditure of more than £100 million. So far as can be ascertained, the actual inventor was a Frenchman called Cartier, who emigrated to England shortly before 1914, changed his name to Carter, and began to make potato crisps on a very small, almost domestic, scale. In 1920 Frank Smith started to make crisps in two garages in Crown Yard, Cricklewood, behind *The Crown* public house, which still stands. He bought up Carter's Crisps and developed the business quickly. In 1921 Smiths moved to a disused canteen in Somerton Road, Cricklewood — it had been built for workers in a wartime aircraft factory — and then, in 1938, to a new factory near Staples Corner, on the North Circular Road, London, which remained their headquarters until the 1960s.

During almost the whole of this period Smiths were synonymous with potato crisps to the British public. But this proved to be the company's undoing. It failed to modernise and overhaul its organisation, with the result that the door was left wide open to its competitors. Two of these, Golden Wonder and Walkers, have now left Smiths a long way behind. The factories built by Frank Smith during the 1920s and 1930s have been mostly sold and converted to other uses — the buildings remaining as the principal examples of potato-crisp archaeology. Smiths Crisps, renamed Smiths Foods, was bought by an American food group, and, its grandeur departed, found new accommodation on a factory estate at Kew.

Most of the technical and human history of potato crisps is locked away in the memories of veterans who worked for Smiths as the empire rose and fell. The story has never been written down. Rosie Weatherley, for example, has 50 years' service with Smiths to her credit. From the time

31 Smiths Potato Crisps: former headquarters building, Brentford, 1930.

32 Smiths Potato Crisps: Bristol factory, 1932. Now used by Radio Rentals Ltd.

Smiths' monopoly of the potato crisp market during the 1920s and 1930s was based on a network of regional depots and factories. Consignments to individual customers were usually small and distribution costs relatively high. At that time a high proportion of the potatoes used came from Smiths' own estates, which was a practicable arrangement so long as the market for crisps remained, by modern standards, small. The present situation is quite different.

In 1960 the British crisp market was estimated by to be worth £13 million. By 1965 it had reached £32 million and by 1974 it had risen to £104 million. This enormous growth within a comparatively short period reflects a revolution in dietary habits, which is illustrated equally well by the sales pattern for nuts and other forms of packaged snacks. A large number of people of all ages are no longer taking what can reasonably be called

meals. They have become compulsive nibblers, and the firms which were early to realise this important social development have prospered remarkably. It is interesting to notice that of the 600 and more hopeful crisp-making companies which mushroomed and mostly died between 1945 and 1955, one, started in 1948 in a small Scottish bakery, survived long enough to become part of the Imperial Group in 1960 and, under its new name of Golden Wonder, won the lion's share of the market by 1970. Golden Wonder now has six production centres in the UK. Its factory at Widnes is the largest in Europe within what can now be considered a highly significant food industry. None of the six factories, however, is more than 20 years old, which means that in this instance the industrial historian finds himself faced with nothing that he can reasonably call archaeology, even by the compressed time-scale of the twentieth century.

when she first joined the Company until the late 1940s the method of turning potatoes into crisps was still very much what it had been in 1920. Each unit was looked after by one girl, known as the fryer. Miss Weatherley recalls that each had:

> a small copper pan which held six gallons of oil, and each pan had its own cutting unit, so that she judged for herself how many potatoes she had to cut into the pan to make the equivalent of two tins of crisps. These took about two minutes to fry and when they were ready she scooped them out with something which resembled a large butterfly net made of wire, and put them up on a draining board on the side to drain, while she chucked the next fry into the pan. When that was cooked, she shot her original fry down a chute into the packing room below.[1]

'Those', Rosie Weatherley says nostalgically, 'were the days when we made a really good crisp.' When the individual pans went out and continuous frying became the rule, 'the crinkle went out of the crisp and it became very much thinner.' But with the new, large-scale techniques of cooking came the extractor-hoods over the machines, so that the girls no longer carried the smell of the factory home with them in their hair and their clothes. The workers of the 1920s and 1930s had to put up with the smell, because jobs were difficult to get. The trade was very seasonal, with furious activity during the summer and very little to do between October and Easter. One reason for this was that the crisps had to be eaten very quickly after they were made. The waxed paper bags were not airtight and until the early 1960s, when plastic film became available, the shelf life of a bag of crisps was reckoned to be one day from the time that the bags were taken from the large square tin, similar to a biscuit tin, in which they were delivered. Public houses, one of Smiths' main categories of customers, tried to extend the period a little by putting the bags into a glass jar placed conspicuously on the bar, but even then the crisps would survive for three days at the

most. Today, a bag of crisps will remain in good condition for three months, which considerably simplifies production and distribution problems.

It is interesting to study the advertisements for crisps which appeared before the outbreak of war in 1939. They are aimed entirely at the middle class and they make it clear that at that time potato crisps were not considered, either by the manufacturers or their customers, to be a substitute for real food. An advertisement in the *Daily Telegraph* of 25 April 1931 reads: 'No hiker's outfit is complete without Smiths Potato Crisps and nuts and seedless raisins. Obtainable in 2d. and 3d. packets from ham and beef shops, grocery and provision stores and village inns.' Hiking, like picnicking, was very much a middle-class pursuit, and so, until the post-war period, was crisp-eating. The modern manufacturer has a classless and far larger public in mind, one which does as little cooking as possible and takes much of its nourishment in the form of snacks.

Pet Foods

This trend towards 'quick foods' has had some curious side effects. Ready-prepared meals and snacks contain no waste and therefore no scraps with which to feed dogs and cats. Occasionally, but much less frequently than even 10 years ago, bones, offal and fish-heads are bought from the butcher or fishmonger specially for pets. An increasing proportion of people never patronise a butcher or fishmonger, however, and buy everything they eat from a supermarket. Among their purchases is pet food, canned, packaged and arranged on the shelves in exactly the same way as the food the pet-owners buy for themselves. During the past 30 years the manufacture of pet foods has been one of the fastest growing industries in Britain and is now one of the largest.

The beginnings of the pet-food industry are very prosaic. Dog biscuits were originally ship's biscuits that had become unfit for human consumption. In the middle of the nineteenth-century James Spratt invented a special 'dog-cake' to provide something more respectable, if not more appetising, and in 1860 he set up a shop in Holborn, with Charles Cruft — later to achieve fame as the founder of Cruft's Show — as his assistant.

The business grew fast and was eventually bought, as a thriving concern, by Edward Wylam, the proprietor of the popular magazine, *Fun*. With his brother and brother-in-law as partners Wylam developed the business enormously, for both dog and poultry foods. A new factory was built in Henry Street, near London Bridge station, and in 1897 the firm added much larger factories at Poplar and at Newark, New Jersey. The millers were well disposed to the boom in dog biscuits, because this provided a welcome outlet for some of their waste product.

Until 1945 the traditional method of feeding dogs and cats continued to hold the field. A cat received fish offal and, if it was lucky, bread and milk; a dog had to be content with biscuits mixed with table scraps and meat unfit for human consumption, with an occasional bone as a special treat. The foundations of the new world were laid in 1934, when the confectionery business established in Britain two years earlier by the American, Forrest E. Mars, bought Chappel Brothers, a Manchester firm which canned second-grade meat and sold it as pet food, under the brand name of Chappie. Production of Chappie was transferred to the Slough Trading Estate, and by 1939 the annual turn-over of the business, then known as Chappie Ltd., had risen to a modest £100,000 and Kit-E-Kat, a prepared food for cats, had been introduced alongside the pioneering Chappie. The business stagnated during the Second World War, but very soon after 1945 it began to boom. By 1951 sales had reached £1 million, and the capacity of the Slough factory was providing unequal to the demand. The company therefore moved to a site, formerly occupied by a textile firm, at Melton Mowbray, Leicestershire. Sales continued to rise, large new buildings were erected, and in 1953 the factory went over to 24 hours-a-day, 7 days-a-week shiftworking. In 1957 Chappie Ltd. became Petfood Ltd., and later, in 1974, Pedigree Petfoods. A second factory at Peterborough was added in the same year and the company, with sales of more than £100 million each year, is much the largest manufacturer of petfood in Britain, using, in its own words, 'protein that is to a considerable degree a by-product of the human food industry'. Its dominant position has

33 Pedigree Petfoods, Melton Mowbray: exterior of plant, showing part of the former mill and the canal which used to serve it.

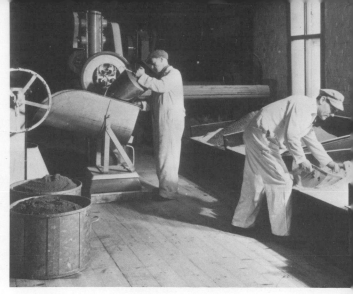

34 Pedigree Petfoods, Melton Mowbray: weighing and blending cereals by hand in the granary, 1951.

35 Pedigree Petfoods, Melton Mowbray: aerial view, 1957, showing the original Paton and Baldwin mill in centre foreground.

36 Pedigree Petfoods, Melton Mowbray: mechanised production and packing of 'Trill' bird seed, 1974.

In the 'primitive' days before 1945, dogs and cats were fed on household scraps, fish-heads and dog biscuits. Those days are long past. In 1977 the average owner spent £1.55 on feeding his dog and nearly £1 on his cat each week, with over 60 per cent of these amounts going on canned pet foods. Since there were 5.3 million dogs and 4.6 million cats, this obviously represented big business.

From the national point of view, the industry fulfils a useful function in two ways — by using raw materials which would otherwise have little use except in the manufacture of fertilisers, and by providing much-needed employment in areas which could otherwise find themselves in difficulties. One can approve or disapprove of the existence of such a huge number of pets in Britain, but feeding them is indisputably part of

the twentieth-century food-processing industry.

Pedigree Petfoods, an American-owned concern, dominates the world market. Its modern factories could perfectly well produce food for human consumption. They rely on large laboratory staffs to supervise the manufacturing process, and they are excellent customers of the Metal Box Co., which supplies them with the cans.

been reached partially as a result of very high expenditure on advertising. Even in 1964 the advertising budget amounted to more than £4 million a year.

The archaeology of Pedigree Petfoods can hardly be called extensive — a factory at Slough now used by another firm and the remnants of an old mill in Melton Mowbray. A comparison between the factory at Slough and the factory at Melton is illuminating, for the difference in size is a dramatic indication of the growth of the British petfood industry in this century.

Frozen Foods

Frozen foods have been available in America for nearly 50 years, but for a good deal less in Britain. In the 1920s an American biologist, inventor and fur-trapper, with the distinctive name of Clarence Birdseye, patented a quick-freezing technique which was eventually to become the basis of a new world-wide industry. The method, in essence, was to place flat packs of food close to two refrigerated plates, one above and one below. In this way the temperature was brought down in a matter of minutes from 32°F to 25°F. This prevented the formation of large ice-crystals, which would break down the cell-structure of the food and spoil it. In 1930 Birdseye opened a factory in Springfield, Massachusetts, and became the first person to sell frozen food commercially. Later, he sold the rights to the General Foods Corporation, which expanded the business throughout the world under the Birds Eye name. The history of Birds Eye in Britain is somewhat curious. In 1938 an understanding was reached with Chivers, the Cambridge company, to try out a freezer provided by the Frosted Foods Corporation, the American quick-freezing subsidiary of the General Foods Corporation. At the same time Wingets, the Rochester firm manufacturing concrete mixers, was licensed to make American freezers. The Second World War, however, brought all British development in this field to a standstill. In 1943 Chivers sold their holding in Frosted Foods to Unilever, and two years later the Ministry of Food allowed Birds Eye, now manufacturing under its own name, to set up a factory at Great Yarmouth. Other factories have since been added at Lowestoft, Hull, Kirkby

and Eastbourne. Today, the British Birds Eye Co. is the largest producer of quick-frozen foods in the world; the sales exceed those of the Birds Eye business in the USA. Some idea of the remarkable growth of this entirely twentieth-century industry can be gained from the fact that in 1946 Britain spent £150,000 on frozen foods and in 1961 £56 million, excluding sales to caterers. By 1979 this total had risen to over £250 million. Fish fingers, the most important innovation brought about by quick-freezing, were first marketed by Birds Eye in 1955.

Chivers are still at Cambridge and Birds Eye are still at Yarmouth, and either or both of these factories can be considered the cradle of quick-freezing in Britain. This seems to be a case, however, of buildings with no more than a symbolic or associative value. Study of them teaches us little about the history of the industry. Rather, the most fruitful fields for historical study of this industry are the experiences of the farmers and fishing companies who have produced the raw materials for the factories, the reactions of restaurants and private customers who have bought its products, the technical equipment and the packaging. The true archaeological relic, worthy of a memorial plaque is not in Britain at all, but at Springfield, Massachusetts.

The Environment of Food Industries

The Birds Eye factories point to a relatively neglected, but very important aspect of industrial archaeology, that is, industrial buildings in their environment. The environmental context of Birds Eye's Grimsby plant, for instance, is partly the immediate surroundings of the processing buildings, partly the port area, and partly the adjacent farmland of Lincolnshire, which produces large quantities of peas for freezing. The port, the farms, and the areas in which the Birds Eye workers live all form the context of the factory and, if he is to do his job properly, the archaeologist needs to be sensitive to changes within this context and to be well informed about them. To concentrate obsessively on the factory itself is to miss much of its true significance. The factory may be the focal point of what one is studying, but to insist on seeing it all

the time in tight close-up is to behave like a horse in blinkers. If one is to become aware of the story as a whole, it is necessary to move constantly between the close-up and the wide-angle view.

The food industry provides some particularly good illustrations of this point. The case of Shredded Wheat is not untypical. An American lawyer, Mr Henry Perky, suffered from acute indigestion, like many Victorian businessmen on both sides of the Atlantic. He discovered — but we do not know how — that wheat, shredded and boiled with cream, solved his problem. He started a factory in Canada to manufacture the wonder-working cereal and in 1908 set up an English company to import and distribute it, with its base at the Aldwych, in London. A successful sales campaign increased British demand to the point at which it became clear that a factory would have to be built in this country. A site was chosen at Welwyn, Hertfordshire, where a new garden city was being planned in the open Hertfordshire countryside. The Shredded Wheat factory, 'a palace of crystal, its great walls of glass held together by slender white-tiled columns of concrete', was opened in 1926 by the Marquis of Salisbury. It was described by the *Daily Mail* of 17 May 1926 as 'a fine example of the new spirit and method which is entering into industry', which meant, translated into ordinary prose, that the factory was light, clean, good to work at, and in surroundings which had a strongly rural flavour. It was, as the Company itself put it, 'an ideal place to produce an ideal food'. The factory served Shredded Wheat well and is still in use, but it no longer has the same effect on the visitor as it did in the 1920s. The open fields have gone and the British home of Shredded Wheat is now surrounded by other industrial plants, producing goods which do not suggest birdsong, sunshine and the countryside at all. Shredded Wheat has inevitably suffered from the change. The factory, considered merely as a manufacturing unit in isolation, is much the same as it always was, but it has completely lost its rural associations. Its image-evoking possibilities are no longer what they were.

The 'new' food industries, particularly those which came to Britain from America, have always set great store by attractive surroundings with plenty of green grass, trees and fresh air. It has not always been easy to manage. In the London area, Heinz, at Harlesden, and Wrigleys, at Wembley, could hardly pretend that they were in the middle of farmland, but they did their best, with a clean, suburban factory in the second case and lawns and trees in the first. In the Wirral, where Heinz eventually situated a larger plant after the Second World War, something closer to the rural ideal has been achieved. It is hardly the fault of Wrigleys that Wembley has gone down in the world since the 1920s, but quite possibly the image of chewing-gum can tolerate decayed suburban surroundings better than baked beans or tomato sauce.

The 'old' food industries, on the other hand, have mostly been content to stay close to the docks and the railways amid the noise and dirt of large cities. There is nothing romantic about the environment of the great majority of flour mills, meat storage depots and sugar factories, which belong to the heavy side of the food industry. The areas surrounding the Tate and Lyle refining plants at Greenock, Liverpool and Silvertown are not ideal places for a walk on a Sunday afternoon in June.

An interesting task for the industrial archaeologist is to observe how firms try to adopt to changes in their environment. Sometimes they have little or no choice; the planning authority makes the decision for them. Sometimes they have simply outgrown their old sites, physically and psychologically. Sometimes they have dreams of grandeur and of going up in the world, or otherwise they have grown tired of urban pressures and costs and opt for a district which seems likely to present fewer problems.

The leading seed-house in Britain, Suttons, is worth examining in this connection. Until very recently the firm was always known as Suttons of Reading, and with good reason. In 1806 John Sutton set up in business in King Street, Reading, as a corn factor and agricultural seed merchant. The firm prospered and received the Royal Warrant in 1858, a privilege it has continued to enjoy ever since. In 1873 the original premises were replaced by extensive offices and warehouses, covering a large area in the Market Place. T.K. Hodder, who visited the firm's headquarters in 1956 on behalf of the Royal Horticultural Society, described the premises in these terms:

The visitor to the Royal Seed Establishment at Reading cannot help but become conscious of the air of old-world courtesy which pervades the place — a rare and refreshing thing today. The traditions which have been handed down from father to son through generations are largely responsible for this atmosphere; however, let nobody misunderstand it and think for even one moment that this firm is old in spirit as well as years. On the contrary, the most modern methods are grasped with eagerness, explored and adapted to the business, and efficiency pervades it throughout its many facets. Few of these visitors will have any conception of the magnitude of the premises behind the Market Place entrance. Over the years, the expansion has gone on, till now when offices, order rooms, warehouses, granaries, packing rooms and laboratories cover nearly five acres in the heart of Reading. The house of Sutton, starting with two or three, was employing seventy by the mid-century and now numbers nearly 700 ... To the traveller, particularly by rail, the Sutton grounds just outside the town and again by the railway at Slough are delightfully familiar. These two trial grounds and experimental stations cover over 150 acres and for much of the year they are a blaze of glorious colour.[2]

This was in 1956; today, both the trial grounds and the headquarters in the Market Place belong to the past. In 1962 the Royal Seed Establishment left its old home in the centre of Reading and moved to its trial grounds on the eastern outskirts of the town. 'These modern buildings', it announced, 'designed on contemporary lines, embody all the features necessary for the economic running of such a great and important seed business. Without doubt these premises are the most up-to-date of their kind in the country.'[3]

In 1976 Suttons left Reading for good and re-established themselves at Torquay. By that time the original building in King Street had been demolished, the Market Place site redeveloped and the business was no longer controlled by the Sutton family. Today, the building of 1962 is used as a general office block, warehouses have been constructed on what were once the trial grounds, and the eyes of passengers by rail are no longer delighted by 'a blaze of glorious colour' as their trains near Reading. The 'Suttons of Reading' label is obsolete; the archaeology of this great business is confined to a 1960s office block on the A4. Fortunately, throughout all its moves and expansion, the firm has maintained an excellent archive of documents and photographs, much of which is now at the Museum of English Rural Life, Reading. Few businesses are easier for the historian to study.

What has happened to Suttons is clear. An important, but by modern standards small, Victorian business has grown into a large, international, twentieth-century concern. Each move has constituted a step away from the nineteenth century towards the twenty-first. Seen in this light Torquay is a more logical centre of operations than Reading. Environmental pollution is not so serious a problem in South Devon as it had become in Reading; labour of the desired kind is more easily available; and the leisure and recreational associations of Torquay provide the raw material for a much better company image than the outer-London suburb into which Reading has been transformed. Furthermore, with the extension of the motorway network to Exeter, transport to and from the South West is no longer as difficult as it once was. The physical context of Sutton's headquarters and activities makes sense of the moves and the new buildings.

On the other hand Reading has continued to be a perfectly suitable base for one of Britain's leading firms of agricultural equipment manufacturers, Gascoignes, which has grown in prominence and prospects as agriculture has become, to a large extent, a branch of engineering. Gascoignes has built its reputation on two types of twentieth-century product: milking machines and silos, which is another way of saying that its fortunes have been closely bound up with those of the British dairy industry.

---

[2] *Journal of the Royal Horticultural Society,* Vol. LXXXI, May 1956, p. 4.

[3] *The Royal Seed Establishment, Reading, 1806-1962* (Reading: Suttons, 1967) p. 3.

Suttons are one of the two largest seed firms in Britain with an important export business. Beginning as corn factors in Reading in 1806, they launched out into the flower and vegetable seed trade in 1837, received the Royal Warrant in 1858 and moved to new offices and warehouses, covering five acres in the centre of Reading, in 1873. In 1962 the business was transferred to a large new building on the firm's trial grounds on the outskirts of Reading, but the twin threats of atmospheric pollution and the eventual construction of a new motorway link caused Suttons to leave Reading and to install themselves more conveniently and expansively at Torquay.

The archaeology at Reading illustrates a number of important economic and social factors in the history of both the industry and the firm. The Market Place site was, by modern standards, congested and gloomy, and represented a serious fire hazard. It occupied a valuable city-centre site in a most wasteful manner and it offered no room for expansion. The replacement of the Sutton complex by a new multi-storey building owned and occupied by the Prudential Assurance Co. is the type of city-centre redevelopment with which everyone is now familiar.

It is also clear that, by the 1950s, it was becoming difficult to find people who were willing to work under the conditions made inevitable by the

Market Place site. Reading was suffering from over-employment and the labour market had become highly competitive. The one advantage possessed by the old site was its central position, which allowed the large number of female employees to do their shopping in the lunch hour. The new building, two miles out, was less popular for this reason, although in all other respects the facilities were immensely superior. Today, Suttons' one remaining link with Reading is a garden centre known nostalgically — but not altogether accurately — as Suttons Garden Centre. It occupies the house and garden of the former manager of the trial grounds.

37 Suttons, Reading: aerial view of Market Place buildings (1873), before demolition in the mid-1960s.

38 Suttons, Reading: survivals of original buildings, Market Place (1873).

39 Suttons, Reading: new headquarters (1962-75).

The business was founded in 1926 by George H. Gascoigne to sell American metal silos, cow stalls and water bowls. He tried selling American milking machines, too, but found the import costs prohibitive and decided to design and market his own machine instead. Gascoignes (Reading) Ltd. was formed in 1927, primarily to develop the milking-machine side of the business. The time was right, because the depressed state of agriculture was encouraging farmers to turn to mechanisation as a way of reducing labour costs. There were, however, technical imperfections to be overcome if the notoriously conservative British farmer was to be persuaded to give up hand milking.

The mechanisation of twentieth-century agriculture has demanded as much patience on the part of innovators as the First Agricultural Revolution had done 150 years earlier. Constant advertising has been essential and a major feature of it in the past was the signed testimonial from satisfied customers. During the early 1930s dairy farmers were writing to Reading about their experiences, and the firm took care to reproduce these letters in their literature for the benefit of other farmers who were still milking cows by hand. Farmers were given the opportunity to convert other farmers by mean of such enthusiastic reports as, 'The milking time was reduced to a little over half the former time with only half the number of milkers. The yields have increased from 10 to 23 lb daily and I am now free from udder troubles', and, 'I feel it is my duty to let you know of one of the cows in our herd — "Logan Mains Ivy 4th", which has just created a new record for an Ayrshire cow in Scotland. This cow has given 2347 gallons in 360 days, and is still giving 4½ gallons daily. "Ivy" has been milked right through with a Gascoigne Milking Machine, so I don't think I need say much more about it.'

The original offices in the Market Place at Reading have been demolished; however, the building into which the Company moved in 1927, at Lynford House, 17 Castle Street, is still there. In 1930, in their continuing search for more space, Gascoignes were to be found at a new address in Castle Street — this building has gone — but in 1933 they were back in Castle Street in larger premises, which still survive. The development of auto-recording milking stalls brought about further expansion and in 1939 a new factory and office block were built in Berkeley Road, Reading, where the Company has remained. If all the buildings at one time occupied by Gascoigne in Reading had survived, a short walk from one to the other would be an excellent and economical way of illustrating the growth of an essential twentieth-century business.

In Britain, as elsewhere in Europe, farmers took a lot of convincing that time is money. As late as 1939, Gascoignes were pushing their machine-milking plants, which weighed each cow's milk separately and allowed the milk to go straight from the cow to be cooled in the dairy, by reminding dairy-farmers that 'Cows come to the milker, and not the milker to the cows. The system may be likened to the endless belt of mass production methods of the factory, which is as it should be, saving countless hours of your men's time! Men's time costs money whereas the cows' does not, a point that is often forgotten!' And Gascoignes' principal competitor, Alfa-Laval, noted that 'even the 1914-18 War, when labour shortage had illustrated the value of milking machines, had not radically altered farmers' thinking.'[4] When they could be persuaded to give up hand-milking in favour of machines, British farmers were unwilling to go beyond the bucket-type, which had to be emptied after each cow had been milked. For many years they would not consider combine plants which took the milk direct from the cow to a single point for processing and storage. The Rotomatic, developed in New Jersey in 1930, had a large circular platform on which 50 cows could be put at one time and revolved in turn to the milking machine; but it was not to the British farmers' taste. Even the simple bucket-machines were slow to catch on. Alfa-Laval sold only 265 of them in 1934, but the formation of the Milk Marketing Board in 1931-3 led to better prices and to a greater willingness to invest in new equipment. Today, it would be hard to find a farm in Britain that milks cows by hand. The practice and the skill that went with it have to all intents and purposes vanished. The bucket-machines, too, have gone, but the milking revolution has taken more than 50 years to accomplish, and the two companies mainly responsible would have gone bankrupt very early if they had been wholly dependent on dairy equipment. Alfa-Laval's milking machines were subsidised in effect by their brewery equipment and by their industrial separators and evaporators.

The growth of this company, like Gascoignes, can be traced in its buildings: two in Grosvenor Road, London, during the 1920s; a new headquarters at Brentford, on the Great West Road, in 1934; war-time factories at Acton and Farnham; and a new factory complex at Cwmbran, near Newport, in 1949. The building at Brentford now functions only as the administrative headquarters and the centre for industrial sales development. It is interesting to note in this connection that when the Brentford headquarters was opened in 1934 it was thought to be inconveniently far from the centre of London, especially for important customers or Board members who, it was felt, could not be expected to make the journey to and from the metropolis by public transport. After much discussion, an 18 h.p. Austin car was bought, at a cost of £372, to provide a comfortable private service between Brentford and the centre of town.

Although they were perfectly satisfactory at the time of construction, the crop of factories built along the North Circular and Great West Roads — and in other parts of the new suburban areas during the 1920s and 1930s — presented great difficulties during the post-war years, when people increasingly abandoned public transport and travelled to work by car. A modern factory allows room for car-parking, although usually not enough room; the previous generation of factories did not, and are consequently ill-adapted to today's requirements. If a company is to be able to grow satisfactorily and to attract and hold the labour force it needs, it is compelled to move further out into the country and often away from the major cities altogether.

[4] *Alfa-Laval: Fifty Years in the U.K.* (Alfa-Laval, 1965).

40 The bucket milker; used throughout the Second World War and until the 1950s, when a centralised storage and weighing system became increasingly widely used.

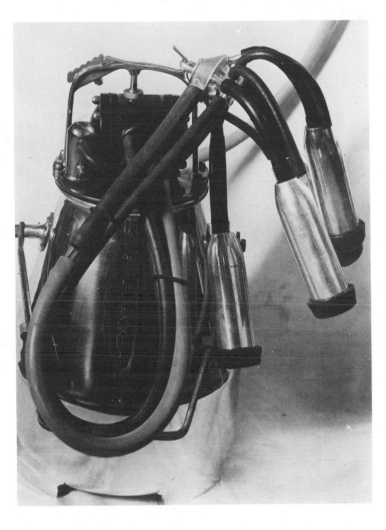

The mechanisation of farming and horticulture distinguishes the First and the Second Industrial Revolutions as much as any other single change. Completely new industries have grown up to supply agriculture with a range of equipment which aims at reducing the number of people employed to the absolute minimum. Modern agriculture could not exist without the internal combustion engine and electricity. There is now no greater farming disaster than a power failure: milking and milk-cooling stop, chickens stifle, automatic glasshouse watering cannot operate. The non-arrival of a fuel tanker has similarly disastrous results. But the archaeology of mechanised agriculture is not plentiful outside museums, and little enough of it survives even there. Old equipment and installations are simply scrapped.

41 Mechanising the cow: Gascoigne milking machines, 1938; each cow's milk being taken to a separate container.

Chapter 3

Retailing and Packaging

The history of retailing in modern Britain has two major aspects. The first concerns ownership and is characterised by the creation of large groups and chains of shops. The second has to do with the appearance, organisation and management of shops and is distinguished by the growth of the self-service system. An essential part of this has been the adoption of packaging for every category of goods — to discourage pilfering, to prevent damage and to allow weighing and pricing to be carried out in advance and behind the scenes. These features of the great changes which have taken place in retailing are closely and intimately connected. Without a highly developed and reliable system of packaging self-service could not have developed as it did, and without large groups, with the finance to experiment and to make substantial investments, self-service would not have come into being.

Retailing

The most important nineteenth-century figure in the development of multiple trading was Jesse Boot. By 1897 he had 126 shops, nearly all in the North and Midlands. A fundamental condition for his success lay in the Victorian fondness for patent medicines, the sales of which quadrupled between 1850 and 1914. During this period there was, for the first time, a substantial number of people with a little money to spare after they had fed, housed and clothed themselves; and patent medicines were, it seems, given a high priority on the list. Doctors' bills were beyond the

means of many people and patent medicines seemed to offer a reasonable alternative. An increasing number of working-class people could read well enough to understand advertisements, and the fact that there was no control whatever over the claims made by the manufacturers of patent medicines provided a heaven-sent opportunity for unscrupulous people to accumulate a fortune in a very short time.

The most successful of the Victorian patent medicine salesmen were Holloway and the Beechams. Both of these geniuses specialised in pills and other medicaments of the panacea type, for which the cost was very low and the profit enormous. There was, however, a more reputable and scientific side to the business in the form of pharmaceutical preparations, which were accurately measured in the laboratory and factory and which could be easily administered. Allen and Hanbury opened their factory in Bethnal Green, London, in 1878 and shortly afterwards Silas Wellcome and Henry Burroughs migrated to England from the USA to introduce the new American 'safe-to-take' system. Burroughs, Wellcome and Co. had an excellent sense of publicity and their business grew so quickly that in the early 1890s they bought Dartford Paper Mills and converted it into a modern pharmaceutical factory. In the early years of this century Boots were buying regularly more than 80 Burroughs Wellcome preparations. Another American firm, Parke, Davies and Co., also played an important part in the development of the British drug industry. They appointed a London agent in 1885 and were manufacturing in Britain two

years later.

Jesse Boot was greatly helped by a legal decision in 1879 which allowed limited liability companies to employ qualified pharmacists. He took advantage of this situation in 1884 at his shop at 16 Goosegate, Nottingham, the founding establishment of the Boots empire, and in that year he began manufacturing on his own account at the back of the shop in Goosegate. In 1887 he set up his first factory and warehouse in an old spinning mill. His shops, however, were more important to him than his factory. He and his wife took a great deal of pleasure in building new shops in medieval and Tudor styles. Exeter, Gloucester, Winchester, Lichfield, York, Shrewbury and other historic towns all received these reproduction facades, and so did a number of towns of no antiquity worth mentioning. A London architect, Morley Horder, was employed to design statues, heraldic devices and stained glass windows to suit the buildings. A number of these Boots-Tudor facades survive, one of the most curious kinds of retailing-archaeology in existence and an interesting clue to the mind of the man who sponsored them.

The Boots business was greatly helped by the National Health Insurance Act, the implementation of which began in 1913. Small, retail chemists found little benefit in the Act because the prescription allowances were very low, but Boots, which had been undercutting the usual rates long before the Act came into force and had attracted a large business as a result, did very well out of it.

Jesse Boot was not, apparently, an

42 Boots, Putney High Street, c. 1910.

Few industries have changed as radically during the present century as those concerned with pharmaceutical products and cosmetics, and the history of Boots in this connection is particularly interesting. Their corner shop in Putney, built in 1907, was very grand and impressive, a temple of variety and reliability in the days when many people were unable to afford visits to the doctor and relied instead on self-medication and chemists' advice. With the creation and development of the National Health Service and the huge increase in High Street rents and property values, however, chemists, including Boots, found it necessary to diversify and sell a much wider range of products. In particular, this process involved a greater dependence on cosmetics and household goods.

43 Interior of an unidentified Boots shop, c. 1910.

over-generous employer and up to the time of his death the firm's manufacturing was carried out in a number of old factories in some of the worst areas of Nottingham. Most of them have now been pulled down. In the late 1920s, however, it was decided to erect a new, large building to house all the headquarters' activities more efficiently and more agreeably. In 1933, two years after Jesse Boot (by then Lord Trent) had died, the present great glass and concrete building at Beeston was opened. The Company's image was greatly improved as a result.

Until the 1960s many of Boots shops retained much the same appearance and arrangement that they had had 30 or 40 years earlier. They had an unmistakeably middle-class atmosphere, emphasised by the lending library which formed part of every major branch. Since then — and partly perhaps as a result of the takeover of the Timothy White chain, which had a more popular image and a more chaotic style — the tone has altered noticeably. The change is an interesting one but since no shop of the vintage period has survived intact, at least as far as the interior is concerned, the difference between the old world and the new can be documented only by photographs and personal memories.

Boots were off to an exceptionally early start in the branch-trading race, but there were soon many close rivals. By 1914 there were 16 firms with more than 200 branches.[1] In the lead were W.H. Smith and the Singer Sewing Machine Co., both of which were to be found in every town of any size, often with more than one branch. The butchery concerns, Eastmans and James Nelson and Sons, each had over 1,000 branches; and the Maypole Dairy, Boots the Chemists, Liptons and the Home and Colonial all had over 500.

Sainsburys were in a rather different league. The founder, John Sainsbury, was a dairyman who started in Drury Lane, London, in 1869. He opened his first new-style grocers, 'all space and clinical opulence', in Croydon in 1882. The choice of town was significant for Croydon at that time was a well-to-do London suburb, if not exactly fashionable, and Sainsbury was after a middle-class trade. The tradition has persisted into the supermarket age and, despite innovations which would have revolted Sainsburys' bourgeois customers of the inter-war period, their shops still carry a good deal of the old image.

Mac Fisheries has had a strange history. In 1919 Lord Leverhulme decided to do something to develop the economy of the islands of Lewis and Harris, then in an ailing condition. Herrings, he thought, were the answer, so he bought a firm of herring drifters and about 300 shops which were supposed to sell, among other fish, the herrings caught by the men of Lewis and Harris. The previous owner of each shop was

[1] For details of this, see Greville Havenhand, *Nation of Shopkeepers* (London: Eyre & Spottiswood, 1970).

usually kept on as manager and was given a more or less free hand to run the business as he wished. Within a few years, however, it had become evident that the original scheme was not working well and a more conventionally controlled and operated chain of shops resulted. Until the 1950s Mac Fisheries continued to sell mainly fish and poultry, but from then on the growing popularity of fish fingers and frozen fish cut increasingly hard into what is known, not very flatteringly, as 'the wet fish market', and the Company moved over into fruit and vegetables. In 1969 Mac Fisheries was receiving only one-quarter of its turnover from fish, and anyone who had been a long time abroad and who went on a shopping expedition in search of fish could have been excused for thinking that he had strayed into the wrong shop. With the arrival of deep-freezing, however, the public demand for what became known as 'wet fish' fell away sharply. Supermarkets took over most of the retail fish trade, and the Mac Fisheries shops, which had been a High Street feature for sixty years, were all closed down. By the autumn of 1980 these once-familiar places had become archaeology.

To anyone born before 1945 the Home and Colonial Stores and the Maypole Dairy are likely to have been a familiar part of the English scene in that person's youth. Both were casualties of a series of mergers which eventually produced Allied Supplies, a giant group in the food trade of which very few people have heard since it operates no shops under its own name. Of the six chains of food shops which were absorbed by Allied Suppliers, only one survives — Liptons. The history of the six spans three generations. The oldest, the Maypole Dairy, was established in 1819 in Birmingham and bought by Home and Colonial in 1924. Liptons, which began its career in Glasgow in 1871, was taken over in 1927 by the margarine concern, Van den Bergh, and then by Home and Colonial in 1931. The Meadow Dairy Co. (1901) was a Newcastle creation. It became part of the Van den Bergh empire in 1912 and in 1929 went to Home and Colonial. Pearks Dairies (1860) was London-based; after a long and successful independent career, it was bought by Meadow Dairy in 1914. Home and Colonial Stores itself was

another London firm. Its first shop was opened in 1885 and in 1919 it was taken over by another international margarine group, Jurgens. In 1959 Home and Colonial, which by that time controlled all six chains, became Allied Suppliers.

What can the archaeology of such a process be said to be, and, more important, what does it tell us that we could not get from a study of the documented history of the individual firms and of the gradual process of the merger? The archaeology of shops can only be the shops and the warehouses that supply them. A considerable number of the buildings which once housed Home and Colonial, Lipton, Maypole, Meadow and Pearks have been bombed out of existence or pulled down during site redevelopment. But many remain — we are, after all, talking of a total of nearly 2,000 shops — and are now shoe-shops, electrical shops, fashion shops and any other kind of shop which can still, today, carry on a successful business in small premises. If, with the help of an old local telephone directory, one locates a shop which was once the Home and Colonial or Liptons, one is likely to be struck by the narrowness of its frontage and by the relatively restricted amount of space inside, by contrast with even the more modest-sized food shops which are now anywhere near the centre of a town. If one then asks why this has happened, one soon becomes aware that what has taken place is not merely a series of take-overs, which could theoretically have led to little more than the closure of redundant shops, but the end of specialisation in the food trade. The dairies and the grocers have gone, and the butchers and the fishmongers are in the process of going, replaced by giant shops selling the full range of foodstuffs. And for this change to be possible the shop with 500 or 1,000 square feet of selling space has had to give way to the shop with 5,000 and 10,000 square feet. Sometimes this has been achieved by extending an existing shop, but more often by starting again with a new building. The archaeology of food shops can make a particularly valuable contribution to the history of retailing.

It is worth pointing out that the rich, or at least the London rich, have been able to enjoy for more than a century the kind of shopping convenience for which the ordinary citizens have had

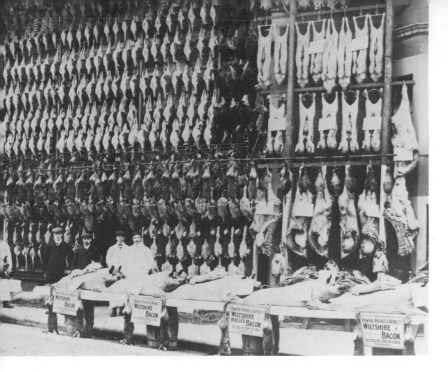

44 Selling meat and poultry in the traditional way: Christmas display in the Market Place, Trowbridge, c.1900.

45 A former Home and Colonial store in Bristol. A casualty of mergers and change, the site was too small for modern food retailing. Now a gift shop.

46 Mac Fisheries, Croydon, 1935. The small frontage and the method of display of fish and poultry are typical of the period.

The predecessors of today's food supermarkets were often remarkably small, sometimes with a frontage of 20 ft. or less. About half of the total width was taken up by a long counter running almost the full length of the shop, with a range of stocked shelves behind. Customers were restricted to the remaining cramped space but, given plenty of assistants, it was an efficient system. Such shops could never be remodelled for self-service and were sold off by the food chains.

Until c.1945 there were, broadly speaking, only two kinds of shops: those selling a single type of product — groceries, meat, flowers and vegetables — and the department stores, every department of which was really a specialised shop. Shops of both types were happy to deliver goods to people's homes, and both depended upon a supply of cheap labour, a requirement which no longer really exists.

After the War, British retailing began to adjust itself to the American system of self-service, not without considerable initial resistance from the public. It demanded an efficient daily flow of goods into the store, much larger working units, smaller staffs in relation to goods sold, and considerable investment.

to wait until the coming of the super-market. Harrods and Selfridges have had their deservedly famous food halls since Edwardian times, with a range of goods at least as wide as that of Sainsburys, Waitrose or Tesco today. The fundamental distinction, of course, is that there is only one Harrods food hall but hundreds of Tescos and Sainsburys. To supply one shop with easy access to Smithfield, Covent Garden and Billingsgate markets and the great London wholesalers was quite different from supplying 200 or more branches scattered throughout the length and breadth of Britain. Without modern packaging and transport systems, a high degree of standardisation and a severe restriction in the number of lines and brands stocked, the food super-market could never have come into being. Compared with Harrods and Fortnum and Mason it may be a second best, but it offers a range of foodstuffs never approached by the provincial foodshops of the 1930s.

Of the three firms which can be said, more than any other, to have brought about the multiple-trading revolution in Britain, two were British-owned from the beginning and one was American. In the 1870s F.W. Woolworth pioneered the walk-around open-display type of store from which everything of the self-service, super-market type has since developed. Woolworth's first store in Britain opened in Church Street, Liverpool, in 1909. During the 1920s Woolworth's were opening stores at the rate of one every 18 days, and they now operate 988 stores in Britain, the largest being at Wolverhampton, which has a mile and a quarter of counter. The firm of Marks and Spencer was registered in 1903. By 1914 it was organised on a national basis and in 1926, when it became a public company, it had 120 stores. In 1977 it had 252 branches and, of the 1976 total sales of £840 million, about 30 per cent derived from food.

Marks and Spencer, like Woolworths, did not come round to the idea of self-service until after the Second World War, and then only in its food department. Tesco's pilot self-service store was a tiny one in St. Peter's Street, St. Albans. It was not a success for some time. Self-service really took off for them in 1950, and by the end of that year they had converted 20 shops to the system. The pressure to do this was increasing steadily. Inflation was

47 A typical Mac Fisheries interior of the 1950s. Most of its open-fronted shops had disappeared by this time, but premises remained small. The emphasis was still on fish, presented in the old way and sold personally by assistants — always men.

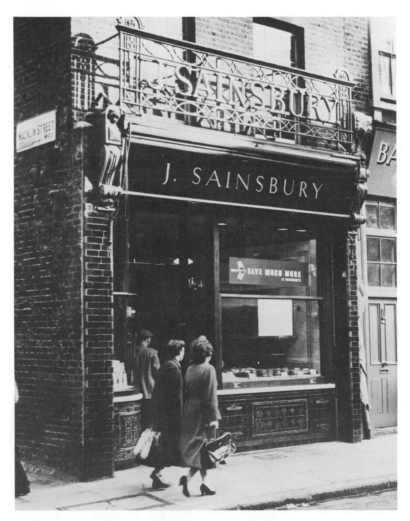

48 Sainsbury, Drury Lane, London. The site was too small for the scale of the Company's activities today, so this little shop was demolished in the 1970s. There was still, in 1981, a similar branch at Peckham Rye.

49 The modern image: packaging and self-service; Waitrose, Ramsgate 1977.

50 Selfridges food hall, 1928: selling the best to the best.

51 Selfridges moves with the times: the food hall today.

34

The changes in the retail food industry are reflected in the parallel revolution in the restaurant field catering for the mass market. So far, the subject has been inadequately studied. Much of the required information, in the form of menus, wine lists, details of staffing, etc., does not survive, but the picture can be partially pieced together from various sources — especially the reminiscences of former workers in the trade. Photographs depicting former interiors of restaurants, cafes, kitchens and hotels — even 20 years ago — are quite rare and probably unrepresentative.

The recipe, as it were, of one company — Berni Inns — has been to provide an environment in which a very broad sweep of the population can feel at home, relaxed. Like the food, this environment is deliberately unsophisticated, and it has been an almost unqualified commercial success — to the taste of the C and D social classes at least.

52 The Old Manor Hotel, Bracknell. Berni Inns bought an old-established hotel and transformed it to fit their image, closing the unprofitable hotel and installing bars and restaurants in the rest of the property.

53 The Berni Inn of the 1970s: the furnishings, decor and style, typified by Gayton Hall, Harrow.

pushing up prices and wages faster than profits and the only way to change the situation was, as the Americans had already found, to reduce staff costs. The first Tesco store was at Burnt Oak in 1932 and the second, soon after, at Becontree. It is interesting to note that the founder of Tesco, Sir John Cohen, always preferred to establish his shops in the new suburban areas around London — Neasden, Rickmansworth, Pinner, and the rest. He worked inwards towards the centre of the city during the late 1950s and 1960s, and at the same time extended his attention to the provinces on a considerable scale.[2] He was a developer's man, not a High Street man.

Tesco can claim the credit for three important innovations in British retailing. The first was Tesco House (1934-5), Angel Road, Edmonton, the first modern food warehouse in the

country with centralised stock control and facilities to serve up to 200 branches. The second was the idea of a store-chain having its own brands. Tesco was doing this in the early 1930s, years ahead of its competitors, with tea, sardines, coffee essence, soap, jam, peas, floor polish, evaporated milk, custard and jellies. The third innovation was the freezing and jam-making business, developed in connection with fruit farms at Goldhanger, Hertfordshire, which Sir John bought during the Second World War. He sold this in 1957 to Mitcham Foods, an Express Dairy subsidiary. Later, Goldhanger Fruit Farms was bought by Schweppes, which by that time controlled Chivers and Hartleys. To-day, much expanded, it is part of the Cadbury-Schweppes Group and the largest canner of 'own-label' fruit and vegetables in Britain, producing five

million cases for Woolworths, Fine Fare, Key Markets and other chains.

In the case of such a rapidly changing system of retail distribution and self-service stores, archaeology has very little to add to the historical record. At the beginning of 1977 Tesco, to consider this group alone, had one hypermarket, 53 superstores, 393 supermarkets, 195 self-service food stores, 63 separate 'Home N'Wear' stores and 19 separate furniture stores. None of these had existed in 1945, although in some cases a new store had been built on an old Tesco site, and none had fittings more than five years old. In this situation, entirely typical of postwar retailing, the archaeologist has little material with which to work. The history of Tesco and its contemporaries can be built up only from the memories of members of its staff and of the public, from trade periodicals and from such records as the company itself may happen to have preserved, which, in the experience of the present authors, usually amount to very little.

[2] It is interesting to note, as an indication of the difficulties which are frequently experienced in documenting the history of our own times, that in 1976 Sir John Cohen announced that, even after the most diligent searching, he had failed to discover a photograph of his first shop at No. 54 Watling Avenue, Burnt Oak. In the hope of finding something, he made a characteristic offer of '£25 worth of grocery, fresh foods and Home N'Wear merchandise' to anyone who could produce a photograph of the shop when he had it.

Packaging

Developments such as those outlined above could not have occurred without corresponding changes in other areas of industry. The growth in the canning industry is one of these, an industry which belongs almost entirely to this century, although 'An important trade', as the 1895 edition of *Mrs. Beeton's Book of Household Management* noted, 'has sprung up within the last quarter of a century in tinned food of various kinds.' It is necessary, however, to make a distinction between canning and putting commodities into tins. Canning is used to prevent food from going bad; tins, which may or may not be airtight, for convenience in transport and storage. In Victorian and Edwardian times a number of home-based industries, such as biscuits, tobacco, cocoa and paint, were good customers for firms making tin-boxes, but the business was on a small scale. It was only the development of colour printing applied directly to the tin which turned tin-box making into an attractive business proposition. By 1914 there were maybe six firms which provided a complete service of design, printing and manufacture. None of them had a capital of more than £150,000 or sales of more than £100,000. In 1922 four of the leading tin-box makers — Hudson Scott, Atkins, Barclay and Fry, and Henry Grant — decided to merge. The new company, Allied Tin Box Makers, later changed its name to Metal Box and Printing Industries. It remained a private company throughout the 1920s.

By 1925 the Americans had been using automatic canning machinery for 30 years. It was unknown in Britain until 1927. In 1929 it was believed that two of the largest American can-making companies were planning to set up factories in Britain. The threat was successively fought off by Metal Box which decided to establish itself as a can-manufacturer on the American scale. A new factory was built at Perrywood, Worcester, to make 'open-top' cans, i.e. cans which leave the factory with their tops open, ready for filling and sealing at the cannery. When Metal Box first went into the open-top business in 1930 they sold 86 per cent of their cans to canners of fruit and vegetables and another 8 per cent to Heinz, for baked

54 Metal Box Co., Reading; headquarters office building.

The Metal Box headquarters, completed in 1974, is one of the few architecturally distinguished industrial buildings to have been designed in Britain since the Second World War. It is also a perfect symbol of a Second Industrial Revolution manufacturing concern. By achieving a degree of technical and managerial efficiency much above the national average, the Company has obtained 75 per cent of the total British business in metal containers. The field in which it operates — packaging — is violently attacked and as strongly defended. Those who attack it accuse it of adding unnecessary expense to the process of distribution, of using scarce raw materials extravagantly, of causing much of the litter pollution problem, and of helping to standardise taste in

food and drink at a very mediocre level. Those who defend it say that without modern methods of packaging and preservation the worldwide problem of supply and demand would be much worse than it is and that many products would find their market seriously, possibly disastrously, restricted.

With these considerations in mind, it was essential that the new Metal Box headquarters should help the Company's image. It had to feel like the modern age, yet be unlikely to date to any alarming extent. It had to be extremely well constructed and finished — no company in any way concerned with the food industry can afford to have either buildings or lorries which look anything but spick and span — and therefore expensive. It also had to feel and look like the centre of an empire, an image which its circular, hub-like shape reflected. The factories are elsewhere.

beans. By 1937, however, the position was quite different, with 45 per cent going to milk and cream, 19 per cent to peas, 8 per cent to other vegetables, 16 per cent to fruit, 6 per cent to soups, 4 per cent to meat and 2 per cent to miscellaneous products. When war broke out in 1939 Metal Box had the most complete monopoly in British industry. They were the main force behind the development of canning in Britain, and for this reason they were worried about the quality of some of the goods that the canning industry was offering to the customer, especially by the chain stores, which, it was said, were interested in nothing

but price.

After the War the can-making industry had to face up to four new trends: the enormous growth of the petfood market, the development of aerosols, the introduction of plastic film and the expansion of frozen food production. The newer and faster-growing methods of food preservation had no use for tins at all. Their requirements for packaging were paper, board, foil and plastics, often in combination. The heyday of the can is already in the past, and for the past 20 years Metal Box have been safeguarding themselves against such a possibility by buying their way into the other

55 British Cellophane, Bridgwater, Somerset.

This section of the factory is substantially as it was when production started in 1937. As the town's pioneering Second Industrial Revolution industry, British Cellophane had to cultivate its image with some care. In the depressed 1930s these buildings told Bridgwater quite unmistakably that a major concern, intent on recouping a large investment, had arrived in its midst. Bridgwater had entered the twentieth century.

packaging fields. It is quite conceivable that the next 10 years will show an increase, possibly a considerable increase, in what one might be permitted to call tin-can archaeology, buildings put up to meet the demand for cans during the 1940s and 1950s and made surplus to requirements during the late 1970s and 1980s. Cans are bulky things to transport and customers carry very small stocks, so that daily deliveries are essential. If even one day's delivery is interrupted or delayed by a break-down or bad weather there could be serious problems at the canning plant. It is therefore prudent to build the can factory as close as possible to the customers' works. Between 1946 and 1961 Metal Box followed such a policy with new factories at Portadown, Sutton-in-Ashfield, Wisbech, Leicester, West Loughton, Carlisle, Rochester and Arbroath. The problem is not only one of declining demand. There is always a chance that a major customer may decide to make his cans on his own premises, which a number have done in the past. The effect of this can be disastrous for Metal Box and for this policy of decentralisation. In 1965, for example, General Milk Products, packers of Carnation Milk, decided to make all their own cans like their associated companies on the Continent and in the USA. They were among Metal Box's biggest customers and the plant at Carlisle had been set up mainly in order to supply them. By 1965, when the break came, they were taking 180 million cans a year from the Carlisle factory, and the removal of their custom left Metal Box with what was virtually a redundant production centre. There is no reason to suppose, however, that such buildings will

necessarily be lost to packaging or to the Metal Box Group. Once the decision is taken to convert them to the production of paper, card, foil or plastic packs, their market territory is greatly extended. Only cans keep them local.

There is no better way of getting an impression of the vast range of customers catered for by the non-can packaging companies than by visiting the Bristol showrooms of the Dickinson-Robinson Group. The Robinson family established themselves as papermakers in Bristol in 1844. By 1914 they had become a large concern, through concentrating on the production of wrapping-papers and containers for which a considerable market existed in Bristol itself, with its important chocolate, tobacco and cigarette industries. Since then they have become established in every branch of film and paper-based packaging. Bristol is also the home of Mardon, Son and Hall, now part of the Imperial Group, which grew big with the cigarette industry and specialises in folding cartons and colour printing. Bristol contains several veteran buildings once used by Mardons, although they have been sadly reduced by demolition. One, occupied until recently, contained a library of all the cigarette cards printed by Mardon's in the years up to 1939, together with the studio where they were designed.

Packaging without cellophane is hardly conceivable nowadays, but its production on a large scale is comparatively recent. Cellulose film, patented in Switzerland under the name of Cellophane, was available in small quantities in 1912, but the cost was

high and the material was not moisture-proof. Research carried out by Du Pont in the USA during the 1920s succeeded in producing a moisture-proof film, which widened the scope of its uses for packaging. In Britain, meanwhile, Courtaulds had been developing a viscose film which they put on the market in 1931 under the name of Viscacelle. In 1935 the original Swiss company, La Cellophane S.A., combined with Courtaulds to set up British Cellophane Ltd. and to manufacture its products under the trade-mark *Cellophane*. A factory was built at Bridgwater, Somerset, and in 1937 it marketed its first film.

Bridgwater had no previous experience of Second Industrial Revolution industries. It was an area of high unemployment and there are many people who remember the hope which the new factory brought to people who had been without work for a long time 'It was', recalled William Hill who was employed by the contractors there when he was 16, 'such an exciting sort of thing to happen in the district that rumours were really wild. One thing I remember quite well is that there was a big haulage contracting company which used to come in quite often; they were called the Ex-Army Transport Company, and that led to the belief that it was to be a secret government factory.'[3] The process-workers who were recruited to get the factory going were mostly in their mid-twenties. Most of them stayed with the Company; the labour turnover at British Cellophane has always

[3]Conversation with the author, 24 November 1976.

been low. When someone left it was usually within the first six months and because he found it difficult to adjust to shift-working for which there was no tradition in the district. Mr Hill, who had spent his whole working life with the Company and, at the time of writing, was Works Personnel Officer, said that the situation had changed in recent years: 'We now find sons coming in for employment with their fathers having already worked shifts, and the position is considerably better.'

Before British Cellophane arrived Bridgwater was a small market town in an agricultural area, with a number of old, run-down, brick- and tile-works to provide what industrial employment there was. Its inhabitants had to get used not only to having a large and rather smelly modern factory in their midst, but also to the completely strange pattern of family life necessitated by 24-hours-a-day, 7-days-a-week shift working. Thirty years later the nearby nuclear power station at Hinkley Point presented another group of local workers with the same problem, but by that time the Second World War had done much to accustom West Country towns like Bridgwater to the kind of social changes which Second Industrial Revolution industries brought in their train.

During the 55 years of its existence the products of the Bridgwater factory have changed considerably. Plastic as well as cellulose film is now made there, together with bonded fibre fabrics. With more than 3,000 people employed at the works, British Cellophane provided a living for one-in-three of the town's working population. This was a satisfactory state of affairs so long as the demand for packaging materials continued to grow, but the one-industry town is particularly vulnerable to recession and economic change.

The close connection between packaging and self-service retailing has already been noted, but a distinction should be made between, on the one hand, packaging which serves mainly to keep goods clean, to measure and price items in advance, and to prevent pilfering and waste, and, on the other, packaging which keeps perishable goods in a usable condition. The link between the two types of packaging is that both can be used to carry advertising material. The introduction of plastic and viscose film made all these aims easier to achieve, but it did not in itself usher in the revolution.

What happens to bread is particularly worth considering in this connection. No other foodstuff which is eaten exactly as one buys it receives the amount of handling that bread does and it would be comforting, but alas untrue, to believe that all these pairs of hands are clean. By the time it reaches one's table or breadboard the unwrapped loaf is not always a good candidate for microscopic examination. In the days of the small bakery the only people to touch the loaf, the bun or the cake might be the baker himself and the customer, but with the extension of large-scale baking and retailing the perils multiplied. The first wholesale baker was the United Co-operative Baking Society of the Clydeside, founded in 1869. By 1900 most of the larger retail co-operatives in Scotland were receiving daily deliveries of bread from the central bakery in Glasgow. The only other big bakery and retailing organisation in the nineteenth century was the Aerated Bread Co. in London, which started business in 1862, and added catering to breadmaking during the 1880s and 1890s, with 100 tea-shops by 1900. J. Lyons and Co. (1894) operated a similar but smaller business.

During the 1920s and 1930s large wholesale baking firms increased their share of the market, but still mainly on the basis of unwrapped loaves. The first really practicable bread-wrapping machine was introduced in 1925; and the first sliced-bread, mostly wrapped, was being sold in Britain in 1928. Mechanical wrapping — until the 1960s this was usually in waxed paper — allowed for brand-names, and this habit grew steadily during the immediate post-war period. The importance of large-scale baking should not, however, be exaggerated. About half the bread and the flour confectionery sold in 1950 was baked and sold by the individual master-baker. The present figure is about one-third, but there are strong signs of a consumer rebellion against the idea of all bread being wrapped and sold in supermarkets, and very recently the number of individual bakers has shown an unexpected and unplanned rise. The smaller unit seems to be on the way back, but whether this is a temporary trend or a permanent development remains to be seen.

Whether the department store has also had its day is difficult to decide on present evidence. Many have closed during the last few years and nearly all now form part of large groups, something which would have been unthinkable in the nineteenth century. The House of Fraser includes Harrods, D.H. Evans, Barkers, and Dickins and Jones in London, as well as a number of provincial stores. The John Lewis Partnership has 17 department stores, four specialist shops and the Waitrose food chain. Debenham's has over a hundred stores, including Debenham and Freebody, Marshall and Snelgrove, Harvey Nicholls, Plummer Roddis and Bobbys, as well as the 70 Cresta shops. All these stores have their history, if not their archaeology, and, in the case of the larger towns, it is worth investigating the name under which the present Debenham store traded 10 or 15 years ago. In nearly every case it was not Debenham. We are involved here with merger archaeology, a significant feature of the Second Industrial Revolution.

Chapter 4

Building Construction and Housing

Two rather different projects — the building of the first rural council houses in Britain, at Montacute, Somerset, and the construction of the Ritz Hotel, London — will serve to introduce some of the themes and significant developments in this area of Second Industrial Revolution archaeology.

In 1909 the Liberal Government's Housing Act empowered local authorities for the first time to build and let houses, and to compel owners of substandard houses to carry out improvements. The situation in Montacute was very bad. The majority of the working-class houses there belonged to the Montacute House estate or to farmers. An inspection carried out on behalf of the Parish Council showed that one cottage, with one bedroom, was vacant; 22 cottages had one bedroom each; 18 had no garden; and 13 had no through ventilation. Altogether 40 houses were condemned as being unfit for human habitation. Armed with this evidence and supported by the fact that houses were urgently needed by masons employed at the Ham Hill quarries, the Yeovil District Council was pressed to adopt the Housing Act.

It was decided to build 12 houses to begin with. They were completed and occupied by October 1912, the material being dressed Ham Hill stone. Each house had a large garden, three bedrooms, sewage, water and gas. The cost was £162 per house, including land, and the rent was 5s. 9d. per week. (The price was kept low by building the houses in two terraces, known together as Fullfoot Terrace.) Subsequent improvements have included the installation of electricity

and hot water and the conversion of one of the bedrooms to a bathroom. It is interesting to note that the next council houses in Montacute, built nine years later, cost six times as much. A plaque placed in the garden wall of one of the houses records that: 'These houses erected in 1912 were the first built by the Yeovil Rural District Council and were among the first Council Houses in the country.'

To the archaeologist, the cottages at Montacute are as important a piece of pioneering as the Ritz Hotel in London — completed in 1904 and the first completely steel-framed building in the metropolis. The negotiations between the Parish Council, the District Council and the Government over Fullfoot Terrace are as significant in their way as the fact that the architect of the Ritz was compelled as a result of the London building by-laws to make the external walls of full load-bearing thickness, even though they carried no load at all. The steel-frame, so far as the authorities were concerned, was little more than an architect's toy and certainly no sub-

stitute for solid blocks of stone. The feature common to both these projects is their significance for the future. Both were significant 'firsts' and as such have claims on the archaeologist's attention. Nevertheless, both remain firmly a part of the preceding industrial age in so far as their substantial construction is concerned, and both *could* have been built considerably earlier as a result.

Peter Jones' store (1936) in Sloane Square, London, on the other hand, could not have been built in the nineteenth century. It contains aluminium, which is a Second Industrial Revolution material, a large area of glass which, in turn demands modern methods of heating and ventilation, an extensive system of lifts and escalators, and without electric lighting and telephones it would have been unworkable. The Ritz had lifts, electric light and telephones from the beginning but the building could, at a pinch, have functioned without them. Peter Jones

56 Fullfoot Terrace, Montacute, Somerset.

57 Ritz Hotel, Piccadilly (1904): the first completely steel-framed building in London.

By the end of the nineteenth century every aspect of the construction of buildings was tightly controlled, the basis being the London Building Act of 1894 and its later amendments. Local authorities throughout Britain came to use the very conservative London Act as a model for their own by-laws, with the result that it was hard to get acceptance of new materials and techniques. The obstacles which architects and builders had to overcome are illustrated by the case of the Ritz Hotel. The load of the building was completely taken by steel columns, but as a result of the bye-laws the external walls had to be constructed of load-bearing masonry, even though they carried no load at all. The earlier Savoy Hotel (1898) has load-bearing walls and no steel frame. Its original terra-cotta facing disintegrated and in 1912, when a large extension was added, it was entirely refaced with reconstituted stone, one of the first major buildings to be finished in this way.

Once architects had learnt to design buildings in which the weight was carried on a steel or concrete frame, instead of on the external walls, it became possible to use much lighter materials for cladding. Glass was an obvious choice. The first building in Britain in which this was done in a thorough-going way was Peter Jones' store in London, where the facade consists of vertical ranges of metal windows, fixed between steel mullions. The casements open to allow the windows to be cleaned from inside. Glass-faced buildings of this kind became practicable only after the invention of the metal extrusion process in 1893 and the development, early in this century, of hot-rolling processes for producing light metal sections.

58 Peter Jones store, Sloane Square (1936): an interesting precursor of the glass curtain-wall technique.

59 Savoy Hotel, London (1898).

60 A tobacco warehouse: Canon's Marsh, Bristol (1922); built of reinforced concrete using the Hennebique technique.

could not, any more than the Woolworth building in New York could have done. In both cases the architect assumed that electricity, lifts and air-conditioning were available and constructed his building around them. This, more than anything else, is what makes them truly modern buildings, instead of mere exercises in style and fashion.

Building Materials

We may look first at the introduction and development of some of the more important of these building materials. Based at Ilminster, Somerset, the Wharf Lane Concrete Works, now known as Minsterstone, illustrates very well the transition from the old building world to the new. It was founded during the First World War by a local builder named Hutchings, who had a passion for quality. Much earlier than most people he saw that natural stone was pricing itself out of the market and he believed that artificial stone or, to use the trade term, reconstructed stone, could take its place. Reconstructed stone can take two forms. One can either cast it — 'it' being a concrete made from whatever crushed stone aggregate one chooses to employ — in solid blocks or panels, to any shape, or one can use it as a facing, bonded during manufacture to a base of coarse concrete. The concrete should be mixed with great accuracy and packed carefully into the moulds, but if it is done badly it will disintegrate as it weathers, a fate which has overtaken a great many buildings faced

in this way. If, however, the workmen are set high standards and are supervised properly, the result can be as good as natural stone and in some ways superior to it.

Wharf Lane made its name during the 1920s and 1930s with a wide range of domestic items in this high-quality concrete and especially with the famous Minster fireplace. Men were sent all over the country measuring up work and fitting the finished product, but the eye of the boss was always on them, ready with a sharp tongue to deal with any imperfection. A retired employee, John White, who began working there in 1914, straight out of school remembers the main cause of trouble. The moulder's job was (and still is) to put wet concrete into the mould, ram it down as hard and as tightly as he could and then, when the mould was full, smooth the top over to produce a fine finish. In the 1920s and 1930s he said:

> they didn't have what they've got today, air rammers. It was all done by hand, you see. If you got so far up the mould and you went to the toilet, you came back and you forgot where you'd left off ramming. So next morning, when you take that stone out, you've got a beautiful stone, but right the way around it you've got a patch that's been missed. Instead of a nice, fine, tight piece of stone, you've got a big rib all the way round where it hadn't been touched.[1]

[1] Conversation with the author, 18 August 1976.

Minsterstone has been chosen for special consideration here, not so much for itself, although its story is full of interest, as because it is a microcosm of what has been happening to the building industry as a whole during the present century. The basic problem which has faced the industry is how to reconcile productivity with quality. In most instances the outcome, if not the decision, has been that quality has been allowed to slip. Roofs leak, walls stain, surfaces break up, woodwork shrinks or fails to fit, cracks appear in distressing places and finishes quickly get grubby. The buildings rarely fall down, although with untried methods of construction, such as concrete beams built with high alumina cement, they sometimes do; but after a few years, if not at the beginning, it is better, for one's peace of mind, not to look at them closely.

To some extent this situation has come about as the result of increasingly elaborate construction equipment, which allows work to be carried out faster and on a much greater scale. Size and speed are not easy to reconcile with quality, as we all know to our cost. Ronan Point and other tower-blocks of flats may consequently fall down, whereas Montacute's 1912 council houses, built in the traditional way of local stone, are to all appearances as good now as they were when they were first put up. One should not, however, over-generalise or become too cynical. Modern equipment can, under the right circumstances, produce a better job. At Minsterstone, for instance, the men with long experience are convinced that what they call 'the air-rammers', i.e. hand-operated rammers driven by compressed air, not only allow the concrete to be packed into the moulds more reliably, more quickly and, of course, with far less effort, but also make it possible to make much larger units. With electric and pneumatic power at their command these men can now cast components weighing up to 12 tons, and with exactly the same high finish as in the old days of hand-labour. 'In the early days it would have made us shake to think of it', one old servant of the Company said.

Supposing one assumes — and it is a fair assumption — that architects, builders and civil engineers have been confronted with the following conditions since the beginning of the First World War, or, in some cases, rather earlier:

1. a shortage of skilled labour;
2. the increasing cost of all labour, skilled or unskilled;
3. the unpopularity of working outdoors in all weathers;
4. Customers whose main concern is with cost per square foot, but who all too frequently want something cheap to look prestigious;
5. the possible need for the building to be used for quite a different purpose in 10 or 20 years' time;
6. certain minimum standards enforced by local by-laws and other regulations.

One would therefore expect innovations in building to reflect these demands, although there is always the freakish or exceptional customer to whom the usual rules do not apply. Buildings of any period always contain technical surprises, and many technical questions can therefore only be answered, or indeed thought about at all, when major structural changes involved in demolition or modernisation are taking place. Until that moment many of the details of construction and of the materials employed are likely to remain hidden from view and quite possibly unsuspected.

Plasterboard

Plasterboard is one such material. This useful invention, consisting of gypsum plaster sandwiched bewteen two sheets of tough paper, originated in the USA.[2] Augustus Sachett's first patent was taken out in New York in 1894, and by 1910 plasterboard was being widely used in America. Its appearance in Britain was delayed by trade union opposition and little was seen of it here before the 1920s. Apart from union difficulties there were two important reasons for its earlier acceptance in the USA and Canada. One was a chronic shortage of skilled plas-

[2] See 'The History of Plasterboard', in *The Gypsum Journal*, April, June and September 1958.

terers and the other was the popularity of timber homes for which plasterboard ceilings and walls provided a much-needed fire-retarding lining.

During the 1930s, in the heyday of the speculative builder in Britain, plasterboard was widely used as a substitute for the old-fashioned lath and plaster in party-walls, as anyone who has tried to drive a nail into a wall of one of these houses knows very well. During the Second World War it was one of the few building materials to be in good supply and it was much used for repairing bomb-damaged premises, and for lining huts. In the years immediately after the War it was an indispensable element of both temporary and permanent houses.

Since its first introduction plasterboard has been greatly improved. One of the earliest developments was to cover one side of the board with a type of paper which would either hold a thin skimming of plaster, to give a jointless surface, or which could be finished with a coat of paint or distemper. In the second case, the joints between the boards had first to be taped or filled with plaster. Other recent techniques have been to fix plasterboard directly to brick or breeze-block walls by means of adhesive or screws and, by using boards with tapered or recessed edges, to leave the joints deliberately unfilled, providing a decorative feature, or to fill them with plaster, without a skim-coat being needed over the whole wall.

The original plasterboard had poor thermal insulation. This was overcome by giving it a facing of aluminium foil on one side. The first instance of this in Britain was in 1949 when the Ministry of Works built 94 houses as married quarters in Canterbury for the War Office. This precedent was quickly followed up. Aluminium-backed board was also used by the National Coal Board in the years 1952-4 when it built a large number of houses in Staffordshire. On major contracts like this the panels were usually made in temporary factories near the site in order to minimise breakage and damage. Admirable as it may be in other respects, plasterboard does not stand up well to rough treatment, and the occupants of a house may not be aware that its walls are lined with plasterboard until a child charges against it and makes a nasty hole.

In 1947 the Sound City film studios at Shepperton, fairly near London,

pioneered a new kind of panel consisting of two plaster faces separated by a honeycomb core. These eventually developed into the well-known Bellrock panels, which are widely used as partitions and wall-linings and can be as much as six inches thick, making it possible for them to be load-bearing. During the 1950s the manufacturers began to market partition units which were made up of two layers or plasterboard enclosing a honeycomb core of plastic-coated cardboard. Plasterboards are also made as room-high planks, to fit into aluminium runners on the floor and ceiling. Apart from its relative fragility, which should not be exaggerated, plasterboard has the serious defect of being a poor insulator against noise, as many of the people who live in post-1945 flats have found to their cost and embarrassment. The difficulty has to a large extent been overcome by using glass fibre as an insulating material.

Fibre-Glass

The manufacture of glass fibre, a completely new industry in its own right, was begun in a small way by chance at Glasgow in 1930. In 1944 the Pilkington subsidiary, Fibreglass Ltd., built a glass wool plant at Ravenhead, St. Helens, and the serious marketing of glass fibre in Britain started at this point. Its range of applications now extends far beyond insulation. It is now increasingly used in concrete technology, both for formwork and as a reinforcing material. Fibre-glass moulding allows concrete to be cast and finished with great accuracy, and alkali-resistant fibre-glass reinforcement seems likely to bring about almost as great a change in the use of concrete as a building material as iron and steel did in the last century. Glass-reinforced cement and concrete is creating many new building components and replacing some traditional ones.

Asbestos

One material which fibre-glass may well replace, at least for some purposes, is asbestos, which has become recognised as potentially dangerous to the people who have to work with it. Asbestos, as a commercially useful material, has a history of a little more than 100 years. In the 1870s this fibrous mineral was being spun and woven into fire-resistant fabrics. The fibres which were too short for

Turner Bros. were among the firms which pioneered the manufacture of asbestos-cement products in Britain. Their works at Trafford Park, Manchester (1913) and at Widnes (1917) were notable development centres for the techniques required to make asbestos-cement sheets and pipes sufficiently reliable for commercial purposes.

The Empire Stadium, Wembley, roofed with Trafford Tiles, is one of the best-known monuments to the new industry.

61 Empire Stadium, Wembley (1923-4): a monument to asbestos-cement roofing.

62 Turner Bros. asbestos-cement factory, Trafford Park: one of the few early Trafford Park companies to remain on its original site.

spinning were thrown away as waste, but in 1893 an Austrian textile manufacturer, Ludwig Hatschek, began experiments to see if they could be used as a bonding agent for a new type of building material. In 1900 he succeeded in making the first asbestos-cement sheets, using a mixture of 85 per cent cement and 15 per cent asbestos, and feeding this as a slurry into a Foudrinier continuous paper-making machine adapted for the purpose. By 1910 asbestos-cement was being made in 10 countries, including Britain.

In 1911 British Fibro-Cement began production at Erith, Kent, and two years later Turner Brothers established their asbestos cement factory at Trafford Park, Manchester, making flat sheets, 'Aegis' slates and corrugated roofed tiles, known as Trafford Tiles. Some of the earliest 'Aegis' slates were used for roofing the Dunlop Cotton Mill at Castleton, near Rochdale: they are still in good condition. Trafford Tiles were made for a number of important contracts in the early 1920s, including the Empire Stadium at Wembley (1923-4). These corrugated sheets were considerably smaller than those in use today, with only five corrugations.

In 1917 a factory was started at Widnes with Swiss capital and machinery. New machinery was installed in 1923 and this was used to make corrugated sheets of the same size and profile with which we are familiar today. The first asbestos-cement pipes were made at Widnes in 1927. Soon afterwards the Ministry of Health approved asbestos-cement water-pipes as an alternative to the traditional cast-iron, and large quantities of these pipes were supplied to local authorities during the 1930s. Their resistance to corrosion was found to be superior to that of iron and

their jointing was flexible enough to absorb settlement or vibration without their cracking or becoming loosened. Asbestos-cement sewer-pipes, first laid in Britain in 1961, have also been found to be very satisfactory, as well as gutters and down-pipes which have, of course, the great advantage of requiring no painting.

Asbestos-cement products are, unfortunately, heavy and bulky in proportion to their value, so that the cost of transport is an important factor. There is also a more-than-average danger of cracking and chipping during handling. For these two reasons it has not been found

economic to centralise manufacturing, as the brickmakers have done, and accordingly there are a number of factories, well-scattered over Britain.

Plastics

Plastics can be transported and handled with very little risk of damage. The market for plastics in building is both considerable and expanding. In West Germany it is the biggest market of all, and in the USA it is second only to packaging. Its main use so far has been for what builders call 'rain water goods', i.e. guttering and down-pipes. Until the 1940s these were almost invariably of cast-iron, although there had been some pre-war experimenting with aluminium and, even more, with asbestos-cement. The war-time shortage of metal provided an incentive to use other materials wherever possible. This usually meant asbestos-cement, large quantities of which were employed to take the rain water away from military camps, hospitals, war-workers' hostels and other priority buildings. Once the War was over plastics began to be used for this purpose. The early makes were not well-designed and the range of colours left much to be desired, but by the 1960s there had been great improvements and the market began to grow fast. Translucent plastic roofing panels also found customers without difficulty. They were, unlike glass, virtually unbreakable; they were light to carry and easy to fix, and they could be made to the same size and profile as sheets of aluminium or corrugated asbestos-cement. For some years they had an unfortunate tendency to yellow in sunlight, but this disadvantage now belongs to the past.

The fire-hazard remains, however. Plastics are by their nature combustible, and the ever-conservative British building industry has shown itself more cautious about the perils of plastics than of traditional materials, notably timber. For many years the fire risk involved in the use of plastics has been under investigation by the Rubber and Plastics Research Association, which is also concerned with long-term research into a problem which continues to worry builders and architects — the ability of plastics to withstand constant exposure to the weather.

Until now, plastics have been used mainly in the finishing sectors of the building industry. The possibilities for plastics in structures are still largely untested, if not unexplored although much research is in progress. An increased use of plastics in building is likely to come partly through improvements in the properties of organic polymers and partly by combining plastic with other materials, such as glass fibre. Fully supported plastic sheet makes a perfectly acceptable roof-covering, and suitably reinforced plastic may in time provide a substitute for structural timber. Other possible applications, still in the experimental stage, are for rapid-setting cement-less concrete and for acoustic insulation foam.

Aluminium

Aluminium has had a long start over plastics, in an age when a few decades is a very long time. It is only since 1945 that aluminium has been generally accepted as a building material, although the first applications of the metal in this field were made in the 1890s, very soon after commercial production became possible. More will be said about the history and archaeology of production later in this chapter. Meanwhile, one can usefully identify one or two milestones. The dome of the church of San Gioacchino, Rome, was covered in aluminium sheet in 1897, the earliest known use of aluminium for such a purpose. The roofing was still in good condition when it was examined in 1949, but the great increase in atmospheric pollution since then may have caused deterioration. The cast-aluminium statue of Eros, in Piccadilly Circus, was set up in 1893 and has withstood the destructive London atmosphere wonderfully well, with no appreciable damage.

The church of San Gioacchino was a freak. Up to 1914 aluminium was used mainly for pots and pans, and more will be said about that in the next chapter. The building industry began to think seriously about aluminium in the early 1930s when the newly-developed extrusion process made it possible to produce aluminium glazing-bars at a reasonable price. This was one of the first applications where aluminium's special combination of strength and high resistance to corrosion were used to the maximum advantage. Aluminium, unlike some other metals, lends itself very well to extrusion, and the production of glazing-bars by this method allows more complex and more efficient shapes to be designed, with condensation channels and glazing devices incorporated in the one extrusion.

Apart from this very successful development most of the aluminium which went into buildings before the Second World War consisted of decorative metal-work, mostly internal. Occasionally, however, architects had the freedom to experiment when expensive prestige buildings were involved. The Friends' Provident and Century Life Office (1933) in Corn Street, Bristol, had anodised aluminium window and door frames, which remained in excellent condition despite war-time damage to the building. The extensions to the Bodleian Library, Oxford, and to the Cambridge University Library, both completed in 1939, have aluminium window frames.

Aluminium is the perfect example of a Second Industrial Revolution industry which owed much of its growth to war, just as the iron and steel industry developed enormously during the nineteenth century as a result of the demand for guns, warships and munitions. In 1945 both the primary producers of aluminium and their customers, particularly in the aircraft industries, found themselves with surplus production capacity. Peacetime uses had to be found for the metal. Housing was one clear answer, and between 1945 and 1948, 78,000 aluminium bungalows were built, mostly for the Ministry of Works. Many of these are still in service, although when they were made they were intended to last for only 10 years. Most of the metal that went into them was aircraft scrap, which was available in large quantities at the time. Two forms of aluminium were used for these bungalows: extruded sections, and what is known as 'clad-sheet', i.e. a strong aluminium alloy which is given extra resistance to corrosion by being coated with a layer of the pure metal. Shallow box-sectioned wall-frames were filled with foamed concrete and faced internally with plasterboard. The roof was made of 'clad-sheet' supported on alloy trusses, which carried a fibre-board ceiling. The window and door frames, too, were of aluminium alloy. Each bungalow contained about 1.75 tons of aluminium.

The bungalows were made by a number of firms and provided experience for a number of successful later developments. One fact was clearly established. Since the cost of aluminium is about two and a half times that of steel the designer has to make sure that the minimum amount of material is used. To achieve this he uses extruded sections wherever possible which do exactly what is required of them. The metal in them can be remarkably thin, in the comforting knowledge that it will not deteriorate as a result of atmospheric corrosion. To use this expensive material as economically as possible, one is justified in taking great trouble over the design and in using sophisticated

63 *Eros*, Piccadilly Circus (1893).

Sculpted by Sir Alfred Gilbert R.A., this winged figure surmounting the memorial to the Earl of Shaftesbury is a notable monument to the ability of aluminium to resist atmospheric corrosion. After over 80 years of exposure to one of the most destructive urban environments in the world, *Eros* is still in excellent condition. The figure is an assembly of separate castings, with the joints dressed so as to be almost invisible. The supporting leg is solid and the remainder of the statue is hollow. The drapery is secured to the figure by rivets. *Eros* is 8 feet high and weighs 3.75 cwt. At the current price of aluminium in 1893, it would have been almost as cheap to make the statue of silver. Aluminium had never before been used in this way or in such a quantity.

64 Aluminium detailing. Friends' Provident building, Corn Street, Bristol (1933).

An early use of aluminium for structural purposes. The facade of the building was made of aluminium-manganese alloy, anodised with an antique silver finish for decoration. The grille was cast from a wooden pattern, finished by hand-carving. The doors, windows and balcony railings were made from extruded sections. In 1941 a bomb fell almost immediately in front of the building and badly damaged it. During restoration after the War, the metal was found to be in excellent condition.

production techniques.

During the Second World War and the years immediately following it a great deal was learned about the ways in which aluminium could be used in structural engineering. It was realised that the advantage of aluminium could best be exploited in large spans, in which the dead weight becomes a much greater proportion of the load. In the experimental stages, aluminium was used for the trusses and steel or concrete for the stanchions, but it was later found to be perfectly feasible to carry out the whole job in aluminium, using extruded box-shaped sections as the uprights.

An important milestone, and one that should certainly be on the industrial archaeologist's list, was the hangar built at Heathrow in 1951 — the first aluminium hangar in Britain. The acceptance of aluminium for this building by the Ministry of Civil Aviation was a major step forward in the campaign to convince engineers, planning authorities and Ministries of its reliability as a structural medium. Since then aluminium has been used a great deal in the construction of aircraft hangars. One of the most striking is the building originally designed as the Brabazon Assembly Hall, at Filton, Bristol. The structure is of steel, but aluminium bars were used for the roof-glazing and for the enormous doors, which would not have been practical in any other material. The 32 folding leaves, weighing 200 tons, can be opened in two minutes.

One of the difficulties experienced for many years by architects who wished to use aluminium as a structural material was the lack of an agreed Code of Practice. Consequently there were no agreed standards or criteria on which to base specifications and to approve designs. In 1950 the Institution of Structural Engineers took a first step towards rectifying this unsatisfactory state of affairs by producing the Report on the Structural Use of Aluminium Alloys in Buildings. The new model by-laws which were then adopted by local authorities included aluminium as an accepted structural material, provided the design and fabrication are in accordance with the Report.

Since 1950 the range of applications for aluminium in building has been greatly extended. Aluminium window-frames, corrugated sheeting and roof-

65 Aluminium can be very useful in structural engineering when an addition has to be made to an existing building. An interesting example of this is the fourth storey added to the Radcliffe Infirmary, Oxford, in 1952. If the framework for this had been fabricated in steel, it would have weighed 20 tons and would have seriously overloaded the existing brick building. The aluminium framework, which performs the task perfectly, weighs only 12 tons, well within the limits which the building could support.

trusses are being increasingly used, especially in corrosive atmospheres, and this trend will probably continue for aluminium is a material which is unlikely to be in short supply since there are large reserves of bauxite ore, well-distributed over many countries. Processing these ores, however, demands great quantities of electricity, so in practice production of the metal tends to be concentrated in areas which have the benefit of cheap hydro-electric power. In Britain, this means that aluminium smelters have been confined to the Highlands of Scotland.

Production here remained a monopoly of the British Aluminium Co. for 75 years. The Company was formed in 1894 when it acquired the British rights of the Bayer process for extracting alumina from bauxite ore, and of the Hérault process for reducing alumina to metal. British Aluminium pioneered the industry in Britain; it also pioneered the development of hydro-electric resources to supply power to its reduction works. It now has an alumina plant, three smelters, two rolling mills, three extrusion plants, a plant for making factory ingot, extrusion billets and anodes, and a powder-and-paste works. Its newest Highland smelter, at Invergordon, began operations in 1971.

Soon after its formation in 1894 the Company bought the Foyers estate on the side of Loch Ness in order to harness the power of the Falls of Foyers. Large storage facilities had to be provided and two lochs, Gaith and Farraline, were dammed and joined to form the 4.5 mile-long Loch Mhor. Water was released from here to flow down the original bed of the Foyers river to an intake about 3.5 miles down-

stream. This water, together with that of the River Fechlin, was taken from the intake by a tunnel, 800 yards long, to a penstock chamber 350 feet above the factory. The water was led down from the penstock to the powerhouse by five 30″-diameter cast-iron pipes. Between 1904 and 1908 a second smelting project was initiated with the construction of the Blackwater dam and a temporary factory, high in the valley above Kinlochleven. The construction of the huge concrete dam — over 3,000 feet long and 86 feet high

in one of the wildest and most remote areas of Britain, was a formidable undertaking. A pier was built at Kinlochleven and most of the material, other than stone, was brought in by sea. A narrow-gauge railway was built up to the site of the permanent factory, and from there transport to the dam was by aerial ropeway. The electric locomotives used on the railway were some of the earliest in Britain.

One of the navvies engaged on the Kinlocheven project, Patrick MacGill, wrote an account of his experiences, which must have been very similar to those of the men who had worked at Foyers a few years earlier.[3] They had no idea of the purpose of what they were doing. 'Only when we had completed the job and returned to the town', MacGill recalls, 'did we learn from the newspapers that we had been employed on the construction of the biggest aluminium factory in the kingdom. All we knew was that we had

[3] *Children of the Dead End: the autobiography of a navvy* (London: 1914)

gutted whole mountains and hills in the operation.' The navvies who built the canals and the railways at least knew what the end product, the aim of their labours, was to be.

Living conditions were bad, especially in the winter: 'Rugged cabins with unplanked floors, leaking roofs, flimsy walls, through the chinks of which the winds cut like knives, meagre blankets, mouldy food, well-worn clothes, and battered bluchers were all that we possessed to aid us in the struggle.' There were many casualties, and the graveyard half a mile west of the dam is a significant item in the archaeology of the British aluminium industry. 'They went there from last shift with the red muck still on their trousers and their long unshaven beards still on their faces. Maybe they died under a fallen rock or broken derrick jib. Once dead they were buried, and there was an end of them.' Each grave is marked by a small cement block bearing the man's name and the date of his death. Some of the inscriptions are nicknames, the real names never having been divulged. One stone has the words 'Not known' and a date. This man, it appears, while walking to the dam to look for a job, was killed before he had a chance to mention his name to anyone.

Production started at Foyers in 1896 and continued until 1967. To supply it with alumina a plant was built at Larne, Northern Ireland — it closed in 1946 — and a rolling mill was set up at Milton, Staffordshire, in a factory which was bought from the Cowles Syndicate. Milton had been built in 1888 for the electrothermal reduction of alumina by carbon in an electric-furnace in the presence of other metals, yielding aluminium bronze and other alloys. Electricity here was generated by steam-power and the process was wholly uneconomic. Even so, Milton has the distinction of having been the first electro-metallurgical plant in Europe. The carbon electrodes required at Foyers were made in a small factory at Greenock, but this was closed in 1909 when the new electrode factory by the side of the new works at Lochleven was able to supply all the Company's needs.

The production of aluminium in the Highlands was not only a matter of hydro-electric schemes and smelters, for the British Aluminium Co. was faced with exactly the same problem that had confronted many enterprises in the First Industrial Revolution. Completely new communities had to be built in places where there had previously been very few inhabitants, a situation analogous to that which had confronted the Great Western Railway at Swindon. The Company found that it had, willy-nilly, to enter the housing and town-planning business. At Foyers it built a village which eventually came to contain 600 people, all dependent on the new industry for a living. At Kinlochleven, which only just escaped being called Aluminium-ville — the name was seriously proposed at the time! — the community

was much larger. The village here is split into two parts by the River Leven. The older half lies on the south bank of the river, with most of its shops and houses clustered near the factory. These lie completely in the shadow of the hills during the winter and for three or four months of the year receive no sunlight at all, which is depressing for the inhabitants. Another unpleasant feature was the yellowish smoke from the carbon factory. Housing on the Inverness side is much better. There has been a school since 1919, a village hall since 1914 and a District Nurse since 1910. There are a few shops and a branch of the Royal Bank of Scotland.

The number of workers employed at Lochleven ranged between about 350 and 650. Whether the production of 100,000 tons of aluminium per year and the employment of this relatively small number of people has justified the disfigurement of a beautiful part of the Highlands is a matter of opinion. There may, however, have been a small bonus. The children's teeth at Kinlochleven are exceptionally good. The fumes from the factory chimneys contain traces of fluorine, which causes a bluish film on the windows of houses near the works, and it is quite possible that the children owe their excellent teeth to the fact that they absorb minute quantities of this.

Since Kinlochleven began operation the British Aluminium Co. has extended its activities in the Highlands considerably with the completion of the Lochaber scheme in 1929 and Invergordon in 1971. These spectacular developments should not, however, cause us to forget the incursion into North Wales by one of the Company's competitors, the Aluminium Corporation, in the early days of the industry. The reduction works at Dolgarrog functioned between 1910 and 1925, using the power available from the water of the Carneddau Mountain in the Conway valley. Dams were built at Llyn Eigiau and Llyn Cowlyd, and, in addition to the electricity generated by the Corporation itself, power was taken from the North Wales Power Co.'s plant at Snowdon. The Aluminium Corporation found itself in serious difficulties after the First World War when there was excess capacity in the industry. In 1925 floods demolished one of the dams, undermined another and drowned 16 people in Dolgarrog. After this the Corporation concentrated on its rolling activities until production ceased during the Second World War. A small village had been built for the accommodation of workers and their families, and this survives as part of the archaeology of aluminium in this area.

66 Workmen laying pipes to Foyers hydro-electric station, 1896.

67 Foyers: interior of plant, c. 1900, showing the cells and electrodes.

Pre-fabricated housing is far from new. During the 1840s and 1850s iron houses were being shipped in sections to California and Australia, where there was a shortage of skilled building workers. Iron churches, commercial buildings and even a theatre were produced in the same way. Iron, however, is a very heavy material and the Victorian designers would certainly not have used it if as strong an alternative had been available at the time. Such an opportunity presented itself first with asbestos sheeting and then with aluminium. During the twentieth century both have been extensively used for general building purposes, but only in emergencies for housing. Immediately after the Second World War, when there was an immense demand for housing, such an emergency existed, and building and planning regulations were given a certain degree of elasticity in order to allow houses to be built from these unconventional materials, on the understanding that they were to be regarded as temporary and to be replaced with something more solid within 10 years. In practice, this 10-year limit proved impossible to observe and even today many 'temporary' houses are still occupied and giving good service. Very few, however, are likely to survive until the end of the century, when we shall have only pictures to document the experiment.

The experience and the techniques now exist to allow factory-built houses, of a light but strong form of construction, to make a useful contribution towards meeting accommodation problems. Prejudice, however, largely fostered by the building industry itself, and the difficulty of obtaining loans on anything but bricks-and-mortar properties, have combined to nip this particular series of housing experiments effectively in the bud.

68 Asbestos pre-fabricated housing, Henleaze, Bristol.

69 Aluminium pre-fabricated house, Hucclecote, Gloucester.

70 Brick-covered aluminium house at Hucclecote, Gloucester. The brick skin is not load-bearing; it was added to make the houses more socially acceptable.

Concrete

This is the century in which reinforced concrete has come into its own. It was not until the 1880s that sufficiently strong and reliable cements were available to make reinforced concrete construction really practicable. Between 1880 and 1900 a number of able engineers and architects, mostly in Germany and France, were able to establish the characteristics of reinforced concrete and to work out calculations for structures using this material. It is not easy to explain why certain countries — France, Switzerland, Germany and Italy in particular — should have taken to reinforced concrete so quickly, so enthusiastically and so successfully, and why others, notably Britain, should have hung back. The tendency in Britain to split off the engineer from the architect no doubt has something to do with it, and so, too, have the British building regulations.

To some extent the critics and sceptics in Britain were right, for much of the early concrete was extremely badly made. Every country is littered with bits and pieces of crumbling, stained concrete dating from 1900 onwards and the position has not, unfortunately, improved a great deal in recent years. There is nothing attractive or commendable about a concrete canopy which has rotted away at the edges, a concrete wall which is stained and blotched, or a concrete bus shelter which is streaked with rust from the steel reinforcing rods.

For more than 50 years attempts to reduce the cost of housing, especially working-class housing, have stimulated experiments to find cheaper methods of building in concrete. During the 1920s a good deal of interest was shown in no-fines or cellular concrete, a special kind of poured concrete in which the proportion of cement to aggregate was exceptionally low. Such concrete needed rendering on both sides to produce an acceptable finish, but it was cheap and it had good insulating properties. The earliest British examples of this technique are 50 two-storey houses in Edinburgh, built in 1923.

Within the past 30 years concrete blocks have become one of the most commonly used of all building materials. Simple, hand-operated block-making machines were on the market by the 1860s, and at the beginning of the present century it was reckoned that blocks made on such a machine were cheaper to buy and lay than brickwork. This is even more true today.

The output of Portland cement in Britain trebled between 1945 and 1970, and the cost of production rose less than that of any other basic construction material, largely as a result of replacing the older, less efficient plants by modern, automated units. The kilns are now all fired by oil and rotated by electric motors, which makes cement a Second Industrial Revolution industry twice over. To reduce costs new plants have been sited away from the Thames-Medway area, in which production was concentrated until the 1950s, and transport of brick by train to regional distribution depots, or by road direct to large contracts, has been used to rationalise supply and handling methods.

The huge and growing demand for aggregate has presented a difficult problem, especially in London and the south-east. The available supplies of gravel and crushed stone are nearing exhaustion in a number of areas, but alternative sources, such as gravel dredged from the sea-bed, have so far made it possible to meet requirements. Considerable ingenuity has been shown in discovering new aggregate. Waste materials, such as fly-ash and screened household rubbish, are now widely used for making light-weight concrete blocks.

The continuous improvement and development of mixing and placing equipment has greatly reduced the labour costs of concrete work. Concrete-mixers have been in use since the 1850s but for many years they were manually operated. Mixers driven by petrol-engines and electric motors belong to the present century, as does the transit-mixer, mounted on a lorry-chassis, which was first used in the USA in 1926. It is now an indispensable item of civil engineering equipment. Small-bore pumping units have come into widespread use since the 1950s for distributing concrete to different parts of a building site, and mechanical vibrators now make it a simple matter to compact large masses of concrete to a degree of efficiency that was not previously possible.

Much attention has been given to reducing the cost of shuttering — an important consideration given the upward trend in timber prices — by designing modular components which can be re-used many times and moved on to new sections of the work as soon as the concrete has set. As concrete technology has advanced the pre-cast branch of the industry — organised since 1918 into the British Pre-Cast Concrete Federation — has greatly increased in importance. The pre-casting of concrete units, made away from the site under factory conditions, offers considerable technical and economic advantages: a high standard of quality control; a degree of accuracy which is possible only with precision-built moulds and formwork; a more consistent and more reliable product; and year-round production, regardless of weather conditions.

The pre-stressing of concrete is now a normal technique within the civil engineering field. The theory of pre-stressing was known at the end of the nineteenth century, but its application was not practicable at that time because the necessary high tensile steel was not easily available. The system did not come into widespread use until the 1930s. It is of particular value in the construction of load-bearing beams. By mechanical stretching of the high-tension reinforcing material, which is often piano-wire, stresses are introduced into the concrete which are able to resist those of the external loading. Consequently, the beams can be made both stronger and lighter.

Brick and Stone

In the process of concentrating on new industries one should not overlook the enormous progress made in some of the older forms of construction during the twentieth century. Brick is a notable example. A revolution in brickmaking took place at the end of the last century with the manufacture of bricks from the Lower Oxford Clay beds began at Fletton, near Peterborough. It was found that the shale-like Fletton clay could be pressed into a brick which could be fired immediately, without any previous drying. An equally important advantage of this clay lies in the fact that carbonaceous material comprises 10 per cent of its volume. This can be made to produce sufficient heat during firing to allow a 30 per cent reduction in the amount of coal required in comparison with other clays.

The success of the highly mechanised methods pioneered at Fletton persuaded other firms within the Oxford Clay area to adopt the Fletton process. During the 1920s many of the smaller firms ran into financial difficulties and the three large companies now dominating the industry came into being as a result of mergers and take-overs. These three — London Brick, Marston Valley Brick and Redland — now produce more than half of all the bricks used in Britain. The London Brick Co. is the largest brickmaker in the world.

Within the Bedfordshire brickfield the 111 chimneys dominate the landscape, which is mainly flat and treeless. The chimneys range in height from 100 to 300 feet. The trend is towards taller chimneys as the most effective way of dealing with the serious pollution problem arising from the waste gases which contain fluorine compounds and sulphur oxides which kill trees and endanger the condition of cattle and other animals. The brick industry has injured the landscape in another way for its vast pits have made thousands of acres derelict. This particular problem, however, is on the way to being solved. Some of the pits are being filled with household rubbish from the Greater London area — each acre takes about 30,000 tons of rubbish — and others are being used for various kinds of water-sport.

If natural stone has a future in the construction of new buildings then it must lie in greater mass-production of standard components and in techniques which allow ashlar-facing to be attached easily and efficiently to steel or reinforced concrete frames. In other words, stone must be able to compete with other and more modern cladding materials. This has been achieved in a number of large buildings completed during the 1960s and 1970s. The Carlton Tower Hotel and the headquarters of Guest, Keen and Nettlefold, both in London, and the extension to Queen's College, Cambridge, are examples. Experiments have also been made with very large stone cladding-panels, prefabricated from standard modules and held together with pre-stressed wires which fit into slots across the back of the panels. The whole slab, measuring perhaps 10 feet by 6 feet, can be transported directly from the factory to the site and fixed very rapidly to the face of the building.

Housing Schemes

The essence of a successful building is that it shall make the occupants happy. A great many twentieth-century buildings have failed to do this. They have leaked, provided poor thermal and acoustic insulation, demanded more maintenance than is reasonable and, worse still, been designed without proper research into the needs of the people who are going to live and work in them. One of the saddest examples of the last kind of failure is the much-publicised Quarry Hill Estate in Leeds which was designed in 1935 but, because of planning and organisational problems, not completed until 1941. After appalling vandalism and misuse the estate was abandoned by Leeds Housing Department, which had commissioned and built it, and demolished in 1976-7.

It was the largest 'complete' estate in England, including flats in blocks ranging from two to eight storeys, shops, a day nursery, a laundry and a communal hall. It covered 28 acres, and had accommodation for over 3,000 people in 938 flats. There were 88 lifts — Quarry Hill was the only council estate built in Britain during the 1920s and 1930s to have lifts — fitted kitchens and a sink waste-disposal system. The City Architect, P.A.H. Livett, was determined that, after generations of living in slums and near-slums, the working-class of Leeds should live in the best possible conditions. He toured Europe for ideas and was particularly impressed by what he saw in Berlin and Vienna. Leeds, he believed, could do even better.

To keep the unit cost at a reasonable level Livett chose the most completely pre-fabricated method of construction then available. This was the Moplin system which had been used successfully for houses and flats in France. Basically, the system involved the fixing of vibrated-concrete slabs to a light, steel-frame, with other vibrated concrete placed in situ. The load was shared between the steel frame, the concrete facing and the concrete filling, thus making a monolithic structure. The method eliminated scaffolding and shuttering and permitted all-weather working. In France it may have worked well, although Livett was possibly given optimistic reports about this, but in Leeds it was a disaster.

The factory production was never satisfactory co-ordinated with erection on the site, and it had not been appreciated that handling and fixing the slabs involved skills of a special kind. As a result the contract dragged on for six years and all the promised savings were lost.

Much worse was the fact that the former slum-dwellers hated Quarry Hill. The lifts, the day nursery and all the other amenities so well-meaningly provided at Quarry Hill did not compensate for the fact that, to a worker in Leeds, a flat was not and could not be a home. In the minds of many lurked the belief that an urban flat could never be a substitute for a suburban house. It might be a transit camp, until one could find something better, but it could be nothing more. Quarry Hill, therefore, came to be occupied by less and less satisfactory tenants who turned the City Architect's dream into a giant slum. Eventually, after only 30 years' use, it became uninhabitable.

The Greater London Council made the same kind of blunder during the 1950s and 1960s with its now notorious high-rise flats, and other local authorities, of course, followed its prestigious example. These unwanted dwellings were built not because the tenants wanted them but because they reflected fashionable architectural thinking. Le Corbusier, Gropius and other 'gurus' of the inter-war period had preached the gospel of tall blocks. The vertical garden-city was to replace the obsolete horizontal garden-city, providing more efficient living accommodation and checking urban sprawl. Post-war British architects, with the full support of the Ministry of Housing, took the first opportunity to put such thinking into practice, selling the new high-rise blocks with such emotive catch-phrases as 'modern living'. Between 1953 and 1959 only 0.5 per cent of all the tenders approved for local authority housing were in blocks of 15 storeys and over. In 1965, the peak year, the figure had risen to 10.6 per cent but by 1970 it had slipped back to 1.8 per cent. The high-rise boom was clearly over, the process of decline being understandably accelerated by the partial collapse of Ronan Point, a 22-storey block in the London borough of Newham. There was a gas explosion in the kitchen of one of the flats on the eighteenth floor, and one corner of the building collapsed like a pack of cards. An en-

quiry showed that there had been a serious defect in the design of the structure and recommended that all blocks built to a similar system should be strengthened.

It is only fair to say that most high-rise blocks, and there are a great many of them in Britain, have not collapsed, unsatisfactory as they may have proved to be in other respects. What has occurred on a large scale, however, is neurosis, vandalism and a generally poor quality of life among the people who are forced to live in these buildings. The Second Industrial Revolution has evolved the techniques to construct these sky-scraping warrens of people; it has not produced a way of ordering or persuading ordinary families to like them. For whatever reasons this century has not seen means much better than those of the last century to solve the problem of housing the poor decently and happily. Whether this represents a social or a technical failure is a matter for argument.

During the 1950s and 1960s the fashion swung from making houses in factories to what became known as industrialised building — tall blocks of flats which embodied factory-made components in their structure.

Until the 1930s the most that tenants could expect from municipal housing was somewhere to sit, sleep and eat in reasonable comfort. The Peabody Flats achieved this remarkably well, by Victorian standards, but neither they nor any other working-class block aimed at architectural distinction or showed much evidence of imagination in design at that period. The solid, low-

71 Peabody Trust, Wild Street Estate, Drury Lane (1896).

72 Kensal House, Ladbroke Grove: a pre-war success and still in use — vandalisation has not occurred.

73 Quarry Hill Flats. Leeds.

maintenance, minimum-amenity approach persisted almost without variation throughout the 1920s and 1930s. Ossulston Flats, Euston (1928) was the first project to try for some degree of originality and even charm, but it was a lone swallow.

Kensal House (1936) — designed by Maxwell Fry, owned by the Gas Light and Coke Co., which had a big gasworks a few yards away, and built by Bovis — was a pioneering venture and had considerable influence. Today, the visitor may well wonder just how and why it acquired such a formidable reputation. Time, style and standards have moved on and much that is now taken for granted was very new and adventurous in the mid-1930s. Kensal House was conceived as an 'urban village', with a nursery school and a club house. It was an experiment in housing poor families from slum areas and the aim, in the words of the architect, was 'to build a group of homes where people whose incomes allow them little above sheer necessity could experience as full a life as can be.' Access was from stairs, not from the more usual outside galleries, which were considered 'unprivate, draughty, barrack-like and loved by nobody.' The three blocks were of four and five storeys. They contained 13 two-bedroom and 54 three-bedroom flats. The construction was framed re-inforced concrete, with four-inch walls lined internally with one inch of compressed cork and finished externally with cement paint. The tile and concrete floors were covered with material known as 'battleship linoleum', cemented to the floor screed.

For the first time, working-class housewives in Britain were given genuinely labour-saving homes. They had a cooker with thermostatic oven control, an instantaneous water heater serving the kitchen and the bathroom, a movable wash-copper, a gas-iron in the kitchen, a gas-ignited coke grate in the living room, a gas fire in the main bedroom and gas points in the others, and switch-controlled gas-lighters. The total fuel bill averaged 4s. 4d. a week, compared with the usual London working-class figure of 6/-. The biggest breakthrough at Kensal House was undoubtedly the abolition of the coal-range in the living room, so that tenants were given evenings

'free from the sights, sounds and smells of cooking and washing up.'

Kensal House is still inhabited and in very reasonable shape. It was a realistic project in that the rents were within the means of the slum-dwellers it was rehousing. Quarry Hill, Leeds, was, by contrast, idealistic rather than realistic. It was allegedly built to house market-workers, on the assumption that market-workers needed to live near their work. In practice, however, no attempt was made to match the rents with the incomes of such people, and only a small number of market-workers ever appeared to have lived in the flats. Since 1945 the replanning of Leeds has left Quarry Hill Flats in a marooned, not to say dangerous position, with new roads running close by and pedestrian access difficult.

The spectacular and much-publicised collapse of one corner of the 17-storey Ronan Point block of flats in 1968 brought public and official anxiety about this type of dwelling to a head. The path to Ronan Point is a sad one. Throughout the 1920s and 1930s, in both public and private housing, the popular ideal was the low-density 'garden suburb.' It was the national slum clearance campaign, begun by the Housing Act of 1930, which finally pushed local authorities into building flats, instead of houses. This was partly to avoid building on green-belt land, partly from the mistaken belief that flats were cheaper, and also from a wish to keep as many people as possible living within the city boundary and thus to hold on to precious rateable value. During the 1950s and 1960s political considerations also became important. What came to matter most was not the quality but the quantity of housing provided, in order to meet the election promises of political parties and to maintain the reputation of Ministers of Housing. The tower-blocks of the 1960s, aimed at getting people out of slum dwellings — the first 11-storey living-towers in Britain were built by the LCC against the background of Wimbledon Common and Richmond Park — are in the process of becoming the slums of another generation. Disliked and feared by their tenants from the beginning, they have been vandalised on an appalling scale and the demolition of many of them within the

next 20 years seems extremely probable. Here, as with pre-fabs, archaeologists may well find material for study to be in very short supply by the end of the century.

The high-rise phenomenon has to be seen in proportion, however. It was a fashion that came and went remarkably quickly, and it was largely confined to municipal housing. It should also be emphasised that, so far as people of modest means are concerned, flats are largely a child of the Greater London area. In 1966 two flats out of three in England and Wales were in the South-East and 29.5 per cent of all dwellings in Greater London were flats.

74 Ronan Point: showing collapsed corner.

Chapter 5

Domestic Equipment

The Census of 1851 revealed that over one million men and women in Britain were employed in various forms of domestic service. Indeed, it constituted the second largest occupational group after agriculture. The number remained fairly constant until 1914, but by 1918 the total had been halved, and has continued to decline ever since. In effect, the decline has meant that middle-class women and their husbands have had to get used to doing the housework that they were previously able to pay other people to do for them, and there can be no doubt that the disappearance of servants has been the main reason for the invention and development of labour-saving equipment and materials of all kinds. Moreover, once the middle-classes had hot-water systems, vacuum cleaners, stainless steel cutlery, washing-machines, central heating and food-mixers, the working-classes not unnaturally demanded and got the same. The growth of new industries to supply such goods has been a major feature of the Second Industrial Revolution.

Electricity Supply

The availability of electricity has been a measure of the change and also a vital pre-requisite, since so many types of household equipment depend upon it for energy and motive power. A brief survey of the growth and development of the electricity supply industry in this country will not, accordingly, be out of place here.

Electric power for domestic use is almost wholly a product of the twentieth century. In 1921, 12 per cent of British households had electricity; in 1971 the figure was 97 per cent. When public electricity undertakings were first set up in the 1880s they could only provide a low-voltage supply, which could be used for little more than lighting and the telephone. It was not until 1900 that most of the electricity companies began to provide the much heavier loads that were needed for the new electric tramways, and it was not until many years after that the new high-voltage supplies were used to any extent for domestic purposes. One reason for this was that until well into the present century electricity was both unreliable and expensive. In the 1890s a unit of electricity cost 6d. in the West End of London, a considerable sum in those days. Coal and gas, on the other hand, were cheap, and therefore electricity was never considered for heating. Nor was there any point in considering it for cleaning since, until the First World War, domestic service was cheap and abundant.

Electricity was, in any case, available only in the main towns. In the first years of this century private companies were, it is true, set up to generate electricity elsewhere, but the supply situation was completely unco-ordinated, not to say chaotic, on the outbreak of war in 1914. Apart from an increase in capacity in the major industrial areas to provide power for the munition factories no improvement took place before the passing of the Electricity Supply Act which provided for, but did not guarantee, a central authority to create a nationwide network of electricity. Even as late as 1925, however, there were still nearly 600 separate supply undertakings. The Electricity Supply Act of 1926 therefore established a Central Electricity Board which had compulsory powers to concentrate the production of electricity at a relatively few stations, which could be depended on to maintain an adequate load, at a standard alternating frequency. The Board was also given the powers, which it began to use almost immediately, to construct a National Grid which, for the first time, would connect up supplies all over Britain. It was then that the now-familiar galvanised pylons began to appear throughout the country. Many of them are still standing and giving good service.

Electricial Appliances

One of the earliest suppliers of electrical appliances was the General Electric Apparatus Co., which set up a London warehouse in the 1880s. At this stage the Company carried out no manufacturing itself and it had to find small workshops that were able and willing to make what was wanted. By 1890 this enterprising concern was selling electric irons, fans, immersion heaters and something described as an 'electric rapid cooking apparatus', which was in fact the ancestor of the electric kettle and boiled a pint of water in 12 minutes — not exactly a record-breaking time! By then, the General Electric Apparatus Co. — it had changed its name to the General Electric Co. in 1889 — had begun to manufacture this equipment at its own factories in Birmingham. It should be emphasised, however, that anyone who used electric appliances at this time was a well-to-do enthusiast indulging in what amounted to a hobby. From a purely practical point of view it was absurd to boil water or do the ironing by electricity. A servant and a coal fire would do such jobs at a fraction of the cost and without the risk of electrocution.

Two other great names first came before the public during the 1890s — British Thompson Houston in 1894 and British Westinghouse in 1899. Soon after, electric heaters were pioneered in Britain by Premier Electric Heaters, established in Birmingham in 1907, and by Belling and Co. which began manufacturing at Edmonton, North London, in 1912. Belling's founder, C. R. Belling, became well-known for his 'instant geyser', which heated water as quickly as gas but at an enormously higher cost. His appliance took 10 kilowatts, and when switched on and working it dimmed the lights of the whole district.

Household vacuum cleaners originated in America, the first practicable machine being David Kenney's stationary model, which was patented in 1903. (The word 'vacuum cleaner' was first recorded in the Oxford Dictionary in that year.) A neat improvement was James M. Spangler's electrically driven suction sweeper, patented in 1908. The Hoover Co. put similar machines on the market soon after this, using the modern principle of a rotary suction fan and a bag for catching the dust. Hoover was a leather manufacturer in Ohio and developed his vacuum cleaner as a sideline. Hoover Ltd. was set up in Britain in 1919 to market the firm's cleaners. Its regional headquarters buildings were a feature of the British scene for many years, until rationalisation and a slump in the sale of vacuum cleaners caused most of them to be closed during the 1960s. English Electric was formed in 1919 but did not enter the domestic appliance field until 1927 when it offered cookers, bowl fires and irons. Electrolux, a Sweden-based concern, began making vacuum cleaners and refrigerators here in 1927.

Until 1945 the increased use of electrical appliances was steady rather than spectacular. Electric cooker sales rose from 75,000 per annum in 1930 to 240,000 in 1935. By 1939 it was

75 10,000 volt alternator under construction at Deptford, 1889.

76 Deptford generating station (1889).

reckoned that there were about 220,000 domestic electric refrigerators in use, compared with 75,000 run by gas. Vacuum cleaner sales doubled from 200,000 in 1930 to 400,000 in 1939, three-quarters of them on hire-purchase. Bank interest rates, and therefore hire-purchase rates, were very low during the inter-war period. Without hire-purchase the manufacturers would have sold extremely little but, even so, the sales for each firm were very small and, one would have thought, unprofitable by modern standards. In 1939 there were, for example, 21 different makes of refrigerator available and it is doubtful if any single company was selling more than 10,000 per year. From a national point of view, however, the situation had improved when Britain went off the Gold Standard in 1931, whereby sterling fell by 30 per cent against the US dollar, making American imports much more expensive. After the Import Duties Act of 1932 put a 20 per cent duty on all imported appliances, foreign firms found it more profitable to manufacture in Britain. By 1935 97 per cent of all vacuum cleaners, the fastest-selling item of equipment, were being made in this country.

Until 1945 it was a middle-class privilege to have electricity in one's home. Gas, not electricity, was considered suitable for the working-classes in the 1920s and 1930s, mainly because electricity was much more expensive, but also because it was widely believed among those in positions of authority that working-class people, especially women, were too stupid and irresponsible to be trusted with electricity. In 1938 a report to the City of Liverpool's Housing Committee expressed doubts as to whether the tenants of municipal flats had the capacity to operate a lift. It was considered that working-class people were not equal to the task, and so, since the cost of an attendant would have necessitated a substantial addition to the weekly rent, Liverpool had no lifts until after the war. One of the biggest and most prestigious of London's housing-blocks of the 1920s, Kensal House, had no electricity laid on at all; even the irons were powered by gas. At the Ossulston estate, Euston, the L.C.C. rented gas-fuelled washing-machines and water-heaters to its tenants for between 1s. 9d. and 2s. 0d. per week. Ossulston had elec-

77 Early electric cookers displayed in the Domestic Appliances Gallery, Science Museum, London. Their solid, heavy quality is evident.

78 West Wiltshire Electric Light and Power Co., Trowbridge: showroom exterior, c.1930.

The Electric Lighting Act of 1882 discouraged the building of central power stations in Britain by limiting the rights of the promoters to 21 years. This was amended by a new Act in 1888, but the original Act was largely responsible for delaying the spread of electricity in Britain. Most early power stations, built during the 1870s and 1880s, were designed to provide a supply for individual premises. Both the Gaiety Theatre and Billingsgate Fish Market, for instance, were lit by electricity in 1878. One of these private schemes expanded to provide a public supply. In 1883 the Grosvenor private schemes expanded to provide a public supply. In 1883 the Grosvenor Gallery, at 137 New Bond Street, was equipped with a Siemens generator — steam-driven, like all the early plant — installed in the basement. The station was extended by enlarging the basement in 1885, in order to serve the district around Bond Street. The equipment gave a good deal of trouble and Dr Sebastian Ziani de Ferranti, later to become a great name in electrical design and manufacturing, was called in. He made radical alterations and in 1887 a new company, the London Electric Supply Corporation, was formed to supply power over a wide area: from Regents Park to the Thames, and from Knightsbridge to the Law Courts. Distribution was by overhead cables fixed to iron brackets on the house tops. (Some of these have survived and can be seen today.) In 1890 the installations in Bond Street were completely destroyed by fire and the building itself severely damaged. By this time, however, Ferranti's new riverside power station at Deptford was under way, on a scale never previously seen.

The Kensington Court power station was set up in 1886 to serve the adjacent block of expensive flats, and it later extended its lines to other premises. Providing a D.C. supply, it functioned until 1966 when its service area was converted to alternating current. A plaque placed above the door records these facts.

There is some dispute as to which was the first *public* power station in the world. The honour probably belongs to one installed at 57 Holborn Viaduct in January 1882, but the Brighton undertaking, which dates from February 1882, certainly has the

79 West Wiltshire Electric Light and Power Co., Trowbridge: showroom interior, c.1933.

longest continuous history of a generally available supply. The original plant was in Reed's iron foundry, Gloucester Road. A new station, next to the old one, was opened in 1886 and a municipal station at North Road in 1891. North Road was closed and replaced by a new station at Southwick in 1906. Nothing remains at Gloucester Road, but there is still evidence of the North Road buildings.

The development of electricity generating in Britain is reasonably well documented by surviving power stations and former power station buildings. Many of the buildings of the 1890-1910 period have been converted to other uses and others

have been kept in service for standby purposes. Some, like Reading, are too small and old-fashioned to be economical in the face of today's coal process, although they date only from the 1930s, and are being closed and demolished.

It is not without significance that the early power stations were set up either in wealthy residential or business areas, or for the benefit of theatre-goers or railway travellers at metropolitan termini. Until the 1920s electricity was far too rare and expensive a commodity to be squandered on the domestic comfort and convenience of the common people.

tric light but there were no power-circuits. The decision of the Leeds Housing Department to put one 10-amp point in each of the living rooms of its new Quarry Hill flats and another in one of the bedrooms was unprecedented. Unbelievable as it may sound now, those who opposed the installation of even electric lighting in working-class homes often did so on the grounds that the cost of running such a system would force the tenants to go back to oil-lamps.

It is not easy to make reliable statistical comparisons between the pre-war and post-war period, but it is clear first, that there was a spectacular growth in the use of electric appliances during the 1950s; and, second, that it was not confined to the pre-war users of electricity, the middle-classes. By 1960 the British population as a whole had not only an electric supply in their homes but a power supply. To have brought this about within such a short time was a remarkable achievement on the part of both the Central Electricity Generating Board and of the various Regional Boards. It required, since the increasing needs of industry also had to be met, an extensive programme of building power-stations and constructing new transmission lines. Within a period of 20 years, it is fair to say, Britain was electrified.

There was considerable expansion on the manufacturing side also. Immediately after the War the Government embarked on a policy of establishing new factories in places which were not in traditional industrial areas. Firms were given the opportunity to take over, on very favourable terms, Government factories that had been built during the War to make munitions, and the electric appliance manufacturers had their share of these. GEC, for instance, moved its production of domestic appliances from Birmingham to Swinton, Yorkshire, and Simplex Electric, which had also been in Birmingham for many years, went to Blythe Bridge in Staffordshire. Hoover stayed at its main vacuum-cleaner base in Middlesex, but opened two additional factories, one at Cambuslang, in the Scottish Development area, and another at Merthyr Tydfil, to make washing-machines, marking a new Hoover departure. Pressed Steel converted a former shell-making factory near its car-body plant at Cowley to handle the production of

80 Two pages from Ferranti's *Catalogue*, c. 1894.

81 Cambridge Electric Supply Co., Mansfield: showroom, 1938.

refrigerators.

Thorn Electrical Industries, which had previously concentrated on making lamps, went into the appliance market in 1946 by buying an old-established appliance company, Tricity Electric. In the same year a new refrigerator company, Lec Refrigerators, entered the field with its factory at Bognor Regis. Lec succeeded in making refrigerators at a remarkably low price, and both its manufacturing techniques and its marketing methods had a great influence on a fairly conservative industry. Dimplex, one of the biggest post-war success stories, was another new firm to make an impact on the rapidly growing market.

Established in Southampton in the late 1940s, it concentrated on oil-filled electric radiators, which made it possible to have something closely approaching central heating but without the installation costs of the normal kind of central heating system.

The 1950s and 1960s was the period during which most British people at last began to keep their homes warm, possibly too warm. The previous pattern had been to have a coal fire in the sitting room and, on very special occasions, in the drawing room, letting the bedrooms and passages look after themselves. An electric fire in the bedroom was a great luxury and so, until the 1950s, when that great comforter, the electric blanket, began to make its appearance, the British were famous for their hot-water bottles.

82 'Tide' and 'Daz' packets and their precursors.

Until the 1920s domestic equipment meant machines, tools and materials for use in conjunction with hand-labour. The revolution came only with the development of the fractional-horsepower motor and with the availability of a reliable electricity supply throughout the country. In Britain, it was not a rapid revolution and until well into the 1950s it affected little more than 20 per cent of the population. The British people took a lot of persuading that electrically-driven equipment was worth buying and the Hoover salesman of the 1920s and 1930s, earning his living from day after day of doorstep interviews, became something of a figure of fun. The vacuum cleaner was the only item of electrical equipment, apart from lighting and cooking, which made any substantial impact on the British market before the Second World War. Refrigerators, heaters, shavers and washing machines only became commercially important during the 1950s and 1960s, and the archaeology of these industries dates mostly from this period. The do-it-yourself movement has produced a boom of an other kind — in power tools for home use.

A second part of the revolution in domestic equipment came with things which required no power, but which simply did the job more efficiently and with less effort. Plastics and detergents are obvious cases in point and the firms concerned with these industries have grown fast.

83 Former Hoover regional headquarters, Bristol: converted from a pair of elegant early nineteenth-century houses.

84 Gillette offices, City Road, London, 1931. The modest size of the building is an indication of the low overheads carried by a leading manufacturer at that time.

85 De-luxe cooking between the Wars: the 'Governor-General' cooker, c.1935. This is now in the John Doran Museum, Leicester.

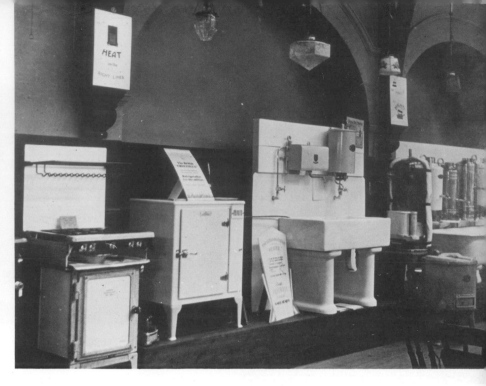

86 (above)
Part of the Gas Co.'s showrooms at Wellingborough, 1940. The equipment here displayed is very similar to that installed in the Gas Light and Coke Co.'s Kensal House flats (see pp. 50–51).

87 (below)
The last days of local works making gas from coal: Doncaster in the early 1950s. Only the gas holders now remain of the buildings in this photograph.

In 1977 the East Midlands Gas Board opened a museum on part of the old gasworks in Leicester. Installed in a skilfully converted office building, it includes a fine collection of what are described as 'gas-related artifacts' drawn from the Board's region. There is a full range of objects — from cookers to meters and from gas men's tools to Board minutes — with a blend of photographs, documents and objects chosen to make the story clear, human and interesting. It is both a museum of technical change and a monument to the five generations of workers who have brought this change about. It has a fair ration of curiosities — gas-powered hair-dryers, resembling the old ship's ventilator; a thermo-electric generator which allows a radio set to work off the gas supply; the 'Governor-General' cooker, handsomely stove-enamelled with a willow pattern design; and an original 1923 disc of Sylvia Willing and the Gainsborough Orchestra performing the 'Trust the Regulo' song. No doubt further remarkable curiosities will be acquired in the future.

88 The John Doran Museum, Leicester: some of the heating, cooking and gas lighting appliances.

Another revolution was brought about virtually single-handed by the activities of one man, Kenneth Wood. He began to make Kenwood toasters and food-mixers in 1947 and deservedly prospered. No man has saved more woman-hours in the kitchen than Mr Wood, and although other manufacturers subsequently made both toasters and mixers, the credit for popularising them has to go to him.

The electric cooker is a story on its own. Before the Second World War the majority of British homes, whether working-class or middle-class, cooked on gas. After the War coal yielded ground to gas and electricity in about equal proportions. The new pre-fabricated houses sponsored by the Government as an emergency measure in the immediate post-war years had electric cookers and this was a pointer to the change that was taking place. Before the War it was extremely unusual for municipal houses or flats to have electric cookers, which demand, it is true, more careful and responsible handling than other kinds, especially if large bills are to be avoided. One should not exaggerate the change in habit, however. In 1939 manufacturers delivered a total of 970,000 cookers; of these, 220,000 (23 per cent) were electric. In 1950 the total was 1,090,000 of which 275,000 (25 per cent) were electric. The difference between the pre-War and post-War figures is very small — only 2 per cent — but in such a highly competitive market this is considered sufficient to indicate a trend, which indeed was continued during the 1950s and 1960s. In 1970 about 35 per cent of the cookers delivered were electric. One cannot assume, however, that the proportion of electric to gas cookers delivered is a reliable guide to the proportion of households which cook by one means or the other. During the 1940s and 1950s many of the gas cookers sold were undoubtedly for replacement — the design of all forms of gas appliances improved enormously during the post-war years — whereas many more of the electric cookers went into homes which had not cooked in this way before. To have a cooker is not, of course, the same thing as using it, and the increasing popularity of convenience-foods especially during the 1960s and 1970s almost certainly means that many cookers are in use for fewer hours in the day than formerly. Likewise, the increasing use of synthetic fabrics probably means that less ironing is done now than 20 years ago. The hardest-worked piece of electric equipment in the average home today, in fact, may well be the kettle.

One casualty on the kitchen front has been the enamel saucepan. It is still made and used and its quality has improved, but its place has been taken by heavy aluminium. Aluminium is an exceptionally good conductor of heat and this, in cooking terms, means faster work and less consumption of fuel. Aluminium pots and pans were available before the First World War, but very few households possessed them. Their use greatly increased only during the 1920s and 1920s, but it is now almost universal.

Since 1945 the kitchen has been transformed more than any other room in the British home.[1] From being a mere workshop it has become, in a great many instances, a place in which meals can be eaten in a more or less civilised manner — certainly a place where children can be fed satisfactorily — and in which one can talk to one's friends in a reasonably hospitable way. New industries have been created to supply the kitchen with special furniture, with suitable and pleasant floor-coverings, with ventilator equipment and, of course, with electrical devices of all kinds. The Second Industrial Revolution kitchen is different in every way from the kitchen of the age of coal and iron. The Victorian kitchen was, in fact, precisely that — a coal and iron kitchen. The kitchen of the 1970s is an aluminium, electricity and plastics kitchen, a microcosm of the industrial revolution which has occurred during the present century.

One of the main agents in this transformation has been Formica, which has eliminated the scrubbing and scouring characteristic of the First Industrial Revolution kitchen. Formica was invented in Britain by the De La Rue Co. during the 1930s. It was a side-product of the phenolic resin and paper laminates made for electrical insulation and of the other laminated plastics developed by the Company for industrial and military purposes. In 1930 the Company designed and built, at its plastics factory in Shernhall Street, Walthamstow, London — one of the industry's most important archaeological sites — a machine to begin experiments with plastic laminates. By 1935 this factory had become impossibly overcrowded and a new and more up-to-date factory was built in Walthamstow Avenue. Machinery was bought in Germany for the full-scale development of plastic laminates, which by this time included decorative materials as well as industrial products.

[1] The development of the basic items of household equipment during the present century can be followed in the interesting, but very inadequately housed, Domestic Equipment Gallery at the Science Museum, London which has an excellent collection of washing machines, cookers, water-heaters and vacuum-cleaners. There is, alas, no catalogue or handbook.

Mr Ernest Davis, who began working with the De La Rue Co. in 1919, was closely involved in the production of the new laminates. His own office at Shernhall Road, he remembers, was 'panelled in 20″ × 20″ squares all round with this wood-grain effect', and at his home in Essex he had a kitchen table covered with a pioneering sheet of similar material.[2] His kitchen contained, too, many examples of the pre-war plastic hollow-ware which De La Rue made under its tradename of Enduraware. It was quite probably the best domestic-plastic museum in Britain, carrying the story of his company's products through the 1950s and beyond. Even its Gas Division, which later became Thomas Potterton and Co., was represented. The kitchen contained a De La Rue 'Warwick' gas cooker and a 'Diplomat' gas boiler.

In 1945 De La Rue acquired the business and factory of Traffolyte, a decorative laminate, from Metropolitan-Vickers at Manchester, and shortly afterwards reached an agreement with the Formica Corporation of Cincinatti to make laminated material under their name. Demand from catering establishments, hospitals, shops and offices, as well as from private customers, was expanding very rapidly, and construction of a large new factory was begun at Tynemouth in 1947. On its completion all production was transferred from Manchester.

By 1963 the development of decorative laminates had reached a point at which there was a problem of finding adequate quantities of suitably strong and cheap materials to which they could be attached as a surface. Wood chipboard seemed to be ideal for the purpose. De La Rue decided that a very large market was opening up for sheet made from wood chips and urea-formaldehyde resin, particularly in the building and furniture industries. Three timber and timber-processing companies on Tyneside were taken over to form the technical and manufacturing base for the new industry. The tables, cupboard panels and working surfaces of the Second Industrial Revolution kitchen are therefore likely to contain two new materials,

[2] Conversation with the author, 5 August 1976.

not one. The hidden material is, in its way, quite as interesting and important as what covers it and attracts the attention. It should be observed that what is known professionally as 'particle board' has developed since 1945 from the original concept of a means of making profitable use of waste wood to a major manufacturing industry, for which wood is specially grown and selected.

It is not easy to decide where the category of domestic equipment begins and ends. Cleaning and cooking are certainly not the limits. One definition might be 'anything which is used within the walls of the home', and this would certainly include devices for shaving. In this, there have been two steps forward. The first belongs to the First Industrial Revolution and the second, appropriately enough, to the Second Industrial Revolution. The traditional method of shaving depended on a piece of sharpened steel and a lubricant or beard-softener of some kind, usually soap and water. The safety razor was no more than a refined version of the specialised knife that had done the job for centuries. It was first marketed by an American with the commercially valuable name of King Camp Gillette in 1904, but although he was the first person to realise the commercial possibilities, its invention, in the strict sense of the term, was patented in 1847 by a Londoner, William Henson. All the essentials of Gillette's razor are to be found in Henson's patent for a 'comb-tooth guard or protector' to be attached to an ordinary razor, and a razor, 'the cutting-blade of which is at right angles with the handle, and resembles somewhat the form of the common hoe.'

The first year sales from Gillette's factory in Boston, USA, amounted to 90,000 razors and 124,000 blades; by 1908 the annual production of blades had passed 13 million. In 1905 Gillette opened his first overseas factory, in London. In 1909 he built a factory in Leicester, and in 1920 he set up a plant at Slough, for manufacturing and distributing throughout Europe. By 1925 his company was making nearly 15 million razors every year and more than 300 million blades. When Gillette died in 1932 he felt able to boast that he had done more than any other person before him to 'change the face of mankind'. This may have been so in the sense that fewer men cut

themselves each year as a result of his and other firms' safety razors, but, for all its refinements and commercial success, the safety razor was no more than a continuation and development of a tool which already existed and in one important respect it was a backward step. What other kind of knife does one throw away as soon as it becomes blunt? The razor-blade is, at one and the same time, a technical triumph and a technical idiocy. The innovations which have been brought in since Gillette's first invention do no more than add a gloss to the basic product — the stainless steel blade, the plastic-coated blade, the adjustable razor, the platinum blade. From beginning to end the safety razor belongs to the age of coal and iron.

The electric shaver works on a completely different system. The original patent belongs to an Englishman, G.P. Appleyard, whose 1913 specification described 'a power-driven shaving appliance', comprising 'a fixed cutter A, having finely serrated edges, co-operating with a reciprocating blade B'. The reciprocating blade, he said, 'may be rotated or osculated and actuated manually, mechanically or electrically'. Appleyard's invention had no immediate success, however, for all its attraction. This was, first, because very small electric motors were not available at the time, and, second, because metallurgy had not yet developed to the point at which the parts of such a shaver could be satisfactorily designed and built. The modern dry shaver allows the hairs to slip through holes in a very thin, tough metal plate, so that they can be sheared off or ground off by the moving cutter. All that has been developed, in fact, is no more than a very small lawn mower which can be used on the face. Such a piece of equipment could be bought, at a price, in the late 1930s, but the electric shaver did not really establish itself until the 1950s. The major developments this time took place in the USA and West Germany, the original British initiative by that time being exhausted. Somewhat curiously, the market for electric shavers is now almost static. Fifty per cent of men, in all the countries of the West use a safety razor and 50 per cent do the job electrically. The subconscious or conscious differences between the two groups are fascinating and go a long way beyond mere technology.

Chapter 6

The Manufacture and Care of Clothes

The history of clothes in the twentieth century may be divided into three parts — the history of fabrics, of garment-manufacturing and retailing, and of laundering and dry-cleaning. All three have an archaeology which illuminates, illustrates and corrects purely documentary history.

There are three particular trends to notice in the history of fabrics since about 1900: the decline of the cotton industry; the steadily increasing price of wool; and the development of synthetic fibres. Cotton and wool are First Industrial Revolution materials; synthetic fibres were created by the chemist and the engineer and belong to the Second Industrial Revolution. It is with the latter that we are chiefly concerned here.

Synthetic Fibres

Rayon

Rayon has a cellulose base. It was first produced commercially at Besancon in 1892. Six years later the New Artificial Silk Spinning Co. began manufacturing at Wolston, near Coventry, which can therefore be regarded as one of the birthplaces of the British rayon industry. There is, however, another place with an equally just claim to be regarded as the first site. In 1892 three British chemists took out the master patent for viscose, a liquid produced by treating cellulose with caustic soda and then with carbon bisulphide. The following year they set up the Viscose Syndicate, which in 1897 became the British Viscoid Co. This compart started a small experimental plant in Station Avenue, Kew,

London, to develop the technique of viscose-spinning. Edwin Beer worked there and in 1962 he was persuaded to set down his memories, which were subsequently published.[1] His reminiscences contain such items as:

> September 4th, 1899. The potman found, like me, that caustic soda dissolved his skin. The clumsy rubber gloves of those days leaked at the seams, soda got in, but couldn't get out. Raw red fingertips in contact with viscose, inevitable in washing jars, doing viscosities and so on, became poisoned,

and,

> Topham invents a gadget for drawing off the CS_2, finds it leaks and tells Baldwin to solder it up. Naturally there was an explosion, which might have been serious, but luckily (says Baldwin) the door was wide open and I found myself lying in Station Avenue near a hot soldering iron. This was on 27th September. Baldwin's wage was shortly afterwards raised from 4½d. to 5d.

These pioneers, one comes to realise, discovered the new techniques by risking their health and lives, as Marie Curie did in the case of radium. Without such reminiscences as Edwin Beer's, the story runs a serious risk of becoming too neat and tidy, too unrealistically straightforward. But Station Avenue, Kew, is still there, and one can go and look at it with Beer's revelations in mind.

[1] *The Beginning of Rayon* (privately printed, 1962).

Courtaulds bought the British rights to the Viscose Syndicate's process in 1904, and the works closed in the following year. Courtaulds built a new plant at Foleshill, near Coventry, on the Coventry Canal. One of the main reasons for choosing the site was the likelihood that the area would provide an abundance of cheap female labour. The labour materialised, but there was an unforeseen problem — the strong smell of carbon disulphide which the process emitted over the district, both from the spinning sheds and the effluent poured into the city sewers. The trouble was eventually cured, but a great deal of ill-feeling was caused in and around Coventry while it lasted. There were also complaints of night work in high temperatures and of temporary blindness among workers at the plant. The local newspaper, the *Coventry Sentinel,* in its edition of 4 May 1910 even went so far as to refer to rayon spinning as 'a loathsome, injurious and degrading occupation.' The new industry gradually settled into place, however, helped no doubt by the fact that in the early part of the present century men and women needed jobs so badly that they were prepared to endure working conditions which would be thought intolerable today. Great improvements in the quality of the yarn led to the use of rayon for industrial purposes, including hosiery manufacture. By 1913 the British output of rayon was 8 million lbs, amounting to 27 per cent of the world's output. Production declined to 3 million lbs during the First World War, but by 1924 all the lost ground had been more than regained and the annual figure had risen to 25 million lbs. In 1929 it had risen to 53 million. Many new firms entered the industry but Courtaulds continued to dominate it, and by 1927 they were responsible for 80 per cent of British production.

Courtaulds had moved over to rayon from silk. Another firm to do so was William Frost and Sons of Macclesfield. Frosts were silk throwsters and they bought Park Green Mills, in the centre of the town, in 1881. When rayon yarn was first received in Macclesfield it was woven on silk machinery and by silk-workers, who were far

from enthusiastic about the new material, possibly because it was, at this time, always called 'artificial silk', a term which was in general use until 1924 when the Americans replaced it by 'rayon'. In 1927 Courtaulds decided to do the same.

Cellulose acetate, the source of the second major cellulose-based fabric, had its origins in Switzerland, where the Dreyfus brothers patented and began to make it in 1911. Their factory was designed to produce celluloid, but during the First World

War they provided the British and French governments with cellulose acetate dope for strengthening the cotton stretched over aeroplane wings. Their company, Cellonite, set up a British factory at Spondon, Derbyshire, in 1917. The operating company, British Celluloid Ltd., had been registered in 1916, and after the War the Company turned its attention to making cellulose acetate, which it began to market in 1921 under the brand name of Celanese. It changed its name to British Celanese in 1923, by

89 The first viscose spinning machine built for Courtaulds by Dobson and Barlow and delivered in December, 1904. The small works at Kew, now demolished, was established in 1898 by C.H. Stearn, who had just patented his process for making viscose thread. Stearn had two aims: to make filaments for his newly formed electric-light company, and to produce 'artificial silk' fibres. Between 1899 and 1904 he sold off all the national patents rights, including the British rights to Courtaulds.

90 Courtaulds' rayon factory, Coventry, 1908. Built in 1905, its output had reached 3 million lb. a year by 1913 and Courtaulds had become much the largest and most successful of all the firms which had bought the national rights to the process.

which time it was making its own fabrics at Spondon. In dress fabrics and women's underwear Celanese became a serious competitor to viscose. Courtaulds started making cellulose acetate yarns in 1927, selling them under the name of Seraceta, but throughout the 1930s British Celanese continued to be by far the dominant acetate producer.[2]

Between 1905 and 1939, 33 factories are known to have been producing rayon in Great Britain. Sixteen of them had already closed down by 1939 and two more have gone since then. Most of the casualties occupied buildings which still exist and which are now used for other industrial purposes. One or two came to a less than honourable end. Bristol was an especially pathetic case. The nineteenth-century Great Western Cotton Mill, in the Barton Hill district, had fallen on hard times when the Western Viscose Silk Co. set up business there in the early 1920s. Both the multi-storeyed spinning mill and the single-storeyed weaving sheds were taken over for the purpose of manufacturing 'Wescosyl; the British-made artificial silk'. Working conditions were not good and there was friction with Courtaulds, who brought an action against them for the infringement of a patent. Judgement was in favour of Courtaulds and Western Viscose were ordered by the Court to 'deliver up the offending yarn'. This was in fact done in 1933 by the firm's liquidator. The spinning mill building has now been demolished, but the weaving sheds remain as the surviving archaeological evidence of a new Bristol industry which failed to establish itself, a last flicker of life in an old building.

It is important to remember that the real success with rayon as a commercial product came only when the textile manufacturers were persuaded by the yarn makers to buy the new material on a major scale. Much of the effort of Courtaulds and British Celanese was devoted to bringing this about. Rayon stockings were a case in point. Courtaulds salesmen tried hard for some years to get stocking manufacturers to use rayon and in 1912 an

---

[2] A new and important market for rayon, the reinforcing threads in tyres, was forecast, rather than entered, just before the outbreak of the Second World War in 1939. The yarn for this purpose had an exceptionally high tensile strength and had taken a number of years to develop.

---

important firm, Wardle and Davenport, agreed to give it a trial. By experiment and research suitable yarn was developed for the knitting machinery, and in 1913 it was reckoned that about 40 per cent of all the yarn produced was being bought by the hosiery industry.

Nylon

Nylon was first produced in America in 1937. In 1939, ICI, which held the British rights to the Du Pont patents, and Courtaulds, which had manufacturing experience obtained in the rayon industry, decided to combine to establish a new company. British Nylon Spinners was accordingly set up to produce and sell nylon yarn, made from polymer supplied by ICI. The Ministry of Aircraft Production was interested in the possibilities of nylon for parachutes and glider tow-ropes, and this meant that production could continue during the War. An old weaving-shed at Coventry was converted for the purpose, and the raw material, polymer, was imported from Du Pont in the USA until ICI was able to make its own. The spinning sheds at Coventry were hit during 1940 by a bomb which caused the start to be delayed until the beginning of 1941, and even then operations were possible only on a very small scale. The first ICI polymer plant at Huddersfield began working in March 1942, and the first nylon to be spun from ICI polymer came from the Coventry factory in the following month. By this time it had become clear that Coventry was very vulnerable to air attacks so a second small plant was built at Stowmarket, Suffolk. This was fully operational by the autumn of 1943. At the end of that year the Coventry and Stowmarket factories together were producing over one million pounds of yarn annually. Very soon after the War British Nylon Spinners built a large new plant at Pontypool, and the Coventry and Stowmarket plants were closed down in 1948. These two wartime factories, however, mark the real beginning of the British nylon industry and deserve the respect of industrial archaeologists for this reason.

British Nylon Spinners opened a second spinning plant at Gloucester in 1953. The buildings had formerly belonged to the Gloster Aeroplane Co. and had become redundant after the War. They were given a very thorough conversion and facelift, and a labour force, almost entirely male as a result of the regulation on night-shift working, was recruited and trained from the surrounding district. A considerable proportion of the new workers were unemployed coal miners from the Forest of Dean, who took to their very different duties at Gloucester surprisingly easily. Like the former silk workers at Macclesfield and Coventry, they mark the transition between the First and Second Industrial Revolutions.

The second major polymer-based fibre, terylene, was a purely British invention, made in 1940 by J.H. Whinfield who was employed by the British Calico Printers Association at their research section at Accrington. By contrast with nylon, which cost Du Pont a fortune to develop, terylene was very cheap, but little was done with it until after the War.

The post-war history of synthetic fibres in Britain is complicated. During the War Courtaulds had been compelled by the British Government to sell off its large American interest, as a means of raising dollars with which to pay for armaments, and in the 1950s the growing competition from nylon and terylene caused great problems in the rayon industry. A number of the smaller works were closed down and Courtaulds bought British Celanese in 1957 together with five other rayon companies between 1959 and 1963. This period saw the slaughter of a high proportion of the pre-war rayon factories. In 1961 ICI, in its turn, made a take-over bid for Courtaulds. The battle went on until the spring of the following year when ICI finally conceded defeat. Afterwards, however, the previous financial arrangements between the two companies came to an end. ICI gave up their 38 per cent shareholding in Courtaulds, and in 1964 Courtaulds sold their 50 per cent holding in British Nylon Spinners to ICI, which then renamed the enterprise ICI Fibres. Courtaulds also sold off the bulk of its remaining overseas interests and decided to concentrate on the British market. In 1964 it acquired two major groups in the British spinning industry — Fine Spinners and Doublers, and the Lancashire Cotton Corporation. By 1965 what had been the Company's Northern Textiles Division controlled 30 per cent of the spindles in Lancashire. The Chairman

91 Aerial view of Courtaulds' Coventry works in the 1930s. The original spinning mill is to the left of the clock tower in the centre of the picture.

92 British Nylon Spinners, Lockhurst Lane, Coventry. This pioneering plant received a direct hit during the air raid of 8 April 1941, only nine weeks after the first nylon in Britain had been spun there.

93 British Nylon Spinners, Stowmarket. First a flour mill and then a paint factory, it was used for nylon production after the bombing of the Coventry factory. After the War, it returned to its original function.

94 The campaign to sell rayon: a group of advertisements from the 1920s.

95 Conversion in progress of former Bristol Siddeley aero-engine factory, Gloucester, to new works of British Nylon Spinners.

96 British Nylon Spinners, Gloucester, as finally converted.

97 British Nylon Spinners becomes ICI Fibres.

As a result of the Development Areas Act (1944), British Nylon Spinners, subsequently ICI Fibres, decided to build its first permanent factory at Pontypool in South Wales. Site clearance began in April 1945 and by the end of 1946 the pilot plant was built and equipped. During 1947 it was used as a training centre for potential foremen and chargehands recruited locally, which allowed spinning in the first part of the main works to begin in April 1948. A large expansion, Pontypool 2, was completed in 1953 and by 1955 BNS were employing a total of 3,700 people there. Since then, world over-capacity in the industry has forced the sale of half of the factory buildings.

In 1953 the Doncaster rayon-manufacturing concern, British Bemberg, went into liquidation. BNS bought the plant and extended it considerably between 1957 and 1965. Demand was still running ahead of production facilities, however, and in 1959 the Company bought the factory at Brockworth, on the outskirts of Gloucester, which had been previously occupied by Bristol Siddeley (Engines) Ltd. It was converted within a year to its new purpose and production of nylon thread began in May 1960.

The Bristol Siddeley aero-engine factory was built in 1939 on a golf course. The old club house, used during the War as a drawing office, still stands. At the end of the War, what had then become Hawkesleys, i.e. Hawker Siddeley, used the buildings to build prefabricated houses, two of which, a bungalow and a two-storeyed house, were erected by the side of the club house and are still standing.

(The old Gloster Aircraft Co. was next door to the Bristol Siddeley factory. Its works was still making Javelin fighters in 1960, but closed down soon afterwards. Those premises, together with the airfield, now form the Gloucester Trading Estate.)

told shareholders in the annual report for 1965 that 'We wanted to ensure that there would indeed be a Lancashire industry to take our man-made fibres in the future'. A very large programme of modernisation and expansion was begun during the 1960s, involving the closure of old mills and the acquisition of further companies in every branch of the textile industry. Courtaulds came to control a major part of British production in weaving, knitting and bonded fabrics, dyeing, printing and finishing, and in the hosiery and garment trades. In the process the old divisions between natural and man-made fibres were broken down. Mixed fabrics became normal and both production and marketing were closely integrated over the whole range of textiles in order to meet changes in demand. In general, however, both Courtaulds and ICI have stayed with the lighter fabrics and yarns. They have not become greatly involved with woollen material, except as suppliers of synthetic yarn to be blended with wool by the clothing manufacturers.

During the late 1960s the manufacturers of synthetic fibres were faced with a very unwelcome situation — a serious and growing amount of excess factory capacity throughout the world. In 1972 it was reckoned that at least one third of the world's manufacturing facilities of these products did not fit into any reasonable forecast of what would be required in five or ten years' time. Existing factories consequently had to be closed and better use made of those which remained. Among the casualties was one half of the ICI plant at Pontypool, which has been sold off to other industrial concerns. These large buildings, opened with such confidence during the first flush of post-war optimism, housed the manufacture of nylon yarn for only 20 years. Their interest, so far as synthetic fibres are concerned, is now purely archaeological. The market has subsequently declined even further, and the amount of redundant factory space, and therefore of archaeology, has correspondingly increased.

There is, however, an important aspect of nylon and terylene archaeology which should not be overlooked. The factories for the manufacture of the first synthetic fibre, rayon, were all in old industrial areas, where buildings were usually packed fairly tightly together with little thought of amenity value. The second generation of fibres, however, was born at a time when manufacturers were much more concerned about their public image. They wanted to build up the reputation of being good employers and good neighbours and they sensibly concluded that such a development was more likely to take place if their factories looked modern and pleasant. British Nylon Spinners, therefore, went to exceptional trouble to landscape the surroundings of their factories. Apart from looking agreeable, this generous investment in lawns, trees, shrubs, flowers and houseplants helped to give an impression of elegance and luxury which transferred itself to nylon and nylon fabrics. Now, when nylon is taken for granted, this probably has less public relations value, but in the 1940s and 1950s, when nylon was still an innovation making its way against old-established alternatives, the gesture was important.

The Clothing Trade

The clothing industry has not operated in the same way. The most elegant clothes are often made in singularly depressing surroundings. One would have to look very hard indeed for a British clothing factory set on a spacious site against a background of trees and flowers. This sad fact has its roots in the history of the industry. Both large and small firms have tended to grow up either in existing factory areas or in run-down, often semi-slum, residential quarters. The odd firm, usually in knitwear, underwear or in some fringe trade — such as button-making or the manufacture of zip-fasteners — has established itself on one of the more pleasant, new industrial estates, but in general the image of clothing manufacture is still that of the smoky, crowded mill-town or of the urban sweat-shop. More important, the manufacturers do not seem greatly to mind, thinking, perhaps, that it is not where the clothes are made that matters, but where they are sold.

Technical Changes

If one compares the clothing trade as it is today with what it was in 1900, three major changes are apparent: the development of clothes which are lighter in weight; an increasing emphasis on easy washability; and an increased proportion of branded goods.

The nineteenth-century achievement was of a different kind and was concerned primarily with the mechanisation of tailoring processes and with the establishment of large wholesale clothing firms. In 1857 the Singer sewing-machine was introduced into England from the USA. Within two years, 30 machines had been installed by John Barrans of Leeds, who were pioneers in this country of the factory production of men's clothing. Increased sewing speeds led to quicker methods of cutting and to the use of the bandsaw, which allowed several layers of cloth to be cut at once and at much higher speed. John Barrans were responsible for this innovation too. By 1900, therefore, there was efficient machinery for cutting in bulk and for high-speed stitching. There were further improvements between then and 1920, notably the development of machines for blind-stitching, button-holing and sewing on buttons. The Hoffmann press, another pre-1914 American invention, made it possible to carry out pressing operations much faster.

Retailing

On the tailoring side of the clothing industry, the principal twentieth-century contribution has been in organisation rather than in the technical processes of manufacturing. Leeds has played a leading part, in this and as late as the 1950s it could be said that Leeds was the only British city in which clothing was the staple industry. In 1939 about one-third of the insured population of Leeds was employed in the clothing industry, and of these 90 per cent were classified as working in tailoring. A high proportion of these people were Jewish. When they first came to Britain as immigrants from East Europe, most of them found work in small workshops in either Leeds or in London, but as time went on they moved to the wholesale clothiers where wages and working conditions were usually better. In the 1881 edition of *Kelly's Directory* 21 wholesale clothiers are listed for Leeds. They include besides John Barran and Son, then much the largest, Joseph Hepworth, which subsequently showed itself to be the most imaginative and adaptable of all the

98 The beginning of mass-produced clothing in Leeds on the grand scale: Barrans' factory and warehouse (1879).

101 The largest clothing factory in Europe: Burtons, Hudson Road, Leeds. Manufacturing gone, this remarkable industrial monument seems destined for demolition.

99 ⎫ Barrans' factory, Leeds, today:
100 ⎭ converted to offices.

Leeds clothing firms. At first, the big Leeds clothing factories sold their ready-made products mainly to small shops scattered all over Britain. The manufacturer's name very rarely appeared on the clothes and, because the retailers operated only small businesses, the range of sizes and styles that could be carried was extremely restricted, a fact which did much to give ready-to-wear clothing a bad name. Some of the larger manufacturers tried to counter this by setting up what was called a Special Order Department, i.e. a section of the factory which dealt only in bespoke tailoring. 'Year by year', said an article in the trade paper *Men's Wear* in 1902[3], 'the Special Order Department increases in importance and some very shrewd men in the clothing trade express the opinion that in the near future the whole industry will be run on the lines of the Special Department; that is to say, the stock garment

[3] April 19, p. 333.

trade will become a thing of the past, or at any rate reduced to very small dimensions. All garments will be made to measure.'

To a great extent this prophecy was fulfilled. The new policy is particularly identified with Montague Burton, who set up in business as a retail clothier in Sheffield in 1900. He was an idealist who wanted to help his fellow Jews and who deplored the dreadful conditions which were then normal in the small clothing workshops and in many of the factories as well. In 1906 he began to set up a chain of shops in the North and North Midlands, together with a factory in Sheffield to supply them. In 1910 he moved to a factory in Concord Street, Leeds, in order to concentrate on wholesale bespoke tailoring. His real opportunity came at the end of the First World War when the demobilisation of millions of men, all anxious to forget about uniforms and khaki, led to a general boom in the tailoring trade. Burtons, with its unique integration of shops and factory, was able to take full advantage of the situation and expanded fast. By 1921, when he was only 36, Montague Burton owned the largest clothing business in Europe and was about to build the biggest clothing factory in the world, at Hudson Road, Leeds. It eventually covered 100 acres and housed 8,000 employees, providing working conditions and welfare arrangements which were unprecedented in the clothing industry. His accomplishment represented a revolution in retailing rather than a revolution in manufacturing.

These developments in Leeds were accompanied by an extensive building programme of new factories and shops. In 1950, when Burtons were at their peak, they could proudly claim that in one way and another they were providing employment for more than 100,000 people. The Burton shops were all built to a characteristic design, palatial but not excessively so. Many of them included a billiard saloon on one of the upper floors, an idea which was the brain child of Sir Montague himself. They were part of his campaign against alcohol and were aimed at giving young men a pleasant club atmosphere in the evenings and at weekends. They flourished throughout the 1930-60 period and were eventually closed and the equipment sold in the early 1960s. It was by far

102 Burtons, Taunton: the more typical and familiar face of Burtons.

The archaeology of the clothing industry falls into three parts — the small workshops, which may have changed hands and names several times, the mass-production factories, and the shops. Of these, the shops, or rather the former shops, are probably in greatest need of attention from the historian and archaeologist.

Twenty years ago, a walk through the shopping centre of a provincial town or a district of London would have revealed a number of well-known multiple tailors and outfitters — Burtons, Rego, the Fifty-Shilling Tailors, Hepworths, Hope Bros. and Hector Powe were the leading

names. Of these, two — Rego and the Fifty-Shilling Tailors — no longer exist, and two others — Hope Bros. and Hector Powe — now belong to Great Universal Stores. The casualties and the invalids, among which Burtons now have to be reckoned, at least on a manufacturing side, resulted mainly from the teenage revolution of the 1950s, which steadily worked its way up the market so that, in order to succeed, a shop had to sell a much wider range of clothes than its own company could possibly provide. Cheap clothes were certainly still wanted, but they were not required to be particularly durable and they had to be immediately available. A different kind of shop, differently stocked, is required to meet the needs of today's market.

the biggest sale of billiard tables ever to take place in Britain, and probably in the world.

Sadly, the Burton business has experienced great difficulties in recent years, mainly because it has failed, for some inexplicable reason, to realise that a generation has grown up with less demand for tailored clothes. To say that jeans killed Burtons would be an exaggeration, but it would certainly be true to say that between 1950 and 1970 the popularity of the made-to-measure suit and the collar and tie declined at a rate which shook the Burton business to its foundations. The old type of Burton customer was remarkably loyal to the company. He

could be depended on to go back to Burtons over and over again whenever he needed a new suit or a new pair of trousers. He was replaced, however, by a different kind of young man who bought his clothes off the peg as and when he saw something that caught his eye, who had different ideas of fit and style and who liked to assemble his wardrobe from a variety of sources. Burtons became aware of the change too late. The old partnership of the hundreds of branches and the great factory at Hudson Road, Leeds, no longer works. Left to buy its goods where it pleased, the retail side of the business could do very well, but encumbered by a gargantuan and obsolete tailoring organisation it found itself crippled and unable to develop along profitable lines. Hudson Road, once the pride of Leeds, may well become the largest industrial monument in the country.

Burtons was the biggest but by no means the only firm of its kind. The made-to-measure market was a rich one at the lower levels and many other multiple firms exploited it. Prices Tailors, another Leeds concern which traded under the name of The Fifty-Shilling Tailors, came second to Burtons, although on a slightly lower level. It was bought out during the 1950s by Great Universal Stores and eventually eliminated from the scene.

The development of the women's clothing industry into a highly organised machine for producing ready-made clothes by factory methods dates from the early 1920s. For dressmaking the date is rather later, about 1930s. One can certainly say that by the 1930s most fashion outerwear was being distributed directly from the manufacturer to the retailer, in contrast to the situation before 1918. The change was mainly due to the greatly increased importance of the department stores and the multiple groups, which had little need of wholesalers and were in a position to tell the manufacturers exactly what they required.

Marks and Spencer was the earliest variety chain store group to undertake the retailing of women's outerwear, and is still the most important. Until 1939 it had a 5/- limit on garment prices, which necessarily limited its activities to the cheaper qualities. Even so, it managed to sell a million dresses in 1930-1. During the 1930s British Home Stores and Littlewoods were also selling the cheaper lines of dresses, blouses and skirts. Woolworths, whose maximum price was lower still, had at this time debarred themselves from selling anything more than very minor items of clothing. Since 1945 all these chains have, of course, broken through their self-imposed price barriers and now sell the full range of both women's and men's clothing. The manufacturers who supply them have to work to very strict specifications: there is no doubt as to who calls the tune.

The specialist chains are concerned mainly with shoes and with fashion goods. Most of them obtain at least part of their stock from their own factories. During the 1930s C. and A. Modes were the most important firm in this field. Other multiple groups at this time included Barnett-Button, Willsons (London and Provinces) and Morrisons's Associated Companies, all of which helped to pioneer specialised techniques for retailing fashion goods by mass-distribution methods and at low prices.

The major department stores were all established before 1930, many of them much earlier. Most department stores tended to concentrate on women's and children's clothing, on fabrics and, to a lesser extent, on household goods. For the most part they had grown from small retail drapery stores, and they catered for two different markets. The main part of the store provided the manufacturer with access to a large middle-class market, and what was known as 'the bargain basement' catered for the lower income groups. In the North and in some of the London suburbs, conditions were often different and there were department stores here which did not aim at the upper sections of the market. In general, however, the pre-war department store was a middle-class institution. The groupings and amalgamations of the 1920s and 1930s increased the extent of centralised buying and merchandising policies and gave the retailer even greater power over the manufacturer. One should not, however, exaggerate this; in 1939 more than half of all women's and children's outerwear was still being distributed by small individual shops.

Clothes' Care

So far as the care of clothes is concerned, the two most remarkable trends of the present century have been, on the one hand, the decline of laundries and the growth of machine-washing at home — a development which would not have been possible without the development of reliable detergents and the installation of hot-water facilities and electric power — and, on the other hand, the enormous increase in the use of dry-cleaning.

Dry-Cleaning

The pioneer of dry-cleaning is usually reckoned to have been a French dyeworks owner, Jean-Baptiste Jolly, who in 1825 accidentally discovered that kerosene would remove dirt from fabrics. His firm, Jolly-Belin, progressed from kerosene to spirits of terebenthine and then to benzol, benzine and white spirit. Mr Jolly's grandson, Henri Petitdidier, spent part of his apprenticeship with dyers abroad, first with Spindlers of Berlin and then with Pullars of Perth. Both of these firms soon introduced a dry-cleaning service, making use of the expert assistance of operators borrowed from Jolly-Belin. Pullars first offered a cleaning service in 1866. Before this, the process had been carried out entirely manually. Pullars mechanised it by adapting existing dye-house equipment, but the first patent for a mechanical dry-cleaning machine was taken out in France in the late 1860s. Other patents followed, including one for the Barbe closed-circuit system of benzine cleaning and another for the Smith machine. Both these systems carried out the processes of washing in solvent, extracting the spirit from the clothes and then drying. The plant was bulky and suitable only for factory conditions.

Between 1890 and 1930 a great deal of experimental work was carried out with synthetic solvents in an attempt to find a method which was safe — the risk of fire and explosion with benzine and white spirit had been considerable which would not damage the colour and texture of acetate and tri-acetate fabrics, and which made it possible to employ relatively unskilled labour. Several types of improved machine were available during the 1930s, the most successful and best-known being the one developed by Burtols and installed in their plants. No example of any of them survives. The early history of what is now a large, flourishing world industry is entirely undocumented by any museum specimens of its machinery and equipment. We have nothing but catalogues and periodical articles to tell us how the job was done. No-one, for that matter, has yet written and published even an adequate history of dry-cleaning.

The economic structure of the industry has developed in an interesting way. It gradually became an essential community service by the establishment of centralised plants with feeder branch shops linked by rail and road transport — Pullars, for example, was wholly dependent, both for its dyeing and cleaning business, on the excellent network of railways which existed in Britain before the slaughter of the 1950s and 1960s. The large capital investment involved made the centralised plants into empires. The installation of smaller unit plant had already begun before 1939, especially with the Burtol machine, which was an enjoyable sight as it spun round full of clothes in the cleaner's shop window — this was known in the trade as 'exhibition cleaning' — but the War put an end to all development for the time being. After the War a large number of demobilised men invested their gratuities in the cleaning industry, usually by opening a shop for receiving customers' goods and farming the work out to centralised plants. These shops gradually bought, first, finishing equipment, i.e. presses, and then actual cleaning machines. A new industry grew up to supply them with the machinery they needed, the leading British firm in this field being Neil and Spencer, which was set up in 1936 in modest premises in Clapham, London. After these works were destroyed during an air-raid a move was made first to Effingham, as a temporary measure, and then in 1947 to a new factory at Station Road, Leatherhead. Neil and Spencer's 'Mark 1 Junior' machine, which was first produced in 1949, had a dramatic effect on the structure and future of the dry-cleaning industry which could hardly have been predicted. Cleaning became almost entirely an in-shop process, although the large centralised concerns fought a long hard battle to resist change.

The archaeology begins to accumulate in the 1960s. By 1960 the Leatherhead works was completely inadequate and another factory was taken over at Horsham, Sussex. This, too, was overtaken by demand and a third factory, at Raynes Park, was opened in 1969. All these are buildings of the standard, modern industrial type, with nothing architecturally or technically remarkable about them at all. Dry-cleaning machinery happens to be made in them today and it could be typewriters or vacuum cleaners tomorrow, with no major modifications required and no loss of efficiency. They are important, from the industrial historian's point of view, because they mark the growth of an industry which only really took off during the post-war period, and

103 Bollom Ltd., Bristol, 1947: a typical receiving shop of the period.

104 The same shop in 1980, under new management and with a very different function.

Bollom, a Bristol-based firm, has been established in the dry-cleaning business for more than fifty years. Like other concerns in the industry it operated for many years on the basis of a central works, where the cleaning process was actually carried out, and a network of small shops, to which customers brought garments for cleaning. Because no cleaning was done on the premises, these shops could be very small. The one illustrated here was on Blackboy Hill, Bristol, and in its size and character it was typical of the period.

As the picture shows, the company offered a number of other services in addition to dry-cleaning. The two women seen at work here are engaged on what was known as 'invisible mending', much in demand when natural and synthetic textiles were in short supply and expensive, but no longer needed a few years later, when market conditions had become quite different.

During the 1950s and 1960s firms found it cheaper to undertake routine dry-cleaning and pressing in the shops themselves, with small, reliable machines designed for this purpose. Many of the old shops, which were too small to take the new equipment, were then sold off. Bollom's Blackboy Hill shop was eventually taken over by Sweeney Todd, the hairdresser, who found its size and position entirely suitable.

because the machine which did more than anything else to revolutionise dry-cleaning was designed and built in the first of the three factories.

The dry-cleaning industry is now big enough to stand on its own feet, but until the 1940s the same firm usually undertook laundering and dyeing as well. Dry-cleaning was still regarded then as a curious American activity by most English people. The blunt truth is that until very recently any clothes which could not be washed spent their life loaded with dirt to an extent which is not pleasant to contemplate. Colours, especially of men's suits and overcoats, were deliberately kept dark for this reason. Lighter colours and the increased popularity of dry-cleaning have gone hand in hand.

The two major British dry-cleaning firms in the industry's centralised days both originated as dyers. Pullars, as we have already noted, was well-established in Perth by the 1860s. Sketchley

was formed in 1885 as a hosiery-dyeing business, and a cleaning and dyeing service for clothes was added a few years later. The name Sketchley was chosen because the first factory at Hinkley, Leicestershire, stood near the Sketchley brook and in the hamlet of the same name. Since 1950 both of these concerns have had to adapt themselves to radical changes in their pattern of working, finding new types of activities — such as the supply and cleaning of industrial overalls — as the old sources of income declined. Their premises are archaeologically significant because they are evidence of the different economic stages through which these old-established, enterprising companies have passed and of the pre-1939 prosperity which justified the size of the buildings in use during that period.

Laundering

The laundry industry, too, has

undergone great changes since the 1950s. The unpopularity of the work, in a period of full employment, and the steadily increasing cost of labour, virtually killed laundries so far as individual customers were concerned. Many laundries closed and the buildings were converted to a multitude of new purposes. An interesting chapter of social history is waiting to be written around the rise and fall of the laundry in Britain. Institutions, of course, continue to make use of laundries, although even here every attempt is made to avoid the need for laundering. Most clothes and household textiles are now washed either in washing machines or in similar machines in launderettes. The first launderette in Britain is believed to have been set up in Falmouth in 1956, to provide a quick service for yachtsmen and the crews of merchant ships. There are now reckoned to be at least 10,000 of them in England alone.

Chapter 7

The Motor Industry

'The Motor Industry' involves a good deal more than the making and selling of cars and lorries. It includes servicing and repairing them, fuelling and garaging them, and providing them with accessories and replacement items of all kinds. A petrol filling station and a tyre factory are both parts of the motor industry, if one is to use the term with any exactness or usefulness at all.

Early History

The early history of the automobile is a confusion of claims and counterclaims. Gottlieb Daimler, with his car of 1885, was early in the field, but it is alleged that an Austrian, Siegfried Narkus, had designed and driven a four-wheeled car as early as 1875. By the 1890s a lot of people were making experimental cars in Europe and America, but it took many years before the would-be motorist could buy a reliable vehicle which he could depend upon to bring him home. Even so, the growth of the market was rapid. In 1897 there were 90 cars on the roads of the USA; in 1906, 100,000; in 1913 one million; and in 1928, 21 million. In 1931 there was one car to every seven people in the USA and one to every 60 people in Great Britain.

One of the best ways of getting the feeling of the industry in its early days is to study the catalogues of the Annual Motor Show. A complete file, from 1903 onwards, is to be found at the London headquarters of the Society of Motor Manufacturers and Traders. The 1903 edition states that:

Nothing is more remarkable but at the same time more natural, than the extraordinary hold the sport of motoring has taken on the affections of all classes of English society since that dreary day in the winter

of '96 when the scanty, mud-bespattered procession of pioneer enthusiasts found their way through many viscissitudes from London to Brighton. This was barely six years since, and the journey of 52 miles was only accomplished by the few entrants who eventually reached their goal after innumerable tinkerings en route with unruly mechanism. Today a non-stop run of 100 miles is happily no uncommon performance. As a natural consequence, the use of the most powerful cars has not only become possible to the mere civilian, as contrasted to the working engineer required to run the unwieldly mechanism of '96, but owing to the rapid strides made in the design and efficiency of the low-priced motor bicycle, the sport has been brought well within the reach of every old cycling enthusiast.

In 1903, it will be noticed, motoring was regarded as a sport, not as a routine means of transport. (If one wanted mere transport, there was the train.) The British, said the catalogue, were backward compared with continental countries. In France, there were 70 firms making cars and in 1902 they produced 12,000 cars. British firms had not made half that number.

The exhibitors in 1903 and in every year up to the outbreak of war in 1914 were mostly manufacturers who have long since disappeared from the scene. Of those which survived into the 1920s, and in some instances later, one might mention Dennis of Guildford, Siddeley of Coventry, Humber of Beeston, Thornycroft of Basingstoke, Daimler of Coventry — 'By special appointment to His Majesty the King and Contractors to the War Office'. Dunlop tyres were represented in

1904, with a charming advertisement. It reads:

Dunlop tyres for motors used to win the Gordon Bennett Cup, running between Paris and Vienna without a puncture. Also used when the kilometre was covered at the rate of 80 m.p.h., world's record. In the Automobile Club Trials, Mr W. Ducross successfully drove 4,000 miles upon one set of standard pattern Dunlop tyres, selected at random from our ordinary stock.

Car Manufacturers

Ten years later there are some more familiar names — Riley, Rolls-Royce, Austin, and Rover. Rolls-Royce simply announced that they made 'the best car in the world', and left it at that. The Company had permanent headquarters much earlier than the other major manufacturers, which makes its archaeology fairly simple to trace.

Rolls-Royce

The Company was established in 1906, as the result of a merger between the engineering firms of Royce Ltd. in Manchester and C.S. Rolls and Co. in London. After launching Royce's beautifully made two-cylinder 10 h.p. two seater[1], the new Company decided to concentrate on a six-cylinder 40/50 h.p. model.[2] There was a most encouraging demand for it and the works at Cooke Street, Manchester, very soon became too small. A new factory was built at Nightingale Road, Derby, and the firm began to transfer itself there in 1907. The premises have been greatly expanded since then, but the original building is still there and Nightingale Road has always remained the Rolls-Royce headquarters.

The manufacture of luxury motor-cars came to a halt during the First World War and Rolls-Royce turned its attention to aero-engines. Its first engine, the 'Eagle', was designed in 1914, and by the end of the War 4,581 'Eagles', together with the smaller 'Hawk' and 'Falcon', had been built, all at Derby. New buildings had to be erected for the purpose and men recruited. During the 1920s and 1930s Rolls-Royce developed its aero-engine business, mainly for civil flying, as best it could and maintained a steady but not spectacular level of production for cars, especially for export. It had no need to expand beyond the Derby works. Once the Second World War had broken out, however, Rolls-Royce ceased to mean simply Derby. Its famous 'Merlin' engine was in small-scale production before 1939 and thereafter it was made in very large numbers in new factories in Glasgow, Crewe and Manchester — the plant at Trafford Park, managed by Fords. The 'Merlin' went into tanks and motor torpedo-boats as well as aero-planes.

In the later stages of the War Rolls-Royce took over the development and production of jet engines from the Rover Co., with a factory at Barnoldswick. This engine, the 'Welland', went into the Gloster Meteor, the only British jet fighter to go into action before the end of the War. Since 1945 mergers and organisational changes within the aviation industry have brought the large aero-engine factory at Filton, near Bristol, within the Rolls-Royce empire. The bankruptcy which overtook the Company in the early 1970s, as a result of its over-commitment to American orders, and from which it had to be rescued by direct Government intervention, is a story on its own. It is worth remarking, however, that despite the troubles of the aero-engine side of the business the major sector, Rolls-Royce cars, has continued to sell well and to be profitable.

[1] There is an example of this, with the registration number AX 148, in the Science Museum.

[2] No. 13 of the six-cylinder model had an aluminium finish to the open body, with all the fittings silver plated. It was christened the Silver Ghost, a trade name which Rolls-Royce kept very profitably for 19 years. The original, one of the great automobile museum pieces, is in the possession of the Company.

Against this general background, what then is the archaeology of Rolls-Royce and in what way does it enrich and straighten the record, bearing in mind that there is no shortage of museum specimens of Rolls-Royce cars — they are a long-lasting and much-cherished breed — and that the Company's records, both on the documentary and the photographic side, are very good? The archaeology can, in fact, help the historian in four ways. First, by studying the growth of the Derby works, especially by means of aerial pictures, one can see very clearly how the huge business of aero-engines grew up around the successful but always relatively small business of high-quality motorcars. Second, by moving outwards from Derby and considering the map of Britain as a whole, one notes what might be termed Rolls-Royce's new territories, acquired and settled under war-time conditions and always very vulnerable to troubles within the 'empire'. Third, and returning to Derby itself, one has the great quantity of housing, of different sizes and prices, built over a period of more than 50 years to accommodate the people who worked at Rolls-Royce. This is Second Industrial Revolution workers' and managers' housing, as historically important and characteristic of the

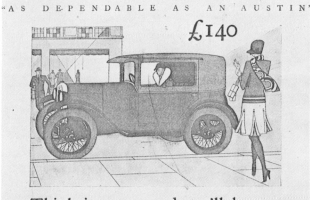

105 'As dependable as an Austin': Austin advertisement, 1930.

107 'All the World Loves a — Ford': Ford advertisement, 1915.

106 'Fit Dunlop the tested tyre': Dunlop advertisement, 1935. (Dunlop Ltd.)

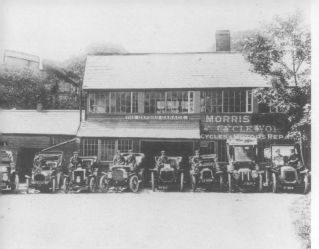

108 'The Oxford Garage' before the First World War. William Morris is seated on the extreme right.

109 Morris, Cowley assembly line, 1934.

111 and **112** (above)
Dagenham plant, Ford Motor Co., in 1949 and 1972. These two aerial pictures show growth and change at the plant over the period, together with the areas reserved for further expansion.

110 (above)
Former Avon Rubber Co. premises in an old woollen mill, Limpley Stoke, Avon.

The assembly plants of the automobile industry present the archaeologist with two main problems. The first is the chaotic nature of the layout of all but the most recent. They grew piecemeal, and the buildings are of a wide range of dates and styles: aerial pictures make the point very well. Such plants are not an industrial planner's dream. The second difficulty is that the emergence of the four major manufacturers since 1950 — British Leyland, Ford, General Motors and Chrysler — has obliterated the names of the original companies which built the factories. In many other cases, as with the Avon Rubber Co., the name continues but the building is no longer used for its original purpose.

period as the Wimbledon villas and South Wales miners' terraces of Victorian times.[3] And, fourth, one should certainly consider the Company's London showrooms in Conduit Street and those of the main Rolls-Royce and Bentley dealers, Jack Barclay, in Berkeley Square. With their solid grandeur and dignified respect for wealth, these showrooms tell one a good deal about the special place which Rolls-Royce has always occupied in the world car market.

Austin-Morris

Austin started making cars at Northfield in 1905, while Morris, graduating via cycles and motorcycles, was selling the first cars of his own design in 1912. They both survived and prospered because, unlike nearly all of their competitors, they could see that making cars was essentially a matter of assembling components made by other firms and that, with so many concerns trying to be car manufacturers, success must inevitably go to those who were efficient organisers who drove a hard bargain with their suppliers. For this reason Birmingham, Coventry and Oxford were good places in which to establish a car-assembly plant; they were conveniently situated in relation to those who provided them with all the bits and pieces that went to make a motor-car.

Looking through the pre-1914 Motor Show catalogues one is struck by the fact that a high proportion of the exhibitors were in comparatively out-of-the-way towns such as Redhill, Lowestoft and Salisbury. They were not in 'engineering country', a fact which put them at a serious disadvantage once the car industry had begun to emerge from its infancy and to enter the competitive phase of mass-production. The lesson had already been learnt by the bicycle-firms from whose ranks William Morris himself had emerged. By the 1890s the Midland bicycle industry had created a network of local firms making, for instance, steel tubing, tyres, wheels and springs. The motor-car industry

[3] The estates created to house Ford workers at Dagenham, Vauxhall workers at Cowley and Austin workers on the western outskirts of Birmingham are, of course, part of the same story. They all illustrate the influence of the automobile industry on the landscape and on the social pattern of Britain.

took advantage of a system which it developed but did not create.

Morris Motors did best before it became too big for Morris himself to control along traditional lines. The Company produced 2,000 cars in 1920, 3,000 in 1921 and 6,300 in 1929. When this point had been reached it proved necessary to buy some suppliers (such as U.S. Carburettors) and to set up others (such as Morris Engines Ltd. at Coventry) in order to be sure of getting the quantity of components that were needed. In 1926 Morris helped to create the Pressed Steel Co., a joint Anglo-American concern, to use new American techniques in the building of all-steel car bodies.

The statistics relating to Morris Motors can be interpreted in different ways. On the one hand, one sees that in 1935 the Company produced one-third of all the private cars made in Britain — 96,000 out of a total of 311,000 — but employed only 8 per cent of the total number of car-workers. This can only mean that productivity was remarkably high and that Morris Motors was an exceptionally efficient firm. On the other hand, by looking at the number of cars produced by each of the major companies in 1929 and again in 1939 one may conclude that Morris were losing their grip, with an increasing share of the market going to their competitors. The percentages were:

	1929	1939
Morris	51.0	26.9
Austin	37.3	24.3
Ford	5.7	14.7
Standard	4.9	12.8
Rootes	—	10.9
Vauxhall	1.1	10.4

Another way of looking at the same figures is to notice that the market grew remarkably during the decade 1929-39 and that one of the causes of this growth was that a wider range of people were buying cars. Given a more heterogeneous group of purchasers, it would seem both inevitable and desirable that there should have been more models to choose from. A more equal spread of sales between the different manufacturers would therefore appear to be a sign of health rather than the reverse.

The buildings occupied by the various companies are an interesting illustration of their history. Morris manufactured cars in a disused mili-

tary training college where, as it happened, his father had been educated. As the business grew more land was acquired and further buildings were erected. The original buildings are, however, still there and still in use. The circumstances of this growth have made what is now the Cowley plant of British Leyland a chaotic-looking jumble of buildings. Much the same can be said of the former Austin plant at Longbridge, which contains buildings dating back to the 1920s and even earlier. The Ford plant at Dagenham and General Motors' at Luton seem, at least to the visitor, rather more coherent and workable. In the case of General Motors there is good reason why this should be so. In 1923 the Company opened a branch factory in the Edgware Road, London, to make first American models and later the British-styled Vauxhall. Frigidaire, a division of General Motors, went into part of the premises in 1931, to make refrigerators, and took over the whole of the site in 1946 when Vauxhall moved into a new factory at Luton.

One has, therefore, the production of the pre-1939 British motor industry, both in museums and, in greater numbers than one might think possible, still on the road. They can be examined, evaluated, driven. We have the premises from the small, garage-like places which did a turn at the beginning of the century to the giant plants which were developed 30 or 40 years later. There is an abundance of statistics, photographs, catalogues and sales literature of all kinds, and these are biographies of several of the pioneers. Yet the possibility remains that this mass of information somehow does not add up to the complete picture, that a dimension is missing. That dimension is the individual and collective memory of the men who actually built the cars.

There is, for example, Mr J.R. Downes, a skilled turner. His first job in the industry was in 1910, at the Maudsley Motor Co., Coventry. 'We used to make one car a week,' he remembers. In the following year he moved to Singers, and then went from one Coventry motor works to another until 1944, when he retired and took over a newspaper shop. 'There was', he says, 'no need to serve an apprenticeship in those days. You could learn the trade better as a freelance'. In other words, one's knowledge and skill

76

developed by going from firm to firm, and 'at the end of six months your old foreman would always give you your old job back if you were any good'.[4] Permanent jobs were scarce in the motor industry, because production was very seasonal. A man could reckon to get six months' work a year; more, with luck, in the toolroom, but for a toolmaker 'the money was not so good as you could earn on piece work'. Sixty years ago the industry had exactly the same problems over differentials which plague it today.

One learns curious things from these old men's memories, things which do not often appear in books. Mr Downes worked at Dunlop, 'on what we called the conversion job. That was turning hubs for all makes of lorries and buses. We then fitted a new rim on the hub for a pneumatic tyre, which lowered the taxation'. These were the days when most goods vehicles still had solid tyres, which did more damage to the roads. By taxing pneumatic tyred vehicles at a lower rate, the Government was trying to persuade owners to go over to the more expensive tyres, despite the risk of punctures which the solid tyres, of course, avoided.

The men were paid in what now seems an extraordinary way — 'out of the hat':

the sections were split up into gangs, run by a charge-hand. On Friday he would go down to the office and get paid for all the work he had sent in for that week. It was tipped into his ordinary cloth cap, gold, silver and copper. He would then come round to you and give you what he thought you had earned and he pocketed the rest, often £7 — £10. It was an unfair system, but nobody would do anything about it, otherwise you would not get another job next year.

Mr J.C.J. Smith began his career in the motor industry on the upholstery side, with the Coventry branch of Fry's, a Dublin-based firm which had been established for many years in the carriage trade. 'I started work there on Armistice Day, November 11, 1918,' he remembers. 'The boss, H.J. Tweedie, gave me half-a-day and half-a-crown.' Fry's works were in Dublin and there were only four people at the Coventry depot:

They manufactured piping, braids, lace and fancy webbing for coach upholstery and also acted as sole agents for hood twills, duck, hides and leather cloth. Our customers included Hollick and Platt, Cheyleswood Bodies, Musson and Friendly, who made cars bodies for Swift, Lee Francis, Standard and Armstrong Siddeley.'[5]

All these companies have now disappeared. They were part of the rich texture of the motor industry in the early days and they provided a fine variety of employment. If one was dissatisfied or ambitious one could always try for a job where the pay and conditions looked better.

Mr Smith found himself attracted to the Standard Motor Co. and in particular to its spare parts section which, unlike manufacturing, had the great attraction of providing all-the-year work. The organisation of such a section in the 1920s was interesting. At Standard:

the Brain was a little chap, Jimmy Griffin. He knew every part number — well, 90 per cent of them — without looking at a parts list. Four typists did the works orders from his paper work. The stores put what we called 'the bits' into trays with the order and a conveyor passed these to six girl packers. Invoices were typed from the duplicate orders and another conveyor took them to the Post Room. We gave customers a very good service, two to three days only.

Today's motorists are likely to find such speed unbelievable. The days of 50 years ago are weeks and even months now.

After a few years Mr Smith found himself obliged to leave Standard, for they built a works on a new site outside the city and transport to and fro was too great a problem for Mr Smith. In common with most other employees of the motor manufacturers at the time he had no car. So he went to Riley and produced their first spares catalogue. Before this, a customer would obtain a replacement part from the works either by sending a description of what was wanted or by posting the broken part itself. The Riley catalogue was a high-class affair, with photographs, but it concealed an impoverished company. 'We were', Mr Smith remembers, 'paid by cheque each month. Funds were so low that we often had to wait until the 10th or 12th of the following month for our money. I was lucky because I was single, but I was always making loans to the other men'. One begins to understand why Riley was eventually taken over by the distinctly more affluent William Morris. But, despite the slow payment of wages, the men at Riley counted themselves fortunate. They made a highly respected car and working conditions were comparatively good. The contrast with Midland Light Bodies, where Mr Smith had friends, was very marked. This was an off-shoot of the Rover Co. and made the 8 h.p. air-cooled car. 'There was a saw-mill, with very little in the way of dust-extraction, a stores about 30 feet square, one wooden office, trim shop, paint shop and assembly'. This was a good deal more typical of the British motor industry in the 1920s than Cowley or Longbridge.

Memories of the early days of Cowley are plentiful. Those of Mr Bob Roberts, who was making body panels at the works there soon after the First World War have been quoted earlier (p.00). How he came to be there in the first place is an interesting story. Morris assembled his labour force from a great variety of sources — men attracted by the high wages of a prestigious new industry and prepared to put up with the insecurity and seasonal working it involved. Mr Roberts 'started as an apprentice at J.H. Grants, Ironmongers, Princes Street, Cowley Road, Oxford, to be a constructional engineer in the year 1913. I worked daily from 6 a.m. to 6 p.m., with half an hour for breakfast and one hour for dinner. Saturday with 6 a.m. to 1 p.m., so I got paid 2s. 6d. per week for a 60 hour week'. In 1917, when he was 16, he joined the Oxford and Bucks. Light Infantry at Cowley Barracks. He stayed in the Army after the War with the intention of making it his career, but in 1925, when he had reached the rank of sergeant, the Geddes Act — and the spending cuts that came with it — decided him to leave, and he had to look around for a job in what was very much an employer's labour market. Influence was required and Mr Roberts was lucky. 'My wife's school pal was Miss Hilda Church, Secretary

---

[4] Correspondence with the author, April-May 1977.

[5] Correspondence with the author, April 1977.

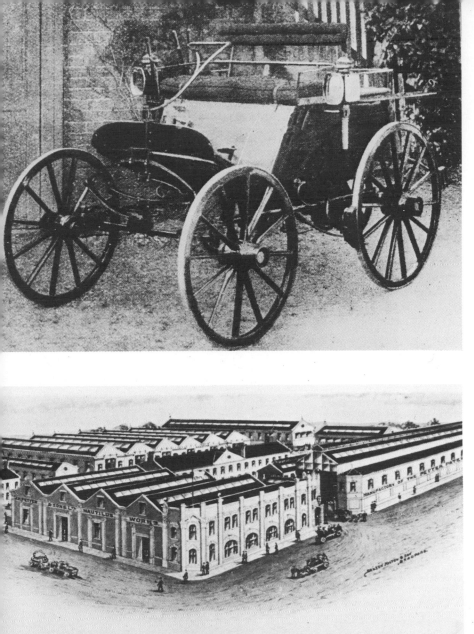

113 The last of 12 Petters cars built between 1895 and 1897. This one was built for *The Engineer's* competition of 1897 in the grounds of the Crystal Palace.

The motor industry is a very fertile and, thus far, largely uncultivated field for the industrial archaeologist. The range of material is embarrassingly large — garages and workshops of all sizes, factories occupied by makers of tyres and components, as well as the assembly plants themselves, filling stations, multi-storey car parks, the homes of Lord Nuffield, Lord Austin and the other tycoons of the industry, showrooms. Every district has examples of the garages and filling stations, some remarkably early, and the need to identify and record them is urgent since the 1970s and 80s will be seen in the future as the main period for the closure of the small servicing and repair units which characterised the industry for most of its history until that time.

Birdseye view of the Nautilus Works, Yeovil, England.

114 First production factory of Petter and Son, Yeovil. Built in 1900, it was the main factory until the move to Loughborough in 1938.

HOUSE, SHOWROOM & WORKSHOP

FOR SALE

Humbert, Flint, Bawlence & Squarey

115 Redundant filling-station, Langport, Somerset, in 1978. Built in the 1920s, this garage — like hundreds of others — was finally killed off by rising costs; now craft workshop and showroom.

116 Chloride Industrial Batteries, c.1900: original battery plate making machine. This method of battery manufacture, now defunct, used lead chloride as the active material, from which the Company derived its name.

117 Yeovil bus depot. Originally part of the Petter factory, it saw the production of the famous 'Nautilus' grates, the Petter Horseless Carriage, lighting sets, cranes, tractors and oil engines.

to Mr William Morris. She said, "Tell Bob to come home. He can start at Morris Motors." I left on the Friday and started the next Monday. I know Hilda Church — now Lady Miles Thomas. She married one of the Directors.'

In 1928 Mr Harold Brooks got in without influence:

I was having a day in Oxford and had just finished a 12 week stint at the sugar beet factory at Eynsham. On the spur of the moment I thought I would try Morris for a job, so, taking a bus to Cowley Works, I was surprised to see a queue and to my surprise I landed a job. I had heard so much about the high wages they were getting and I thought myself very lucky. I was in my early twenties.

They gave me a card and sent me down to the machine shop, to see the supervisor, Mr Jack Beasley who, I may mention, was a very fine and fair man indeed. 'Yes', he said, I would do and could I start now? Being in my best clothes, I suggested the next morning, and he happily agreed. I started in with a gang of chaps assembling back axles, which were delivered from a factory in the North, Rubery Owen. There were about a dozen chaps in the gang.

My first week's wages completely spellbound me. I had never held such money before. Our wage was 1s 3d., plus bonus, an hour, and our bonus was always more than our hourly rate, which amounted to between £5 and £6 a week. That was more than a bricky, carpenter or any other sort of tradesman was getting. I was single then, but after leaving 30/- a week in the bank, I managed quite easily to get married in a twelvemonth.

One thing Billy Morris would not have was a union of any description in his factory, and the majority of workers were not in the least worried, as they were getting more a week than any other worker in all Britain. I shall never forget what my dear old mother-in-law said, 'It's never right for you to get all that money', and I had to agree with her. It wasn't right, especially when farmworkers were getting about £1 a week and other tradesmen only £3 5s 0d. at the most. As

far as I can recollect the toolroom men who had to put in seven years' apprenticeship were only getting 1s. 6d. an hour in those days, while we semi-skilled men were getting 2s. 6d. to 2s. 8d. an hour, and that is what the toolroom men are still fighting for today, and I must say I am in full agreement with them.

After a while the Morris machine-shop was moved to Coventry, and four men, including Mr Brooks, were transferred to spotwelding on the wings.

Piecework had been introduced then, but the timing of the jobs was quite easy. After a week you could earn an hour's wage in less than half an hour, and when there was a shout for more wings, well, you just had to do them and not book them in, as there was an understanding between us not to book more than a certain amount, as if we earned too much we might have had the job retimed. I know I did hours and hours of work for the firm for nothing, rather than have it retimed.[6]

[6] Correspondence with the author, May 1977.

118 Multi-storey car park in Fairfax Street, Bristol (1958), believed to be the first in Britain.

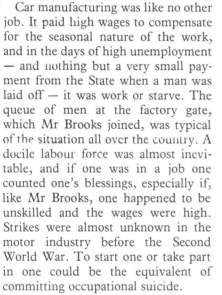

Stacked car parking came late to Britain. The earliest known example was built at Cambridge, Massachusetts, USA (1928), but Britain had no public car park of this kind until the 1950s. The pioneer town is believed to have been Bristol, where unimaginative post-war replanning had produced a degree of traffic congestion ahead of the national average at that time. The design and construction of multi-storey car parks has changed considerably since the 1950s but hardly for the better.

Car manufacturing was like no other job. It paid high wages to compensate for the seasonal nature of the work, and in the days of high unemployment — and nothing but a very small payment from the State when a man was laid off — it was work or starve. The queue of men at the factory gate, which Mr Brooks joined, was typical of the situation all over the country. A docile labour force was almost inevitable, and if one was in a job one counted one's blessings, especially if, like Mr Brooks, one happened to be unskilled and the wages were high. Strikes were almost unknown in the motor industry before the Second World War. To start one or take part in one could be the equivalent of committing occupational suicide.

If the employment situation had been different it is doubtful if the mass production of motor-cars would have started so easily. After all, a factory is fed with people as well as with materials and technology, and the expansion of the market for cars depended on using working-class people as efficiently as possible in order to be able to sell to middle-class people as cheaply as possible. William Morris and Herbert Austin knew how to do this and prospered. Most of their competitors, however, failed to deal adequately with the problem and went under. It remains doubtful whether many of them, being primarily engineers, really understood what the problem was.

When the reminiscences of the motor industry's old-timers have been gathered together, one is struck by the way in which they moved from one kind of job to another within the company concerned. Demarcation lines and disputes were virtually unknown, and a man did whatever had to be done, provided it was judged to be within his capacity. The point is well made, perhaps unknowingly, by Mr George Crook who went to work at Cowley in 1915, straight from school. His first job was in the Spare Parts Department and, in order to prove himself, he had to agree to work for a week for nothing. After that he was paid 5/- for a 59-hour-week. The orders, about a dozen a day, were passed on by the factory office. 'If an order was for a large piece, it would go by rail. The other lad and I would make a suitable box or crate — we later had a part-time carpenter for this — and it would be taken to Oxford Station by van. The smaller orders I would parcel up and take to the local post office.'[7] This may have been all very well in 1915, but it would be unthinkable today. Box making, parcelling and posting are now three distinct and clearly defined jobs, each with its own specialist staff. If a member of the Post Room or Dispatch Department were to start making boxes nowadays a

strike would be as certain as if someone working in the Crate-Making Department had so far forgotten himself as to put parts into the crates he had just made.

Even more difficult to imagine now is the kind of career which Mr Crook took for granted. In 1916, after his short period in the Parts Department, he went to the Engineering Department, making mortar bombs on the night shift. He was 14 at the time and his war-time experience led to a permanent career as a toolmaker. By the time the Second World War came, he was an expert at Universal Grinding and in charge of the night shift.

It is interesting to ask men like this about the atmosphere of the Works during the 1920s and 1930s. 'Discipline', says Mr Crook, 'was good. If a man *did* offend, he was told that there were plenty of men outside who would like his job. There were, too. But most of us were local men and Morris had a sort of sentimental effect on us. We were hard up, but we were happy. Mr Morris was a very active Managing Director and he was always available to discuss problems'. Times have indeed changed, and one is entitled to wonder how successfully and by what methods William Morris, with or without his later title of Lord Nuffield, would have run first the British Motor Corporation and then British Leyland, which inherited his kingdom. Would he have found a great deal to please him at Cowley today?

[7] Correspondence with the author, April 1977.

Car Component Industries

Many of the companies which supply the car factories with components have become large concerns in their own right with a wide range of products and many international interests. Dunlop is a good example. The first practicable pneumatic tyre was invented in 1888 by John Boyd Dunlop, who was neither an industrialist nor an engineer, but a Scottish veterinary surgeon practising in Ireland. The curiously and cumbrously named Pneumatic Tyre and Booth's Cycle Agency was formed a year later to develop and market his invention, mainly in the first place, to the cycle trade. To begin with, the tyres were made from material made by existing rubber firms, but Pneumatic Tyre soon found it prudent to acquire a rubber manufacturing plant of its own, and bought Byrne Brothers of Birmingham, which gave it a base in the heart of the bicycle and, as it later happened, the motor-car country. A second factory was established in the Birmingham area in 1900, and in that year the firm began making car tyres, changing its name to the Dunlop Rubber Co. in order to remove the previous association with cycles. This name remained until 1967, when it became simply the Dunlop Co., an acknowledgement of the fact that Dunlop's interests now extended a long way beyond rubber.

The history of Dunlop, from the point of view of the motor-car industry, can be seen to fall into four phases. The first, lasting from 1889 to 1920, established the Company as the major British supplier of tyres; the second, from 1906 onwards, added wheels to tyres, with a separate wheel manufacturing unit in Coventry. The third, beginning in 1909, gave Dunlop its own source of rubber. It invested heavily in Malayan estates and by the 1920s it was the largest owner of rubber plantations there. The fourth phase was marked by the opening of Dunlop's first cotton mill to provide a supply of tyre cord. Today, the subsidiary company, Dunlop Textiles Ltd., still has its main factory in the old cotton area at Rochdale, although production there is now confined to the rayon, nylon and polyester cords, which have succeeded cotton. In 1910 the company began to build aircraft tyres and in 1916 the construction of Birmingham's landmark factory, Fort Dunlop, got under way.

During the 1920s one of the pioneering British rubber concerns, the Manchester-based Charles Macintosh group, was added to the Dunlop interests, and so was a racquet factory at Waltham Cross, which led to the formation of the Dunlop Sports Co. 'Dunlopillo' latex foam, a Dunlop invention, was introduced in 1929 and began a new industry of its own. The remoulding business of Tyresoles was acquired in 1953, the John Bull group in 1958 and the Slazenger group in the following year. The result of this long process of developments and mergers has been that tyres, with which Dunlop started, now account for less than half of the Company's business, despite the vast growth of automobile and air traffic throughout the world.

Other car component firms have not shown the same degree of diversification as the old-established tyre manufacturers, but the same policy, freeing these companies from over-dependence on car makers, has been pursued by most. What has happened to the major battery-makers illustrates this. The chargeable battery was invented by Planté in the 1860s, consisting, as it still does, of lead sheets in dilute hydrochloric acid. The first major British battery factory began operating in 1893, at Swinton, Manchester. This factory, known throughout the trade as Swinton Junction, has produced a high proportion of the batteries which went into British-made cars, under the brand name 'Exide', which concealed the Chloride Electrical Storage Syndicate. Much of the original works still exists, although hemmed in by extensive later additions, but for some years it has made only industrial batteries, the manufacture of car-batteries now being concentrated at Dagenham.

Neither the history nor the archaeology of the motor industry can be confined within tidy limits. A car factory is the centre of a spider's web and, no matter which point one begins at, one's attention is always led elsewhere. To begin with body-work leads to a consideration of steelworks and paint-factories. Tyres take one on to synthetic fibres, sulphur and to that filthiest of all industrial substances, carbon black. Car interiors at one time implied tanneries and now suggest mainly textile factories. And, thinking of the vehicle as a whole, a car takes one's thoughts to garages and to petrol pumps, which also have their own archaeology. The location and recording of buildings which once functioned as garages is a major task, and one which gets more difficult each year. By the time one reaches the vantage point of the year 2000 it will probably be seen that more garages closed during the 1970s than in any other decade of the century. Centralisation and the creation of the big unit has hit the servicing and distributing side of the British motor industry much later than its factories but with equal force.

Chapter 8

Aviation

The largest preserved industrial monuments in Britain are the two great airship hangars at Cardington, Bedfordshire. The first, originally built in 1917, was extended from 106 feet to 155 feet in 1927 to accommodate the R.100 and R.101; the second was built to its full length in 1927, the year of the R.101's maiden flight. They are reminders, first, that aviation history is not only about aeroplanes and, second, that the archaeology of air transport is likely to be inconveniently large. For this reason the development of flying is poorly documented by the buildings and airfields associated with it.

As with automobiles, one has to consider not merely aeroplanes and airports but the whole business of making and operating aircraft — the factories, the town-terminals, present and former airfields, passenger and freight-handling buildings at the airports, etc. And, like the motor industry, the aeroplane industry has generated a wide range of component industries. In the days of propeller-driven aircraft the manufacture of propellers was a separate sub-industry, and since the 1930s the design and production of landing-gear has been a highly specialised affair, which one British firm has made peculiarly its own. The archaeology of this company, Dowty, is as much a part of the story of the British aircraft industry as the surviving buildings of the 1920s and 1930s in which the aeroplanes themselves were assembled.

The study of aviation history, in its broad sense, presents three special problems. The first is that the many people who have written about it have concentrated to an overwhelming extent on aeroplanes and on flying; they have had little attention to spare for such prosaic matters as airport buildings, organisation and passenger handling. The second problem is that, in Britain, hardly any passenger-carrying aircraft of the 1920s or 1930s has been preserved; there is nothing for us to look at, sit in or compare with modern aeroplanes. The third difficulty is that during the early years of aviation — which means, for the most part, up to 1939 — both civil and military aeroplanes operated from grass airfields. Even when fully loaded, they were light enough to take off and land from a reasonably level, well-drained and adequately mown field. Most of these fields, however, have now been built over, turned into sportsgrounds or, in one or two instances, returned to agricultural purposes. Even as an experiment in a light aeroplane, it is difficult for us to fly from a grass airfield and recapture the experience of the pioneering pilots and passengers. But it can be done, given the willingness to use one's imagination.

Flying Before 1939

The best place to visit to gain an impression of early flying is probably Shoreham, in Sussex. The pre-war airfield, with no hard runways and with its terminal buildings intact, gives a good idea of the scale and method of operation in pre-war days, when an airfield and its buildings resembled a golf-club with its club-house more than anything we are likely to recognise as an airport today. There is the very small lounge-reception area where passengers assembled, the bar, the door leading straight out of the waiting-room to the waiting aircraft, the single telephone box for those who felt a need or an inclination to communicate with the outside world. A more modern, but no larger form of the same basic arrangements, can be seen at places where only a small number of passengers have to be carried each day. Penzance and St. Mary's, Scilly, are good examples. A few minutes at one of these allows one to recapture the flavour of the majority of European airports as they were before 1939, when flights were few, an aeroplane was very large if it carried more than 50 people, and baggage was taken direct to the aircraft on hand-trucks.

No major British airport — Heathrow, Gatwick, Manchester, Birmingham, Prestwick — has anything to offer the archaeologist whose concern is with civil aviation in its pre-war days. Heathrow did not then exist, and the other four have either been completely re-built or altered out of all recognition. Military airfields and bases have fared somewhat better, although the installations here are not normally accessible to the general public. Of the two great names among British civilian airfields in the 1920s, Hendon now has the RAF Museum, but nothing of any operational significance; Croydon has been reduced to part of its 1928 terminal building, the airfield completely gone.

Croydon

The history of Croydon airfield goes back to the First World War when it

The fascination
and comfort of
Silver Wing Travel

TWO and a half hours from London to Paris—150 minutes. Punctuality is part of efficiency, and British efficiency in the air is the standard by which aerial standards are set. It is a fascinating and glorious experience to sit in the comfortable embrace to itself wings. You have the same comfort, the same safety and the same convenience even down to the same light refreshments on the way.
Ventilation can be adjusted to each individual passenger's liking. If it is cold, the air is warmed. Outside you can hear the hum of

Loading the Baggage.

The London Air Port.

IRISH SEA AIRWAYS
OPERATED JOINTLY BY
Aer Lingus Teóranta & WEST COAST AIR SERVICES LTD.

REGULAR DAILY SERVICES (including Sunday)
IN COMFORTABLE CABIN TWIN ENGINED AIR LINERS
CONNECTING
——DUBLIN——
with—
BRISTOL · ISLE OF MAN · BLACKPOOL · LIVERPOOL · MANCHESTER · CARLISLE · etc.

Time Tables are so arranged to give best possible connections with other Air Routes and Surface Transport.

119 Advertisement for Imperial Airways (British Airways)

120 Advertisement for Irish Sea Airways (Aer Lingus)

was established as part of the air defence of London. Aircraft from Croydon went up to attack the raiding Zeppelins in 1916 and the enemy bombers which came over during the following year. A training squadron was also based there. In 1918 the National Aircraft Factory was built on a site adjoining the airfield, in what is now Purley Way. Croydon aerodrome was formally adopted as the Customs Airport for London in 1920 in succession to Hounslow and for the next few years the original Royal Flying Corps' buildings in Plough Lane was used as a temporary airport, until a proper terminal could be established in 1928.

Between 1932 and 1937 the number of passengers passing through the airport each year increased from 70,000 to 140,000, an average of less than 200 a day in the first year and less than 400 in the second. By modern standards the figures are comically small, yet it was reckoned as early as 1934 that, if traffic continued to double every five years, an alternative to Croydon would have to be found. Nothing could be done before the Second World War, and during the War Croydon became an important centre of RAF operations. The terminal escaped lightly from bombings, but the hangars and other buildings were badly damaged and extensive repairs were necessary once the War had ended.

Croydon finally ceased operations in 1959. The terminal building was put up for sale and during the 1960s the airfield was covered by a housing estate. The estate agents' notice marks the end of the first period of British civilian flying, and is a useful source of information about the premises: 'The familiar landmark known as the Terminal Building, Purley Way', it said, was 'suitable for the headquarter occupation of an important organisation or for multiple occupation.' The area of the building was 66,500 square feet, 'exclusive of staircases and lavatories', and there was reckoned to be parking space for 120 cars. 'Originally built as an Air Terminal', the notice continued, 'the building contains spacious main and secondary entrance halls, with many well-proportioned office rooms. The buildings are of steel-framed construction with concrete block walls, the blocks having an imitation stone facing. Parts have brick infilling, the whole presenting a handsome appearance. The main entrance hall and the adjoining former buffet are mostly panelled in oak and contain a number of oak counters which will pass with the property.'

When the new buildings at Croydon were opened, it was announced that 'all services will start from the fine expanse of paving which takes the place of the tarmac of the old aerodrome. On entering the domed Booking Hall, one realises that air services have now taken their place in the civilised world as a recognised means of transport, no longer limited to a few adventurous

'Passengers had very little distance to walk from the check-in counter to the aircraft. The walk across the tarmac from the exit door to the aircraft was a particularly proud moment for most passengers, as they were in full view of the crowd of visitors on the control tower roof, who paid 3d. for the lower level and 6d. for the upper level viewing.' (Eric Engledew: correspondence with the author, 8 June 1977.)

Pre-war passengers would never have tolerated the enormous and exhausting walking distances which have to be endured at most major airports today.

spirits, but used daily by business men as well as those travelling for pleasure.'[1]

There are a number of what one might perhaps call 'fringe survivals' of the Croydon era of British civil aviation. One is the Croydon Aerodrome Hotel, the flat roof of which used to be a favourite place for watching the aeroplanes take off and land. It has many framed photographs of people and events connected with the airport. Another monument is Victoria Air Terminal, very much a building of the Modern Movement in architecture of the 1930s and, until the

[1] *Imperial Airways Monthly Bulletin*, January 1928.

The numerous histories of aviation have nearly all concentrated on the aeroplanes, the pilots, the hazards and operational matters generally. The handling of passengers has been neglected to an extraordinary extent, and a full-scale study of pre-1939 airports is long overdue, partly to do justice to one of the most interesting aspects of aviation and partly as a means of recalling and recording the very small scale of the airline industry during the inter-war period.

The memories of retired airline staff are essential, if the archaeology is to be brought back to life. At Croydon, for instance, 'the counter was highly polished and the Traffic Clerks in their navy blue RAF-type uniforms, polished buckles and crested buttons certainly helped to create the Imperial Airways image of ''The P. and O. Service of the Air''. On the airport bus London, 'one got an indication of the opulence of the passengers from the smell of Balkan Sobranie cigarettes'. (Patrick Gillibrand: correspondence with the author, 22 May 1977.)

121 Croydon aerodrome; main entrance in the 1930s.

122
Croydon aerodrome: main entrance hall, today used as a cash and-carry furniture warehouse.

123
Croydon aerodrome: the Aerodrome Hotel. The main block shown in the photograph dates from the late 1920s and is original, but the buildings have been considerably extended in recent years.

124 Former Imperial Airways town terminal at 13 Charles Street, Berkeley Square. Now renumbered 12A for superstitious reasons, No. 13 is the building with the three upper windows and the van outside.

creation of British Airways, the London terminal of British Overseas Airways Corporation. It operated until 1980 as a terminal for long-distance passengers from Heathrow. The original Imperial Airways town-terminal, in Charles Street, Berkeley Square, a small town house in a fashionable area, has since been converted into flats.

There is no great difficulty in reconstructing at least some aspects of aviation during the 1920s and 1930s as it was experienced by both passengers and pilots. The early London-Paris services from Hounslow used converted wartime aircraft and took only two or three passengers. The pioneering flight on 14 July 1919 had only the pilot and Major Pilkington, of the St. Helens glass firm. Both sat in open cockpits and, despite bad weather, the journey took only 2 hours 45 minutes, which was a very creditable time in view of the fact that in the early 1930s the Imperial Airways service was scheduled for 2 hours 30 minutes and

not infrequently required longer. The details of these flights are important to the archaeologist, partly because they indicate what the limits of the tangible evidence are likely to be, and what consequently has to be looked for in other directions, and partly because they help one to see the archaeology in its proper perspective. If one knows that Croydon was built to take 200 passengers a day, the buildings and facilities provided spell great comfort, which is almost inconceivable to anyone brought up to regard Heathrow as the norm. The veterans almost inevitably have nostalgic memories. One of them, Mrs Leonie Smith, made frequent flights to European cities before 1939. After the War, when flying became possible again, she much preferred to go by train. 'Having flown in comfort, with VIP treatment of every passenger', she said, 'I couldn't bear to be herded like cattle.'[2] She admitted, also, to suffering from claustrophobia under today's flying conditions, with so many people crowded into such a small space.

There are many details about the history of aviation which can only be gathered from the reminiscences of people who were personally involved. They have not found their way into any kind of official document and they are badly needed if one is to explain why civil flying developed in the way it did. And the plain fact is that if industrial archaeologists fail to collect these memories the probability is that nobody else will, since aviation enthusiasts are obsessed with aeroplanes, pilots and performances and have little time for the human aspects of the story, while specialist historians are generally busy with other matters.

The small things are important. Consider, for example, two stories which reached the author from Mr Robert Newman in response to a letter in the *Croydon Advertiser*. In 1918 he flew a military aeroplane, absolutely unofficially, from the Western Front to Croydon in order to buy some sports prizes from a local store. Having got the articles he wanted, he flew them back to France again. This tells one that military discipline was not as tight as one might have expected, that traffic control and security at Croydon were virtually non-existent in 1918, and that flying at that time had a delightfully amateurish quality about it, which gradually

diminished and disappeared as the scale of air travel increased. Pilots were neither grand figures nor highly paid in those days. Mr Newman well recalls, for instance, a pilot in the early 1920s who cycled each morning from Thornton Heath to Croydon in order to fly a consignment of newspapers and other cargo to Paris. He left as early as possible, turned round quickly and arrived home in time for breakfast. One cannot imagine a pilot of today either wanting or, indeed, being allowed to behave in this way. These, however, were relatively un-motorised, un-unionised days, when people still kept the use of their legs and had different notions of their own worth. In 1919, before Hounslow gave way to Croydon, a passenger on the London-Paris service usually went by the District Railway to Hounslow Station and then boarded a tram, which took him and his luggage to a far from convenient point just outside the aerodrome gates. This method of getting to one's aeroplane was soon found to be a problem so passengers were taken by car direct from central London to what was termed 'the departure platform' at Hounslow. 'There was', one of the first year's passengers suggested, 'something incongruous about reaching one's aircraft in this very slow and unremarkable way, before being whirled through the air to France at a hundred miles an hour,' and he is not the first person to notice the difference in time and speed between travelling to the airport and making one's journey by air afterwards.[3]

There is no difficulty in reproducing the first part of the 1919 London-Paris air link. One can still take the District Railway to Hounslow with one's baggage and note the time required and the journey's relative convenience and comfort. The tram, however, no longer exists and this stage has to be supplied by the imagination. So, too, do most of the other features of travelling by air 50 or 60 years ago such as waving to one's friends through the window of the aeroplane as it was taxiing away from the airport building, flying low enough to see everything on the ground very clearly, being weighed

---

[2] Conversation with the author, 9 June, 1970.

[3] Captain Bruce Ingram, in *The Illustrated London News*, 6 September 1919.

with one's baggage and being personally shepherded through the Customs by one's pilot.

In 1922 Handley Page put its new 12-seater aircraft on the London-Paris route. They had wicker seats and, for the first time, an in-flight lavatory, which was a British innovation. Considering the primitive navigational aids, a remarkably high degree of regularity was maintained, although one of the staff at Croydon between 1926 and 1929 recalled a number of unpublicised facts from this period, at a time when the public was being assured that flying was as safe as travelling by train. Once, when acting as a relief telephonist, she heard a distress call from a pilot over the Channel: 'I am coming down in the ditch.' He landed on the sea seven miles off the Varne lightship, with a dozen passengers on board, including women and children, and a Pekinese dog. They managed to clamber out of the plane and sat patiently on the wings, waiting for a boat to pick them up.[4]

Imperial Airways

By this time the British operating companies had merged to form a single airline, Imperial Airways, which carried the British flag until the outbreak of war in 1939. Both the British and the Dutch began operating services to the Far East in the late 1920s, with the South Africa route following soon afterwards, and these long-distance flights demanded a different standard of comfort and equipment, despite the fact that there was always an overnight stop. Broadly speaking, Imperial Airways aimed at attracting, on both the short and the long flights, the kind of people who normally travelled first-class by train and boat, and who were not prepared to tolerate hardship or inconvenience. They could see no reason why they should experience poorer conditions at Le Bourget or Croydon than at the Gare du Nord or Victoria, and the major national airlines did their best to provide the amenities required. The post and telegraph office, the row of telephone kiosks and the restaurant — not as good as Le Bourget or Amsterdam — brought Croydon up to the best railway standards.

The 'Heracles' aircraft introduced in the early 1930s emphasised the Pullman image, with its inlaid woodpanelling, comfortable armchairs, five-course meals and a passenger-regulated system for heating and ventilation. 'In "Heracles",' reported someone who had experienced the pleasure for himself, 'the occupant of each seat controls an inlet of cool air and a heating device that sends warm air up the legs of the sitter; most gratifying, I assure you.'[5] The greatest comfort of all, however, was provided by the 'Empire' flying boats, upon which Imperial Airways relied almost entirely for the Africa service after 1937. A contemporary description supplies some of the internal details:

The midship cabin is located behind the mail compartments, kitchen and toilets and accommodates three passengers by day and four at night. Then, further astern, comes the big promenade cabin seating eight or resting four. On the port side is a rail for elbow resting by the windows and a surprising amount of space for promenading. Leg stretching space — always welcome on long trips. Above this cabin is a loft for bedding stowage, and behind it a further cabin with six seats for daylight flying or sleeping accommodation for four.[6]

The later 'Frobishers' offered even greater refinements, but carried about the same number of people. Neither the 'Empire' flying boats nor the 'Frobishers' could match the airships with their pianos and showers for passengers, but they certainly gave everything which the railway Pullman, sleeping and refreshment cars supplied. Most regrettably, no example survives of these splendid aeroplanes. We cannot see or feel the amenities and the space for ourselves, so we must take the descriptions of passengers and of Imperial Airways on trust. There are black and white photographs but nothing in colour, so that much of the magnificence of the décor and fittings cannot be communicated to us. The aviation museum and the airlines between them have done virtually nothing to preserve the spirit and flavour of passenger-flying in the 1920s and 1930s.

There is not even a museum specimen of Imperial Airways' adjustable chair. Imperial Airways were extremely proud of this chair; they had researched and patented it themselves. It was manufactured under licence by Accles and Pollock and later, in 1938, by Junkers in Germany. Many thousands of travellers to Africa and the East had reason to be grateful for it. The Company attached great importance to it. 'By sea', said the Traffic Manager of Imperial Airways:

an outside room with bath is demanded, but by air the passenger's time is spent chiefly seated in a chair and depending upon his mood, that chair must enable him to sit upright when taking his meals, or to loll back in luxurious comfort to read, and in it he must be able to recline or doze or sleep. All this must his chair fulfil, and that independently of his fellow passenger, who may require his chair to do quite the opposite and at the same time.[7]

Visitors to museums with collections of historic aircraft and the equipment that went with it are likely to find that the story of military aviation is documented quite well and the story of civil aviation extremely badly. The history of the two overlaps to a considerable extent, of course, but the fact remains that aeroplanes flown by the RAF between 1920 and 1960 are remarkably well represented in museums, while the aeroplanes of Imperial Airways have disappeared almost completely. Much the same is true of airfields and bases. At places like Halton and Locking one finds the complete range of buildings erected from the 1930s onwards, sometimes earlier, in a way that Imperial Airways cannot match, even with the help of such romantic and largely unchanged sites as the former seaplane base at Hythe, on Southampton Water. RAF bases, however, are subject to the same criterion of size. All over Britain, one finds abandoned Second World War fighter and bomber aerodromes, many with their rusty, corrugated-iron

---

[4] Mrs Mary Hayman: conversation with the author, 15 June 1970.

[5] Stuart Menzies, *All Ways by Airways*, 1932.

[6] *Imperial Airways Monthly Bulletin*, December 1936.

[7] *Some Aspects of the Organisation of Empire Air Services*, being the Second Brancker Memorial Lecture at the Institute of Transport, 23 November 1936.

hangars still standing — more or less — and nearly all with little concrete pull-ins and parking places dotted about the airfield to thwart enemy attempts to destroy the aircraft on the ground. When one looks at these survivals one's first reaction is likely to be 'How small everything used to be.' To stimulate such a response is one of the prime values of archaeology.

Aircraft Manufacture

By comparison with the operating side of aviation the history of aircraft manufacturing is extremely complicated, with enormous expansion of facilities in wartime and equally striking contraction during the years of peace. The rise and fall of the Gloster, Handley Page and De Havilland companies illustrates the kind of problems this presents to the industrial archaeologist.

Handley Page

The origins of Handley Page were the aeroplanes first made at Hendon soon after 1900 by Everett, Edgcumbe and Co. of Colindale. They were flown from a field later bought by one of the great British pioneers, Claude Graham-White, and this became the nucleus of Hendon Aerodrome. Graham-White aeroplanes were made in factories adjoining this airfield after its opening in 1911, and production rose considerably after the outbreak of the First World War. More than 1,000 men were employed at Hendon by 1915. New factories were built in 1916 and by 1917 the plant covered 50 acres. When the War ended Graham-White turned his attention away from aeroplanes towards motor-cars and furniture, but in 1922 the Government took over both the factories and the airfield and aeroplanes were made there once again. Graham-White had, in his later years, been manufacturing Handley Page designs and after 1922 all production in this part of London passed into that Company's hands. Handley Page themselves had begun at Barking, Essex, at about the same time as Graham-White at Hendon. In 1912 they left Barking and moved to Cricklewood, then on the edge of the open countryside. Pioneer military aircraft were built at Cricklewood during the First World War and flown from the Handley Page airfield by the side of the works. In 1929 the airfield was closed to be developed for housing, and a new one was built further out, at Radlett. Aircraft continued to be built at Cricklewood until the mid-1960s, when the premises were sold for conversion into the Cricklewood trading estate. In the case of Handley Page, then, the archaeologist is concerned with a small factory at Barking, which has gone, factories of various dates at Hendon, parts of which survive, largely unrecognisable remnants of a factory at Cricklewood, and a more or less intact factory and airfield of the late 1920s at Radlett. The story is as much that of the growth of the London suburb as of the aircraft industry.

De Havilland

The equally famous De Havilland company owed its foundation to the collapse of the Aircraft Manufacturing Co. (AirCo) which had been founded in 1912 at Hendon. During the First World War it extended its premises and added an airfield, but it failed to come to terms with peace-time conditions and in 1920 it sold out to the Birmingham Small Arms Co., which had no direct interest in aircraft. At that point a group from AirCo first leased and then bought a 76-acre site at Stag Lane, Hendon, from two men who had been using the airfield for flying instruction. Factory buildings for both engines and fuselages were built west of Stag Lane, along what later became De Havilland Road. The rest of the site, to the north and west, was occupied by the airfield. In 1932 all but 14 acres were sold for house-building and a new factory was opened further away from the congestion of London, at Hatfield, Hertfordshire. Manufacturing, especially of propellers, continued at Stag Lane and between 1939 and 1945 other factories were requisitioned, including some in Carlisle Road and Honeypot Lane. In 1946 the original works at Stag Lane was bought by the Hawker Siddeley Group, which made Rolls-Royce engines there until 1969 when the whole site was sold off to the Brixton estate and its aeroplane period came to an end.

Gloster

The monuments of the formerly prestigious Gloster Company have been a little more fortunate, although

125 Westland Aircraft, Yeovil: women applying fabric to aircraft wings during the First World War.

The southern half of Britain is abundantly endowed with buildings which were at one time used for making aeroplanes and parts of aeroplanes. It is difficult to decide where the archaeology of aircraft manufacturing begins and ends, since so many firms have been involved as sub-contractors, especially during the two World Wars. The pattern of the industry has been two great bursts of growth, in 1914-18 and 1939-45, a precarious existence combined with considerable technical progress during the 1920s and 1930s, and a jerky and uncomfortable decline during the 1950s and 1960s. Many of the buildings used were put up in a great hurry and others have been redundant, as aircraft factories, for most of their life. Those, such as Westlands of Yeovil, which have continued to make aircraft throughout their lives are very exceptional. Conversations with people who spent many years making aeroplanes and then had to turn to other forms of engineering in the same works make it clear that these men felt depressed, down graded and even insulted when the change came. A toolmaker, who had worked at Vickers Supermarine works at Southampton until it was destroyed by bombing in 1940 and then moved to South Marston, spoke for thousands of other men in the industry when he said that the end of aeroplane production there made him 'very sad'. Many men, he believed, 'lost interest'.

126 Westland Aircraft, Yeovil: wing shop, 1936.

127 (below)
Hucclecote, Gloucester: former hangar of the Gloster Aircraft works, now part of the Gloucester Trading Estate.

128 (below)
British Aircraft Corporation, Filton; aluminium doors of the former Brabazon assembly hall hangar, now used for maintenance.

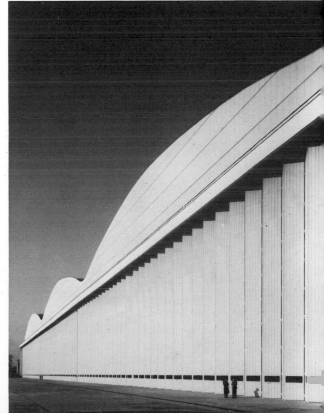

the Company's history is shorter. The story begins in 1911 when George Holt Thomas, founder of the Aircraft Manufacturing Co., obtained the exclusive British licence for building French 'Gnome' engines. Sensing the approach of war, he formed his own company and took over three factories, at the Hyde, Hendon, at Walthamstow, where the building of 'Gnome' engines was concentrated, and at Merton, for the construction of balloons and small airships. Early in 1914 Holt Thomas appointed Hugh Burroughs as manager of the Aircraft Manufacturing Co., and Burroughs in his turn took on Geoffrey de Havilland as chief designer just before war broke out. More factory space soon became needed and, since aircraft at that time were made of wood, the obvious people to help were woodworking companies. Burroughs went for H.H. Martyn and Co., of Sunningend World, Cheltenham. Martyns specialised in woodwork for ocean liners and had, in addition to a large, well-equipped works, a highly skilled staff. By the end of the War Martyns, operating under contract, had a very efficient production system and were turning out aircraft as fast as any factory in the country.

Hugh Burroughs provided the author with the kind of information about early aircraft manufacturing which does not generally find its way into published histories, most of which are written for people who are interested in aeroplanes and not in the history of the industry as a whole. In particular, there is the important matter of recruitment. Where did the people who made aeroplanes in the early days come from? What jobs had they done previously? Those who, like Mr Burroughs, knew the industry personally in those days are in a position to give us the information we require, and where documentary evidence is lacking their testimony is of supreme importance.

Before the First World War, it appears, 'the majority had been motor mechanics or came from small engineering firms. Ninety per cent were men who had served an apprenticeship'.[8] The situation soon changed:

> By 1916 the net was widely spread and the skilled men were soon mopped up. Trainees were taken on and the pre-war 90 per cent skilled had become a negligible proportion by the middle of 1917. The men in the aircraft factories came from everywhere and had done everything. Before 1914 the men who entered the industry were enthusiasts, people who had watched the flying displays at Hendon, Brooklands, and Bournemouth and who were keen to get into what they regarded as a prestige occupation.

The prestige became even greater when air-fighting was publicised in the press. From 1915 to 1918, however, men in the aircraft and engine industries were exempt from military service, and after the slaughter of Passchendaele and the Somme working in an aircraft factory became very attractive indeed. The women and girls employed were a good solid mixture:

> The women were domestics, shop girls, laundry workers and the like in the works, but for the offices, drawing office and tracing, and the clerical planning and progress department, the lower middle-classes were attracted. There were some women from the upper middle-class, daughters of doctors and lawyers, for instance, but not a lot. The proportion of them never rose to more than 5 per cent, except in the clerical grades.

> A high proportion of the women employed in the aircraft industry during the first 25 years of the century worked as dopers. In those days the whole of the wing, aileron, elevator and tail-plane areas were covered with linen, which was treated with tetraacetate of cellulose, known as dope, to waterproof and toughen it. The dope was brushed on, and during the process the acetone solvent evaporated. Nearly all the women engaged on this work were allergic to acetone vapour, and to keep them reasonably healthy and cheerful they had to be given milk as an antidote, a pint in the morning and a pint in the afternoon.

The links between an industry's labour force, its location and its premises are always important, and this is particularly true of the aircraft industry, especially during the period 1905-25 when its special skills and needs were becoming better understood. It is interesting to notice, for example, that its early development took place to a marked extent in the London area, where there was a long tradition of furniture making and plenty of skilled woodworkers, and where both men and factory space were readily available as soon as the War produced severe cuts in joinery manufacture and cabinet-making. It was in the Home Counties, too, that the pre-war flying displays had generated the largest number of aeroplane enthusiasts.

There were, even so, some freakish things about the supply of aircraft workers, which only personal memories are likely to reveal. Propellers are a case in point. For many years, until the coming of metal propellers in the 1930s, propellers were made by cutting a block of laminated wood into the complex shape required. It was very much a craftsman's job, and it was very time-consuming. Until 1914 this was unimportant, since there were so few aeroplanes and the annual British demand was for no more than 500 at most. Under wartime conditions, however, the need was for many thousands of propellers each year. An ingenious solution was found to the problem. Skilled woodcarvers, who normally earned a living by ornamenting public buildings, churches and the homes of the rich, were conscripted and sent to work in Cheltenham. There, they rough-shaped the blocks very quickly by eye, leaving the finishing stages to the practised propeller-makers, with their accurate measuring instruments. The supply bottleneck was removed and the aeroplanes got their propellers.[9]

The Gloucestershire Aircraft Co. was established in 1917 as a result of an agreement between the woodworking concern, Martyn, and the aeroplane concern, the Aircraft Manufacturing Co. The demand for military aircraft became so great that the Gloucestershire Aircraft Co. had to place sub-contracts with other engineering firms in the district, notably Savages

---

[8] Letter to the author, 5 January 1977.

[9] I owe this information to Mr A.J.J. Ayres, one of the carvers involved. At the height of the War he was transferred by Lord Curzon to his newly-rented mansion at Montacute in order to make the woodwork there more acceptable to the taste of Lord Curzon's friend, Elinor Glyn.

and Daniels, of Stroud, and the Gloucester Carriage and Wagon Co., of Gloucester. The premises of these companies can therefore be properly considered to form part of the archaeology of the aircraft industry.

Gloucestershire Aircraft became the Gloster Aircraft Co. in 1926, and two years later it bought the hangars and airfield at Hucclecote, on the outskirts of Gloucester, which the Company had been using for flight tests since 1915. By 1930 its interest had shifted to aluminium aircraft, but there was extremely little work to be obtained and other means had to be found of keeping the Company afloat, while development work continued on a new type of fighter aeroplane. Some of the hangars were rented out for pig and mushroom production, the Sheet Metal Department carried out a considerable amount of work for the motor industry, and other departments produced roll-down shop fronts, milk churns and gas-fired fish-fryers.

In 1934 Gloster Aircraft was taken over by Hawker Aircraft and ceased to exist as a separate company thereafter. The Hawker works was transferred to Hucclecote, which was expanded between 1934 and 1937, and more than 7,000 'Hurricane' fighter aircraft were built there during the Second World War. The first jet-engined aircraft, the Gloster E.28/39, later to become the 'Meteor', was made there in 1940. During the 1950s, with military orders at an end, the Hucclecote factory switched to automatic vending machines, forage harvesters and control equipment, in an attempt to keep the skilled labour force employed.

Thereafter the history of Hucclecote becomes very complicated and, in many ways, typical of the fate which has overtaken the British Aircraft industry as a whole. In 1961 the Gloster Aircraft Co. merged with Armstrong Whitworth Aircraft Ltd. to form Whitworth Gloucester Aircraft. In 1963 the name Gloster finally disappeared when the company became part of the Avro Whitworth Division of Hawker Siddleley

Aviation. It reappeared for a short time in a new company, Gloster Saro, which produced vending machines and road tankers, and in Gloster Design Services, established by former members of the Gloster Aircraft design office. Finally, in 1964, the Hucclecote factory was sold to Gloucester Trading Estates and has subsequently been converted to other industrial uses.[10]

Helicopters

The helicopter side of the industry is in a relatively more prosperous condition, although this may well be short-lived. Its largest concern, Westland Aircraft, of Yeovil, grew out of a company which came into the production of aeroplanes almost by accident. In the 1880s James Bazeley Petter was the proprietor of an iron-monger's shop in The Borough, Yeovil, which now functions as a supermarket. He also ran the Nautilus Foundry, a short distance away, which made the famous 'Nautilus' stove, bought for the comfort amongst others of Queen Victoria at Osborne and Balmoral. By 1900 Petters had given up ironmongery and were making internal combustion engines. An advertisement of 1906 describes them as 'Manufacturers of Stationary, Portable and Traction Petroleum Engines, Combined Pumping Engines, Electric Lighting and Power Transmission Plants.'[11] The Nautilus works, close to the centre of the town, soon became too small and in 1912 a large site was bought in open country, near Hendford railway goods' station, where both a new factory and a garden village were built. Westland was chosen as the name for the new estate and works. In 1913 a power station was built there, and for many years provided electricity for the town of Yeovil as well as for the works.

During the First World War, Petters built a major aircraft factory at Westland — parts of it still survive — and produced 1,100 aeroplanes there. A wide range of aircraft continued to be made there during the 1920s, and in

1934 this branch of Petters was formed into a public company as Westland Aircraft Ltd. The production of oil engines in Yeovil ceased in 1939 when Petters became part of the British Group. Manufacture of these items was moved to Staines, and since then the Westland site has been wholly given over to fixed and rotary-wing aircraft, air-conditioning equipment and industrial doors.

In 1957 the Government encouraged the British aircraft industry to reorganise itself into specialist groups. Westlands then became the centre of the helicopter and hovercraft group, absorbing Saunders-Roe, the Helicopter Division of the Bristol Aeroplane Co. and the Fairey Aviation Co., which was developing VTOL aircraft. By 1960 it was the third largest manufacturer of rotary-wing aircraft in the world.

The process of Westlands' growth has made Yeovil into that very vulnerable community, the one-industry town. Aeroplanes have transformed what was, at the beginning of the twentieth century, a small market-town, with glovemaking to provide a measure of industrial employment, into a place which is almost entirely dependent on a single firm for its livelihood. The recent decline in the international demand for military helicopters, Westlands' bread and butter, has brought a long period of security and expansion to an end, and it is anyone's guess as to how much of the Westland site in the near future will be devoted to the production of aircraft and how much will belong to the realm of aviation archaeology alone.

---

[10] Among the buildings preserved on the Estate are three interesting hangars of the First World War period, with the roofs supported by fine latticed wooden trusses.

[11] Their first tractor was made in 1902.

Chapter 9

The 'Media' Industries

Photography has a long history, the most significant inventions taking place between 1839, when Daguerre perfected his process for producing a silver image on a copper plate, and 1885, when George Eastman produced a machine for manufacturing coated photographic paper in long rolls. In 1888 the first film and the portable roll-film camera were on the market, and by the mid-1890s the Americans were showing their first movies. Photography, however, is essentially a means of recording, and it is no coincidence that the first roll-film and the first gramophones should have been marketed at almost exactly the same time. Both represented success in overcoming problems in a field which had fascinated inventors for generations: how to freeze time, how to prevent sounds and sights from vanishing for ever. Having proved that both sight and sound could be preserved in this way, the next stage was to disseminate the performances of people with an urge to speak, play, act and sing to their fellow men in distant places. The cinema achieved this first and radio second. Television eventually brought the skills and the advantages of the cinema and radio together, and new forms of recording were discovered which obviated the need for broadcasts, whether of sound or pictures, to take place at the same time as the performance. The link between all four media, and what makes them inescapably a part of the Second Industrial Revolution, is electricity. Without it, broadcasting would not have existed at all, and cinema and sound recording could not have progressed beyond the early stages of development in the way they have.

Photography

Eastmans were manufacturing their Kodak film and cameras in Britain by 1903. In 1911 they opened their majestic Kodak House in Kingsway. Designed by Sir John Burnet, it remained the Company's principal shop window in London until the 1960s, when it was pulled down and the site sold. The British factory was established at Wealdstone, near Harrow, in 1905, and, much extended, it remains the centre of Kodak's operations in this country. It is an excellent example of the way in which the location of a factory can suggest useful information about a company's methods and its treatment of staff.

The archives relating to Kodak's activities in Britain are poor. The Company museum at Wealdstone is strong on cameras, catalogues and other material relating to the technical history of the Company, but it is very weak on the kind of records which provide details of the workforce, the management style and the place occupied by Kodak in the local community. Until the 1920s Wealdstone was still semi-rural. The great wave of suburban building that, by the 1930s, was to swallow up the green fields of this part of north-west Middlesex was only just beginning; there was no tradition of factory work in the area and wages were low. The district was grateful for Kodak, and Kodak was grateful for a cheap site, close to a railway station, and for a docile, inexperienced labour force. Most of the work it had to offer was unskilled and demanded little but never-ending concentration. The processing of film and the assembly of cameras are not exciting jobs.

Mr Leonard Millen went to work with Kodak in 1928. Before then he had been a cinema pianist. In 1924 the Harrow Coliseum was included in his regular circuit. He played there and at the local Broadway Cinema on Saturday afternoons and evenings, and for the rest of the week he was busy at various London cinemas. This was an occupation that died very fast once talking-pictures took over and, with so much unemployment in Britain at the time, Mr Millen counted himself lucky to get a job at Kodak, where his wife was already working. He was assigned to the Paper Darkroom Store and stayed there until he went into the Army in 1939. After the War he returned to Kodak to do routine clerical work in the Despatch Department. Meanwhile, his wife had been working first at cardboard-box making and then in the Paper Sorting and Labelling Department and in the Plate Department. On one occasion her appendix burst while she was at work, and she was taken to the Middlesex Hospital by a Kodak lorry, since no ambulance was available.[1]

The management was tough. It always contained a number of Americans, and the factory was run from the beginning on American lines. Until after the Second World War, Kodak was a rigidly non-union concern and discipline was maintained by a policy of hire and fire. 'In my time', remembers Mr Millen, 'very few left of their own accord, as the job situation out-

[1] Correspondence with the author, 12 May 1977.

side was by no means good.' One can interpret both Kodak House in Kingsway and the Kodak factory at Wealdstone in different ways. On the one hand they are symbols of successful pioneering in a new industry and, on the other, temples belonging to a company which intended to develop and apply the new American concept of industrial efficiency all over Britain. To the people who handed in their films at the local chemist to be developed and printed, Kodak's Wealdstone factory, with its huge, well-tamed work-force, was as remote and irrelevant as if it had been in the middle of Siberia. The quality of the finished work was all that mattered to them. But to the Company's employees, the name 'Kodak' and the factory stood for something rather different.

129 HM Stationery Office,
Wealdstone, Middlesex (1896).

These two factories — the first concerned with printing and the second with the production of sensitised film and photographic paper — sit side by side and were built within five years of each other. Both came into existence at the beginning of the age of recording, copying and large-scale transmission of information. Indeed, they are symbols of it. When Kodak first went to Wealdstone the 55-acre site seemed adequate to meet all future requirements, but with the enormous growth of the photographic industry it was soon outgrown and the Company now employs thousands of people at three other locations.

In the 1890s Harrow was a small country town and Wealdstone, on its fringe, looked out over farms. These two important concerns established themselves in the area for three reasons — a clean, dust-free atmosphere, good railway communication with London, and, certainly not least, a docile labour force, for the most part unaccustomed to factory ways and grateful for the chance of a job. Ringed as they now are with suburban estates, these factories operate within a completely different environment from what was so attractive at the turn of the century. This is now an area in which a high proportion of people earn their living from various forms of manufacturing, nearly all of it of the 'clean' twentieth-century kind.

130 Kodak, Wealdstone, Middlesex
(1891).

The Cinema

Kodak was, of course, concerned with the cinema almost from its earliest days. Without film the cinema could never have come into being, and Kodak's entry into Britain coincides very closely with the opening of the first purpose-built cinemas here. The first 'picture palace' in Britain was the Balham Empire in Balham High Street, London, which received its first patrons in 1907. Between then and the outbreak of war in 1914 an enormous crop of cinemas sprang up all over Britain. A high proportion of these early buildings has survived and are worth seeking out in order to get an idea of the style which was considered appropriate to the new art. Many of the pre-1914 cinemas were stuccoed with a good deal of ornamental plasterwork both inside and out. This, however, has usually deteriorated badly, especially when the building has been converted into a furniture store, a garage, a carpet warehouse or some other use which has not required the maintenance of the fabric in its former glossy and appealing condition. However, only a minority of the early cinema shows took place in buildings constructed for the purpose. A more usual setting was a variety hall, theatre, or some other kind of public place. Leeds Public Library has a special collection of pre-1914 cinema posters which illustrate the system very well. In the week beginning 26 October 1914, for example, New Century Pictures presented *The Sign of the Cross,* at the Assembly Rooms, Leeds. This 'Masterpiece of Picture Plays of all times' and 'accompanied by Full Choral and Orchestral Effects' and had four showings a day. In the following week the Assembly Rooms would have been used for quite different purposes; *The Sign of the Cross* was an exceptional picture and an exceptional occasion.

One of London's grandest cinemas, namely the Stoll Picture Theatre, Kingsway, has now been demolished. It was erected in 1910 as the London Opera House, by Oscar Hammerstein of New York, at a cost of £200,000. As an opera house it was a failure, but it did much better as a cinema. The film industry, in fact, was a great stimulus to the property market throughout the inter-war period. Hundreds of new cinemas were built, many of them very large, and there was a considerable amount of conversion of other types of building, especially theatres, into cinemas. In general, these enterprises continued to prosper until the 1950s when television took over the attention and the money of the public, and since then the story has been one of closure, demolition, division of one large cinema into two or more small ones, and, even more frequently, of films yielding place to bingo. The archaeology of bingo shades off into the archaeology of the cinema.

The Cinema Industry

From the beginning, the British cinema industry relied heavily on films made in the USA, but there were film-makers in Britain as early as in America. Nothing very elaborate was required to make a short film of the type that was acceptable in 1900, and the job could be carried out effectively and at a very low cost either in the open air, which was preferable since it avoided lighting problems, or in a small hall. The term 'film studio' was coined at a time when films were, in fact, being made in rooms not a great deal bigger than a photographer's studio and it was carried over into Hollywood days. It is interesting to notice that during the first few years of the present century many small firms were apparently in the habit of faking topical events for news-reel purposes. The London-based Warwick Trading Co., at that time the largest film company in the world, took the trouble to explain that their news-film was taken 'on the spot, and not on Hampstead Heath or in somebody's back garden.' Indeed, they sent their Bioscope men to the Boer War in 1900, the first war to be covered by the new skill of cinematography.

The first major British film-making centre, at Lime Grove, Shepherds Bush, London, was built just after the First World War. It continued in use for its original purpose throughout the 1920s and 1930s and in the late 1940s passed into the hands of the BBC, which has used it for television production ever since. Ealing and Elstree, the two other important British groups of film studios, both belong to the 1920s. Riverside Studios, Hammersmith, were built in the 1930s and taken over by the BBC for the television in the early 1950s.

Mr Alfred Roome went to work at Elstree in 1927 as one of a small batch of young men recruited by Herbert Wilcox to train as film-makers fit to compete with the Americans. They were paid £1 each week, but this was sometimes delayed as Wilcox made his films on a hand-to-mouth basis. With no union restrictions to keep their activities within bounds they learned to do everything. Before British International built their own laboratory, processing at Elstree was carried out by Olympic Laboratories at Acton. One of the jobs Mr Roome had in his days as Junior Property Boy was to take the day's film to Acton. 'I went by train with this bundle under my arm to Cricklewood station, and then took a tram or a trolley-bus to Acton. I got off at School Lane, walked up to the laboratory and delivered my parcel. I could have been run over or lost it, which is a nightmare, when you think of the amount of money there was in each reel of film.' At Elstree, Mr Roome remembers, were 'the first post-war studios really built for the job. The others had been factories and things like that which had been taken over. Elstree was built for the job, as the "Hollywood of England." '[2] There were 'two vast, barn-like structures, built of steel and asbestos sheeting, with three productions going on at the same time.' This was just possible in the silent-film days, but, as Mr Roome recalls:

> you had to have quite a lot of liaison between one production and another. Once we were doing a drama of some sort, and somebody else was doing a comedy, and they were making so much nòise that they were upsetting what we were doing at our end, so that we had to have a sort of pact, that while they were doing their noisy bit, we were rehearsing or having tea or something. You had to dovetail with each other. When sound came in, they tried to make sound pictures in the same big open space, but it simply couldn't be done.

So, with the coming of sound films in the early 1930s, one of the vast hangar-like structures at Elstree had to be divided up with thick walls, to make three smaller sound stages. The other was left undivided, 'so that you could do the big stuff in it.' There was,

[2] A comprehensive list of these premises has never been made. It would be a useful document.

The British film industry and the British cinema industry have always been two separate entities, closely connected and with a good deal of interlocking ownership but with the prosperity of the second by no means dependent on the success of the first. Small-scale production, using makeshift premises, existed in the very early years of this century, but permanent cinemas, built specially for the purpose are rare before 1910. The first large cinema in Britain was the Rialto, in Leicester Square, London.

After the First World War there was a great wave of cinema-building, which intensified during the 1930s. Between 1935 and 1939, the boom period, between 100 and 200 cinemas were built each year. More than 300 cinemas were destroyed in wartime air-raids — they were particularly vulnerable to fire-bomb attacks — and during the 1950s and 1960s the rise in the popularity of television brought about wholesale closures. Of the cinemas which existed in 1939, it is estimated that not more than one in twenty is still operating as a cinema. The rest have been pulled down, bombed or converted to other uses, bingo being an ex-cinema's more usual fate. The archaeology of the cinema industry is plentiful and nationwide, and anyone who has grown up in the television era may well wonder how it was ever possible to finance, build and equip the great cinema-palaces which the 1920s and 1930s took for granted.

The great days of British film-making also lie a long way in the past. Most studios were built between 1920 and 1935 and closed during the 1940s and 1950s. The pioneers among the big studios were Gaumont at Shepherds Bush (1914), which had four stages; Lime Grove (1915), also belonging to Gaumont; Stoll Studios (1921) at Cricklewood; Islington (1924), built by Paramount; the British National Studios at Elstree (1926); British International (1927), also at Elstree; Ealing (1930); and Denham (1934).

131 Lime Grove studios: exterior, c. 1915.

132 Lime Grove studios: interior, showing production in progress, c.1920.

133 Elstree studios, 1927.

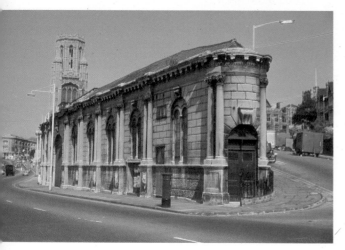

134 Former cinema, Park Row, Bristol (1912).

135 (below)
Walpole Picture Theatre, Bond Street, Ealing. Built in 1912, this little cinema was a casualty of the contraction in the film industry in the 1960s. Now demolished.

136 (below)
Former Ealing film studios: now the BBC Film Centre.

however, another problem. The silent-film studios were literally barn-like; the actors looked straight up at the roof, and 'before you could start filming each morning you had to go round with a shotgun and get rid of the sparrows. They were all up in the girders, going cheep, cheep, cheep.'

When the British National Co., which built the first Elstree studios, went into liquidation, British International took over the premises and built proper sound studios. Meanwhile, Herbert Wilcox had started up his new British and Dominions Co. in new buildings immediately adjoining those of British International. These studios were designed for sound from the beginning. They were unfortunately gutted by a disastrous fire in the mid-1930s, so the building one now sees there is largely a reconstruction.

Mr Roome worked at British National, British International, British and Dominions, for Gainsborough

Pictures at Islington and for Gaumont-British at Lime Grove. He was therefore in a good position to compare facilities at the different studios. Lime Grove, by contrast with Elstree, was 'a beautifully built structure' for Gaumont-British had a lot of money to spend, but its working conditions were somewhat proletarian. 'At Elstree we were rather snooty in a way. We felt we were a sort of Eton of the film business.' To leave Elstree and move to Lime Grove or Islington was to go slumming. In London, 'everyone in the cutting room had to wear white coats, you see, which wasn't done at Elstree. We worked how we liked. Another thing we didn't like at Lime Grove was that we had to clock in and out. We didn't at Elstree. You came and went more or less as you pleased. Nobody ever let anybody down.'[3]

Without memories and details like these, old film studios, like any other kind of industrial building, are dead.

One can place them within their historical context, describe what can still be seen and link the premises with the films that were made there and with the producers responsible for them. But, shorn of the reminiscences of the people who worked there and to whom the building was a daily reality, essential details are inevitably missing. Consider for example the camera booths, long since superannuated, but an essential feature of production in the early days of sound film. No example of these booths survives and the historians of the film industry have shown no interest in them. Mr Roome and his contemporaries, however, are most unlikely to forget them:

We had two cameras for everything in those days. The reason was that you had to have two negatives, one for England and Europe, and one for America. The laboratories hadn't perfected duping.[4] They could do it, but it was very poor quality. So we had two cameras, side by side, taking roughly the same shot. As soon as sound came in, you had this noise trouble. To start with, we had to cover everything with old mattresses and cushions, but it still made a bit of a noise. The microphones weren't all that accurate or sensitive, so they didn't pick that up particularly, but, as the mikes improved, they designed these small booths. The cameras were put in them. That was standard practice for several years.

The booths were simply boxes made of three-ply. The padding on the inside was kept in place by chicken-wire. You had this optical glass front, so there was no distortion, and there was a big door. Three of you could get inside, but there were usually only two men inside each booth. With a hand-cranked silent camera, the reels of film were 400 feet, but for sound purposes they were increased to 1,000. So, with the motor warming up the atmosphere and two or three

<hr>

[3] Conversation with the author, 1 April 1977.

[4] The making of duplicate negatives.

137 Former Gaumont film studio, Lime Grove, Shepherds Bush: now BBC Television studios.

of you breathing inside, it was infernally hot. There was the camera-operator, there was somebody altering the focus — this had to be done by hand, with no remote control — and very often there was a third man operating the panning handle. There was no ventilation. The booth had to be as airtight as possible, to stop any noise getting through to the microphones.

On jobs like filming a Tom Walls' farce, we sometimes had five cameras on a set, each in its own booth. They were placed in a half circle, with each camera getting its planned piece of action, just as early television did 20 years later.

The Gramophone Industry

The technical history of the gramophone is excellently documented, both in print and in museums. One of the finest collections used to be in the possession of EMI. It was sold off piecemeal in 1980. The items in this collection ranged from American-made Edison phonographs of the 1870s and 1880s, through to the refined clockwork models of the 1920s and 1930s, before electric motors and electric recording took over. But, like nearly all museum collections which illustrate the history of recording, the catalogue entries and the captions were purely technical. There was rarely any reference to price, and no indication of what kinds of people were buying these machines. They were presented, one might say, in a social vacuum. Apart from the fascination of looking at the instruments themselves, we had to content ourselves with this kind of description:

11. The 'Pigmy Grand' was introduced in 1909 and was the Gramophone Company's first portable model, with internal horn measuring 15 × 12¾ × 7½ inches. The gooseneck tapering tone-arm gives on to a wooden internal horn opening behind the grille designed in one of the trade marks of the Company. It has a large single-spring direct screw, vertical drive motor. Mahogany case. A carrying case was available. The Pigmy Grand design lasted scarcely one year. Examples are found with

different brakes and speed controls and also the plain 'His Master's Voice' transfer.[5]

We were not told how much it cost nor why it remained in production for only one year, an equally interesting consideration. There was no hint at all of the fact, known from other sources, that up to at least the First World War new gramophones were sold almost entirely to a middle-class market. With gramophones, as with pianos, bicycles and motor-cars, the working-class acquired second-hand what the middle-classes had bought new, and consequently had to be content with something less than the very latest technological developments. It is therefore extremely interesting and important to examine very carefully the advertising of both gramophones and records at different periods in order to judge what the nature and size of the market was conceived to be. It soon becomes evident that, although the social basis of the industry undoubtedly widened to a considerable extent during the 1920s and 1930s, the working-class, the truly mass-market, became important only during the late 1940s and early 1950s.

The history of the gramophone industry in Britain is so bound up with that of EMI that one needs no excuse for concentrating on this company. It was formed in 1898, and the first recordings were made in the basement of 31 Maiden Lane, London, the Company's first headquarters. Only the master-recordings were made here; for some years the pressings were manufactured by the Company's German subsidiary. By 1902 expansion had been rapid and a move was made to 21 City Road. Soon afterwards it became clear that the original pressing plant in Germany had reached its capacity and in 1907 construction began at Hayes, Middlesex, of a new works for what at this time was called The Gramophone and Typewriter Co.[6] The studios at 21 City Road continued in use throughout the 1920s, but in 1930 the decision was taken to build new studios at the back of a house which the Company had just bought — 3 Abbey Road, St. John's Wood. In 1971 these studios were virtually rebuilt, and in the following year EMI opened a new factory at Uxbridge Road, Hayes, to replace the 1907 works, which could no longer cope with the enormously

increased demand for disc and tape recordings.

In 1920 Robert Dockerill went to work as an office boy in London for Columbia, which in 1931 merged with The Gramophone Co. (Columbia was the company founded by Thomas Edison.) Observing the success of The Gramophone Co. in Britain, Columbia decided to establish themselves in what was clearly a growing and profitable market. 'In 1906 they bought a factory in the Bendon Valley, at Garrett Lane, Wandsworth, operating under the name of the Rena Manufacturing Co., with a sales and distribution centre in Workshop Lane, in the City of London. In 1911, the Rena Co. came to an end, and Columbia established itself in Britain under its own name, at 102-8 Clerkenwell Road.'[7] He worked a 12-hour day and was paid 17s. 6d. a week, plus 1/- tea money each week. Living at home in Barking, he used to pay 7d. a day for a workman's ticket to Fenchurch Street. 'I used to walk from Fenchurch Street to Clerkenwell Road, which is a matter of three miles backwards and forwards, every day for many years. Quite apart from saving money, it was good for your health.'

The recording studios were on the fifth floor, and the rest of the building was devoted to offices and storage. When the recordings had been made, 'the van used to call twice a day for the waxes, for processing in the factory at Bendon Valley. The test pressings were brought back to Clerkenwell Road, listened to there and okayed for manufacture.'

Columbia's system of distribution and selling was very different from that of their main competitor, HMV:

HMV used to appoint dealers in selected areas, and, unless they thought the dealer wasn't doing his job, they would never appoint another dealer in that area. Columbia had what we called factors, that is, wholesalers, who used to take bulk supplies. Most of the time, there were 12-15 factors

[5] *Catalogue of the Collection*, EMI 1974.

[6] The Gramophone Company was always known to the public as HMV, after the famous listening-dog trademark was first used on records in 1909.

[7] Correspondence with the author, 16 November 1976.

like this up and down the country, who used themselves to employ reps.

This system continued even after The Gramophone Co. took control of Columbia's activities in Britain, 'but in the mid-60s Sir Joseph[8] had other thoughts, and said, "Why should we give factors a wholesale discount, when we could perfectly well do the job ourselves?" So that was stopped, and direct shipment to retailers went from Hayes.'

In 1920 an office boy was quite unable to buy a gramophone, even with the one-third discount which Columbia allowed all its employees. Consequently, Mr Dockerill has good reason to be grateful to the kindly American head of the London business, Louis Sterling, who lent him a gramophone for his first Christmas with the Company:

> The day before Christmas, I was asked, 'Have you a gramophone at home?' 'No.' 'Would you like one?' 'Yes.' 'OK, go to the showroom and choose one. There's not many there; we've loaned them all out.' I chose a darned big horn model and a dozen records and I took them home for a fortnight. That was the measure of the place; the attitude went from top to bottom, emanating from Sterling, a marvellous man.[9]

When the merger with HMV took place in 1931, Robert Dockerill had graduated from being an office boy to writing what was called 'label copy', i.e. information used both for advertising and for the labels which went on to the records. 'The copy for the labels was all sent to Bendon Valley, because they had a printing plant there, overprinting the outline labels.' This practice soon came to an end; the Bendon Valley factory was closed down soon after the 1931 merger, after which all production was transferred to Hayes.

There were many curious differences between Columbia and HMV. One was the method of manufacturing the records which, as Mr Dockerill rightly points out, seems to have been largely forgotten:

> The Columbia record was laminated. It was rather thicker than the HMV version. It had really nothing more than gum and muck in the middle, but there was a fine coating of first-class shellac on

either side. The HMV record, on the other hand, was solid shellac, the idea being that HMV could punch out the centre with the label and re-use the shellac, whereas you couldn't do that with a Columbia pressing.

The HMV-Columbia merger came at a time when there was fierce competition in the industry, with nine companies, all bent on quick turnover and small profits, trying to survive in a market which was clearly not big enough for all of them. Apart from the genuine rationalisation which the linking of HMV and Columbia produced, there were great advantages on the technical side. Columbia had had the services of the one of the most remarkable technical geniuses of his time, Isaac S. Schoenberg. He joined Columbia in 1928 and when EMI, the joint company, was formed, he became director of the EMI Research Laboratories, supervising the work of a number of notable scientists, including Alan Blumlein, who had come to Columbia in 1929. Blumlein developed a new and highly efficient electrical recording system, which bypassed the American patents, and in 1931 EMI filed his patent for stereophonic recording.[10] He later worked on radar, and was killed in 1942 when the Halifax bomber in which he was testing new equipment crashed. The Greater London Council has put a plaque on his Ealing home to commemorate his achievements, a house which certainly has a place in the archaeology of the electronics and gramophone industry.

A large proportion of the master-recordings made during the first 50 years of the gramophone industry have been destroyed, some by accident, some because the quantity had become impossibly large. EMI, like other companies, have done their best to preserve at least the master-tapes made since this method of recording was introduced. In 1976 these filled a large store at Abbey Road, overflowing into two squash courts opposite, an underground tape vault at Perivale, and a store at the Hayes factory. In 1977 all these were amalgamated by taking over one of the redundant film studios at Elstree, an interesting example of how one industry takes over the remains of another.

Retailing

We have emphasised above (p. 72),

in connection with the motor industry, that the archaeology of any manufacturing industry must embrace both the places where goods are made and the places where they are sold and serviced. Both are required in order to make proper sense of the development of the industry. It is therefore important to study the way in which the gramophone companies sold their records and equipment, and the people who were their customers.

George Fenwick was responsible for many years for HMV's London shop window. This began as the West End Gramophone Supply Co. at 94 Regent Street. It was pulled down when Regent Street was rebuilt after the First World War. HMV then moved to 363 Oxford Street, taking over the premises from a far-from exalted company which traded under the name of Our Boys' Outfitters. It was completely remodelled to make it suitable for this new purpose, with, in Mr Fenwick's words, 'Sheraton style fittings and large, well-furnished rooms, to impress the trade and to bring the gramophone on to a higher plane than what was suggested by the second floor of a piano showroom or an ironmonger's premises.' Mr Fenwick comments that:

> It has to be remembered that in the Twenties and early Thirties the West End was very 'Mayfair', and we, together with the other stores there, served an élite trade. In those days, about 80 per cent of our record business was in classical music. City men, Royalty and famous people from abroad would spend many hours with us and bought large quantities. An assistant would stay in the room

---

[8] Sir Joseph Lockwood, Chairman of EMI.

[9] Sterling's generosity became proverbial. He lived in Avenue Road, Hampstead, 'Millionaires' Row', where his house contained a hall in which he gave Sunday celebrity concerts. To celebrate his fiftieth birthday in 1928, he distributed £400,000 among his staff.

[10] While he was still with Columbia, Blumlein set up a studio for electric recording at Petty France, Westminster. Clerkenwell had proved to be impossible because of interference from the trams. The Petty France studio continued in operation until the merger with HMV in 1931.

WHAT WILL YOU DO IN THE LONG, COLD, DARK, SHIVERY EVENINGS, WHEN YOUR HEALTH AND CONVENIENCE COMPEL YOU TO STAY INDOORS?

WHY!!! HAVE A PHONOGRAPH, OF COURSE.

It is the FINEST ENTERTAINER in the WORLD.

There is nothing equal to it in the whole Realm of Art.

It imitates any and every Musical Instrument, any and every natural sound, faithfully:

the HUMAN VOICE, the NOISE OF THE CATARACT, the BOOM OF THE GUN, the VOICES OF BIRDS OR ANIMALS.

From £2 2s.

THE GREATEST MIMIC.

A Valuable Teacher of Acoustics. Most Interesting to Old or Young. A Pleasure and Charm to the Suffering, bringing to them the Brightness and Amusements of the outside World by its faithful reproductions of Operas, New Songs, Speeches, &c.

EVERY HOME WILL sooner or later have its PHONOGRAPH as a NECESSITY.

HAVE YOURS NOW; you will enjoy it longer.

Brought within the reach of every family by Mr. Edison's last production at £2 2s.

Send for our Illustrated Catalogues to

EDISON - BELL CONSOLIDATED PHONOGRAPH CO., LD.,
Or to our Licensees— 39, Charing Cross Road, W.C.
EDISONIA LD., 25 to 22, Banner Street, and City Show-Rooms, 21, Cheapside, E.C., LONDON.

138 Advertisement for the 'Edison Home Phonograph' (*The Illustrated London News*, 30 December 1899).

During the past 40 years what used to be called the British gramophone industry has changed in two major ways — the discs and the tapes are no longer played on equipment made by the recording companies, and EMI, which was already dominating the recording business before the Second World War, now has interests which extend a long way from making and selling records, although this still represents a substantial part of the total business. The Group is now involved, for instance, in film production and distribution, the operation of bingo and social clubs, the manufacture of electronic equipment of all kinds, and in television. It also makes musical instruments, publishes music and runs a group of theatres.

Archaeologically, the main interest must be with the recording side of its activities, partly because these cover a very long period and partly because they represent the biggest contribution made so far by the EMI Group to the progress of the Second Industrial Revolution. It is worth pointing out that, at the time of writing, the proportion of EMI's historic premises to survive is remarkably high.

139 Record library at HMV, City Road, London, c. 1904.

140 Choosing records at City Road, London, 1906.

141 Former HMV (The Gramophone Co.) headquarters, City Road, London.

142 Opening of the HMV Abbey Road recording studios, 1931. Seated on the staircase are Sir Walford Davis and George Bernard Shaw.

144 Nos. 102-8, Clerkenwell Road, London: former headquarters of the Columbia Record Co. and now occupied by the Bell Telephone Co.

143 EMI recording studios, Abbey Road, London.

100

and put records on for them. The staff stayed with us for very long periods. They were not the ordinary run of shop assistants, but mostly young ladies of good families, who kept their regular customers for years, advising and guiding them through all the new issues. They had a special knowledge of music and wonderful memories. Most of these girls received wonderful Christmas presents from their customers.[11]

Even in the 1930s, however, things were changing. In 1935 the show-rooms were reconstructed to cope with the new pattern of trade. More listening rooms were installed: 'smaller and plainly furnished, to cope with an ever increasing public, which liked to be left alone to choose for itself'. In 1937 the building was completely destroyed by fire. When it re-opened in 1939 it was to meet the needs of a much wider public than had existed even two years earlier. The character of Oxford Street itself was very different in 1939 from what it had been 10 years earlier. The Mayfair set, the wealthy and the social élite had come to prefer Kensington and the Brompton Road. 363 Oxford Street mirrored the changes taking place, and a series of photographs of its interior, which, alas, do not exist, would undoubtedly make the point very clearly.

Radio

There have been many gramophone companies in Britain, each with its own history and archaeology, but, until the 1950s, the story of British broadcasting is virtually the story of a monopoly. The transmission of speech and music only became a practical proposition during the First World War, with the development of the thermionic valve. The War provided exceptional opportunities for technical experiment, a major achievement being the American success in transmitting speech from Washington to Paris by radio. After 1918 research in Britain was centred on Chelmsford, Essex, where the Marconi Co. had its works and laboratories, and in particular on a former army hut at Writtle, near Chelmsford, which might fairly be regarded as the birthplace of British broadcasting. It still stands. A low-powered transmitter was set up at Chelmsford for test purposes, and radio amateurs from all over the

country sent in reports on the speech, gramophone records and live concerts which they received from it. The transmissions aroused a great deal of public interest, but at the end of 1919 the Post Office brought them to an end on the grounds that they were 'interfering with important communications'.

The establishment at Writtle, with its versatile staff of engineers, most of whom subsequently found their way to the infant BBC, then took over. They petitioned the Post Office for a licence to operate a broadcasting station and eventually, in 1921, were permitted to do so for half-an-hour each week. These improvised programmes, from 8 to 8.30 pm on Tuesday evenings, were the first regular and advertised transmissions in Britain.[12] In 1922 the Post Office licensed three more transmitters, including another Marconi station, the famous 2LO, at Marconi House, London. The building, at the junction of the Strand and the Aldwych, survives, although it no longer belongs to Marconi. The other two transmitters, 5IT at Witton, Birmingham, and 2ZY at Old Trafford, Manchester, were operated by Western Electric and Metropolitan Vickers. All three were soon to pass into the control of the newly-established BBC, and within a year five more stations had been built and commissioned — at Newcastle, Cardiff, Glasgow, Aberdeen, Bournemouth and Belfast.

In London, Birmingham and Manchester the studios and the transmitters were in the same building, but elsewhere the two were separated by anything up to two or three miles. Most of the aerials were slung from or between the chimneys of power stations. As the scope of broadcasting developed the original studio premises became inadequate and all the stations had to move.[13] In 1923 the BBC in Birmingham took up its quarters over the New Street cinema, but in 1926 the growth of broadcasting in the city produced a brand-new building opposite the Prince of Wales Theatre in Broad Street, with two studios, one of which was the largest in the country. Manchester's first move to the fourth floor of a cotton warehouse in Dickenson Street, took place in 1923. The studio was reached by a goods hoist, in which staff and visitors had to heave themselves up and down. Understandably, this was found

unsatisfactory and in the following year new and larger premises were found in Orme Buildings, The Parsonage. Orme Buildings, however, was unpleasantly situated, three floors below street level and overlooking the dark, smelly waters of the River Irwell.

Newcastle moved from Eldon Square to New Bridge Street in 1924; Cardiff enlarged its premises at 39 Park Place in the same year and Glasgow was able to house itself much more satisfactorily in a handsome house in Blythswood Square. In London, the search for a new headquarters proved very difficult. Marconi wanted the BBC out of Marconi House: 'It is objectionable to have bands of strangers coming in and out and to have Engineers of other Companies working amongst certain of our experimental gear, and moreover the present installation is by no means a show-piece or as safe as one would like', while the Air Ministry complained that the BBC transmitter was causing interference to its own station in Kingsway. Eventually, in 1924, the transmitter was installed on the roof of Selfridges, with two 125 foot towers for the aerial and two huts for the transmitter. Meanwhile the BBC had transferred its studios and offices to Savoy Hill in March and April 1923. It had taken a lease of the second and third floors — it subsequently had to spread further — on the west wing of the Institution of Electrical Engineers building, facing the Victoria Embankment and Waterloo Bridge. The building, dating from 1886, was originally the Medical Examination Schools. It now carries a plaque recording the BBC's tenure. With its seven studios, Savoy Hill was able not only to provide for a wide range of broadcasts — from talks to performances by small orchestras — but also to carry out technical experiments, especially with acoustic treat-

---

[11] Correspondence with the author, May 1977.

[12] The Writtle transmissions are excellently described in P.P. Eckersley, *The Power Behind the Microphone* (London: Cape, 1941). Eckersley himself, later to become Chief Engineer of the BBC, took a leading part in them.

[13] The early premises are well described by Peter West in *BBC Engineering, 1922-1972* (London: BBC Publications, 1972).

ment, microphones and control equipment, which had been previously impossible. There is now nothing inside the building to remind one of the BBC's period of occupancy, but from photographs — all, alas, in black and white — and contemporary descriptions, one can get a reasonable impression of what the BBC was trying to achieve, and of the conditions under which the staff and the performers had to work.

We will visit first of all the large studio on the first floor. This is the newer of the two, and was constructed in the late autumn of last year, when experience had shown that the first studio, two floors above and immediately under the roof, was really too small for the variety of performances then being given and also too heavily damped with drapery to please the average listener. The new studio, which is about 45 feet by 30 feet in size, has only one thickness of drapery, and has just a suspicion of resonance. But what instantly strikes the visitor is not only the ample dimensions, but the unusual and pleasing decorative scheme. The walls, about 18 feet high, are draped in a French grey, an almost neutral colour. On each of the longer walls have been built two full-length dummy windows, draped with long curtains of a fascinating emerald shade. The windows have a background of silver foil, and in front of the window-frame there hangs an orange-coloured network. Surrounding the windows and hidden by the emerald drapery are numerous electric lamps, giving a blaze of light. The total effect is one of a flood of golden sunlight. The carpet is patternless, but of a deep, restful blue, whilst overhead is a canopy of stone-coloured canvas, supported by a framework of Florentine colonial carving, representing garlands of flowers and fruit. Two grand pianos, differing in 'brilliancy', are there for the choice of artistes. A set of tubular bells stands in one corner. Various lounge chairs and divans are placed against the walls, and at intervals are tables carrying vases of quaintly designed artificial flowers.[14]

Savoy Hill was conveniently on the doorstep of the Savoy Hotel, which was to the advantage of the BBC in two ways — the hotel's bands could be very conveniently broadcast, and its refreshment service was available to the announcers who were involved in these broadcasts. The Savoy Hotel might, therefore, be considered in part as an extension of the BBC premises. Stuart Hibberd recalls that:

We announcers used to enjoy going over to the Savoy. We could dance if we wanted to, but most of us were content to change after closing down in the studio at 10.30, and get to the Savoy just before 11, in time to announce, back-stage, the numbers which had been played. An excellent supper was provided by M. de Mornys, the Savoy Entertainments Manager, in a private room upstairs — my mouth waters as I think of the food of those days, especially the omelettes and sweets — and we came down again to make two further announcements, one at 11.30, and one just before Big Ben at midnight. Generally the two bands — the Savoy Orpheans and the Savoy Havana Band — changed over at these times.[15]

Broadcasting took four years to outgrow Savoy Hill, and in 1928 the Corporation decided to build a new headquarters in Portland Place, opposite the Langham Hotel, which was almost as socially distinguished as the Savoy. Broadcasting House, with eight storeys above ground and three below, was built for the job. Its 22 studios included a concert hall with seating for more than 700 people. Before the move to Portland Place in 1932 an empty warehouse at the southern end of Waterloo Bridge was taken over and converted into a large studio, and in 1934 an old skating rink in Maida Vale was brought for the same purpose. Both of these buildings belong to the archaeology of broadcasting.

There were members of the BBC staff and its public who considered Broadcasting House an absurdity from the beginning, a symbol of the 'Great Stuffed Shirt' era. One such critic, Maurice Gorham, who joined the Corporation in 1926, was both amused and appalled by the new building. He noticed, for instance, the famous Speaker's Studio on the third floor,

with Arnold Bennett's Chair, the walls lined with bookshelves full of leather-backed volumes bearing solemn titles; quite unlike a radio studio, except of course for the microphone, clock and cue-lights, and very modern thermostat projecting from the wall. The idea was, I believe, that the donnish, scholarly critic who was put in a flutter by machinery would feel quite at home here and get comfortably relaxed before the red light called him to the air.[16]

Then there was the coal-fire in the Director-General's office, the modernistic furniture, 'in unpleasant but fashionable woods', the busts in the foyer, the 'floral decorations by a lady of title', and, most remarkable of all, the Chapel, on the third floor:

This really monstrous bit of make-believe was supposed to provide a fitting setting for religious broadcasts and chamber music, which was then practically classed as a religious activity by the BBC. This studio reminded me strongly of a Paris night-club seeking to be original at all costs. Amongst gay pastel shades lurked ornamental crosses: there was a sort of pseudo altar-recess, and into this, by the manipulation of switches in the Control Room, could be thrown the shadow of a cross. I was told that by using other switches a Star of David could be thrown there, instead, but I have no evidence of this.[17]

Most of the décor and furniture of the 1930s has now gone, casualties of years of hard wear-and-tear, air-raids and changes of fashion. What now remains is only the shell of the building into which the BBC moved with such pride in 1932, when Broadcasting House was very much the BBC instead of, as nowadays, the poor relation of Television Centre. As a piece of broadcasting archaeology it has to be interpreted with a great deal of imagination, fed by the reminiscences of those who worked in it. One

[14] A.R. Burrows, *The Story of Broadcasting* (London: Cassell, 1924), pp. 88-89.

[15] *This — is London* (London: McDonald and Evans, 1950), p. 5.

[16] *Sound and Fury: 21 Years in the BBC* (London: Percival Marshall, 1938), p. 43.

[17] *Ibid.*

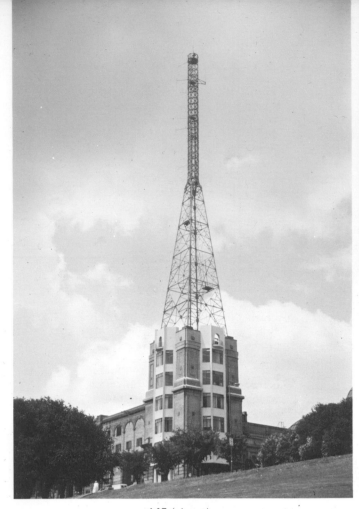

146 Former BBC headquarters, Savoy Hill.

145 (above)
Alexandra Palace, site of the BBC's first regular television transmissions: afterwards used for preparing programmes for the Open University, and now restored after a disastrous fire in 1980.

147 Original 2LO control room, Savoy Hill, 1924.

148 Marconi-EMI studio, Alexandra Palace, 1936: *Mr Pickwick*, the inn scene.

149 Studio 7, Savoy Hill: opened in 1927.

150 Part of the collection of early and historic broadcasting equipment formed by the BBC and now regrettably dispersed: the Blättnerphone recording machine (1931).

The archaeology of British broadcasting is not extensive, partly because a high proportion of the premises used by the BBC during the 1920s and 1930s no longer exists and partly because the interiors of those buildings which have survived have been continuously modified to bring them up-to-date and in line with current technical standards and aesthetic preferences. A series of photographs and technical drawings showing the continuous development

of even one studio and control room at Portland Place over the years from 1932 to the present time would be extremely valuable; it might fill a considerable gap in our knowledge of how, when and why such changes took place.

The BBC operates from many types of building; former cinemas, theatres, old film studios, rented office blocks. Its own premises have never been adequate to meet all the demands of a growing organisation.

Where, however, broadcasting or anything associated with it takes place in a building originally constructed for some quite different purpose, one is in some difficulty in deciding whether that building can fairly be said to belong to the history and archaeology of, say, the film industry or the broadcasting industry. Perhaps it does not matter. More important is that its career has been varied and properly recorded and documented.

prominent detail of the building is as clear and unscathed today, however, as it was in 1932, and serves as a reminder of the extraordinary degree of seriousness with which the Director-General and Governors of that time regarded their task and that of broadcasting. The giant Latin inscription, seen if not read by everyone who enters the reception hall of Broadcasting House, conveys the spirit of the Corporation of the 1930s in a way that could hardly be bettered. 'Deo Omnipotenti', it begins, and goes on, in Latin, to dedicate the building and its operations not to the Muses but to God.

Television

When television began to make its influence felt, the days of Latin texts were over and modernistic design was taking quite different forms. The BBC began its television experiments as early as 1929, using the Baird studios in Long Acre and the medium-wave transmitter at Selfridges. In 1932 a studio in the new Broadcasting House was made available for television, but in 1935 the Postmaster-General's Advisory Committee recommended Alexandra Palace as the site of the London Television Station. The BBC accordingly leased 30,000 square feet

of the Palace, which stands on a hill 306 feet above sea-level, and built a 300 foot mast on top of it. A public television service from Alexandra Palace began in February, 1937, using the Marconi-EMI system. It was technically successful, but few people bought sets. In 1937 a television set cost half as much as a small car.

The television service closed down for the duration of the War and re-opened in May 1946. Progress was, however, slow so long as reception was confined to the London area. In 1948 there were only about 50,000 receivers in use, all tuned to the Alexandra Palace transmitter. The situation

151 The offices of *The Times*, Queen Victoria Street, London: demolished in 1945.

152 (above) *Daily Express* offices, Fleet Street, London.

153 Former *Times* premises, Printing House Square, London; vacated 1974.

In a section devoted to the media it may be useful to point out that newspapers, too, have their archaeology and that without such Second Industrial Revolution developments as recording machines, telex, aeroplanes, transmission of pictures by wire and by radio, and a greatly improved international telephone system, modern newspapers would not be able to function in the way they do.

There have been numerous casualties among newspapers during the past half century — one thinks particularly of the *News Chronicle,* the *Daily Herald* and the *Star* — and whenever a newspaper dies its editorial and printing building usually becomes redundant to the industry. The former *Daily Herald* premises were demolished to make room for flats and offices. *The Times* has moved twice since 1945. The old buildings in Printing House Square were torn down and replaced by an exceedingly undistinguished glass and steel structure, shared with the *Observer*. In 1974 these premises were given up and *The Times* transferred itself to New Printing House Square, in Gray's Inn Road.

The *Daily Express* remains in its 1932 avant-garde Fleet Street building, faced with black toughened glass, the only London newspaper to be installed in offices of any architectural interest whatever. There are those who have said that the building reflects the newspaper, which may well be so, but suggested links between the management and policy of a paper and the building within which it functions have to be treated with some care.

changed completely within the next 10 years, when the building of 11 more transmitters brought 97 per cent of the population within the range of television coverage.

In 1949 the BBC bought a site at White City for the construction of a new studio centre. At that time Alexandra Palace had only two studios, but between then and 1956 eight new studios were opened in different buildings in West London. One, the Television Theatre on Shepherds Bush Green, had been a variety theatre, and the rest, at Riverside and Lime Grove, were converted film studios. The intention was to give them up as the new studios at the Television Centre came into operation — from 1960 onwards — but in practice the Television Centre, like Broadcasting House before it, was never big enough and outside studios have continued to be needed. Television News moved to the Television Centre in 1966, but Alexandra Palace was retained to make programmes for the Open University. It was seriously damaged by fire in 1980.

In 1954 the situation was radically changed by the establishment of a commercial television service, in competition with the BBC. The ITN premises, of all kinds, now have to be added to those of the BBC, to form the pool of potential broadcasting archaeology. Curiously, ITN has established something which the BBC has so far failed to create — a museum of television. Until very recently the BBC possessed a fine collection of historical material, in addition to the excellent archives relating to the development of both radio and television, but, as the Corporation was unable or unwilling to display the collection itself, it languished for a while in the stores of Bristol City Museum, where it had been deposited on loan. It has since been dispersed. The first 2LO transmitter has been miraculously preserved, and is stored at the BBC's Brookmans Park transmitter although it is not accessible to the public.

Once again it has to be emphasised that 'industry' is a portmanteau term. The history and archaeology of broadcasting are to be found on a wide front. The hundreds of firms who made valves, cabinets and components for the radio industry during the 1920s and 1930s are just as much a part of that industry as the BBC itself. Some firms did this kind of work for a while and then switched to something else; others, like Mullard, have continued with it. There is, for example, the case of the Ercolani family, which came to Britain from Italy in 1898. The Ercolanis made high quality picture frames, at a factory in Walthamstow Avenue. In 1933 they converted part of their works to the production of wooden radio cabinets, supplying various radio manufacturers including Pye. Just before the War Victor Ercolani, who controlled the factory, saw the dangers of overproduction and cut-throat competition in this branch of cabinet-making and sold out to Pye for £1.25 million, which was, in those days, a very considerable sum. The money was then available for re-investment in the Ercolani family furniture business at High Wycombe, which makes the well-known Ercol range.

Next door to the Ercolani works in Walthamstow Avenue was the plastics factory owned by De La Rue, to which reference has already been made on page 59. De La Rue were anxious to get full value from their expensive new German presses and throughout the 1930s made high-quality plastic radio cabinets, especially for Phillips and Ekco. Ekco, who made the radios, De La Rue, who made the cabinets, and the BBC, who made the programmes, were all equally part of the radio industry, and their premises equally constitute its archaeology.

Chapter 10

Computers and Office Equipment

Computers

Mechanical computing devices of varying degrees of complexity have been in use since the seventeenth century. Pascal and Morland in the eighteenth century and Babbage and Scheutz in the nineteenth all made valuable contributions towards the design of machines which would carry out the processes of calculation more rapidly and more reliably than the human brain. The first commercially successful calculating machine, however, was the Comptometer, invented by the American, Dorr E. Felt, and patented in 1886. It was a reliable machine and sold well for many years.

An improved type of adding and listing machine was patented by another American, William S. Burroughs, in 1885. With two partners he founded the American Arithmometer Co., and within 25 years the Burroughs calculator had been installed in 175,000 business houses throughout the world. The Comptometer and the Arithmometer did not, however, have the field to themselves. By 1900 nearly 100 different types of calculating machine were reckoned to be in use throughout the world, some of considerable ingenuity. For special purposes it was possible to combine and adapt standard machines, so that one had, in effect, a multi-unit computer. This was done, for instance, at the Nautical Almanac Office in 1914 to compile astronomical tables, and in 1931 at Woolwich Arsenal to perform ballistics computations.

The office calculator was particularly valuable when it was used in combination with punched cards. These in themselves were not a novelty; they had been used in France as early as 1728 for operating a Jacquard silk-loom. Their application to tabulating tasks, however, dates from 1890, when Herman Hollerith used them to compile statistics for the US Bureau of Census. In 1896 he set up his Tabulating Machine Co. to promote his equipment commercially and hired his machines to the US Government again for the 1900 Census. Soon afterwards, the Department of the Interior decided to break away from Hollerith and to develop its own machines. Hollerith's foreman, James Powers, was appointed to carry out the necessary research and his first machine was patented in 1908, in time for the 1910 Census. Thereafter, the history of calculating machine companies becomes complicated.

Powers started the Powers Accounting Machine Co. in 1909 and set up the Accounting and Tabulating Co. of Great Britain in 1914. The best British customer for Powers' machines was the Prudential Assurance Co. During the First World War the Prudential bought the Power patent and manufacturing and marketing rights for the British Empire, and in 1919 the British company formally severed its connection with Powers in America. Soon afterwards, the British-based company changed its name to Powers Accounting Machines, which became Power-Samas Accounting Machines in 1929, after a merger with its French distributor. In 1945 the Prudential sold the organisation to a consortium formed by Morgan-

Grenfell — the merchant bankers — and Vickers. Ten years later Powers-Samas became a wholly owned subsidiary of Vickers, and in 1959 Powers-Samas and the British Tabulating Machine Co. came together·as the nucleus of ICT.

The American Powers organisation merged with a number of other companies in 1927 to become Remington-Rand. A second merger with Sperry Gyroscope in 1955 produced the Sperry-Rand Corporation. Meanwhile, equally far-reaching changes had taken place within the Hollerith organisation. In 1904 Hollerith's company became part of the Computing Tabulating Recording Co. This very successful concern changed its name in 1924 to International Business Machines (IBM).

Throughout the 1930s, and especially during the Second World War, there was intense competition between the major companies to produce machines that would solve increasingly complex mathematical and statistical problems, and to carry out these tasks fast. Most of the very elaborate equipment was produced in a single version, nearly always in co-operation with a major university or government research laboratory. Electro-mechanical computers had been developed in Britain, Germany and the USA by 1942. The most famous computer of this type was the IBM Automatic Sequence Controlled Calculator, now known to technical historians as the Harvard Mark I. It was developed between 1939 and 1944, and when it was eventually completed IBM gave it to Harvard, where it was used by the US Navy. It weighed 5 tons and was 50 feet long

154 International Computers Ltd., headquarters, Putney: a symbol of change and mergers in the British electronics industry.

built in 1947 at Birkbeck College, London, for the British Rubber Producers Research Association, but the real beginning of the electronic age, so far as business enterprises were concerned, can be said to be Christmas Day 1951, when LEO[4] started work in the offices of J. Lyons and Co. LEO worked successfully for Lyons for 12 years, its labours ranging from the computation of payrolls to the calculation of optimum mixes in tea-blending. At this time LEO was the only business computer in the world. By 1956, however, American companies were spending $100 million a year on computers and $4 billion by 1965.

The history and archaeology of the British computer industry is extremely complicated. Buildings have changed their owners and functions with bewildering frequency.

ICL has the blood of nine companies in its veins. In 1959 British Tabulating Machines and Powers-Samas merged to form International Computers and Tabulators (ICT). This organisation then proceeded to buy up the computer sections of other companies — GEC in 1961, EMI in 1962 and Ferranti in 1963. A similar process of rationalisation elsewhere in the industry led to the formation of English Electric Computers. In 1963 Leo Computers (Lyons) and the data processing and control systems division of English Electric amalgamated to form English Electric Leo Computers. In 1964 Marconi's computer interests were absorbed, and finally in 1967 Elliott Automation Computers were added to the group, not known as English Electric Computers.

ICL was created by the merger of English Electric Computers with ICT in 1968. The archaeology of ICL therefore comprises the factories, offices and research premises of the original nine companies, along with the factory and headquarters of ICL itself.

Office Equipment

The archaeology of modern business has been very inadequately studied. We need to know the buildings occupied by a particular company at a particular period, what facilities these buildings provided, how many people worked in them and under what conditions, and what the reasons were for moving from one building to another. Much of this information can only be gathered from talking to people who have worked for the company concerned over a long period. In the case of computers and office equipment generally, this must involve both the firms who have made and supplied the equipment and the firms and individuals who have used it. Such conversations can lead to unexpected results. One discovers, for instance, that ICI (at their Millbank headquarters) were one of the earliest British customers for Muzak — commercially provided music-while-you-work — and that the large room in which their noisy office machinery was located at this time, the mid-1950s, took a different Muzak feed from the quiet office areas. The noisy office received Muzak-with-brass, to cut through the din of the machines, while the quiet office had Muzak-without-

and 8 feet high. It was dismantled in 1959, some parts being preserved at Harvard and some at the Smithsonian Institution in Washington.

The first electronic computer (ENIAC)[1] was built, with Army money, at the Moore School of Electrical Engineering at the University of Pennsylvania, and completed in 1945. ENIAC received a number of improvements and modifications between then and 1955, by which time it had performed more than 80,000 hours of work. It dwarfed the Harvard Mark I as it weighed 30 tons and required 1800 square feet of floor space. It used 18,000 valves and had 500,000 soldered joints. Although it performed calculations a thousand times faster than Harvard Mark I it had one great disadvantage — it could not store programmes and each new problem meant that the machine had to be reset, a task which took hours at best and days at worst.

The first stored programme computer (EDSAC)[2] was British and began operating at Cambridge in 1949. During the next few years the joint efforts of Manchester University and the Manchester electrical firm, Ferranti, proved very fruitful. The University installed its Ferranti Mark I in 1951 and in the same year Ferranti's 'Nimrod' computer was a star attraction at the Festival of Britain. The first computer to use a magnetic drum for storage was (ARC)[3],

[1] Electronic Numerical Integrator and Calculator.

[2] Electronic Delay Storage Automatic Computer.

[3] Automatic Relay Calculator.

[4] Lyons Electronic Office.

155 The original Gestetner premises in Sun Street, London.

156 The Gestetner offices and works, Tottenham, 1906; the office block on the right is still standing.

Study of the archaeology of the office equipment industry reveals the remarkable increase in its scale. As bureaucracy developed, commerce and industry discovered an insatiable appetite for processing paper and for making and keeping records of all kinds. The First Industrial Revolution was content with very simple records; the Second apparently cannot have enough, and the office equipment industry has not discouraged the trend.

157 The pre-1920 office: a replica, using original equipment, at the Gestetner Museum.

brass. Punched-card machines and duplicating machines make a great deal of noise, and the modern office, or at least parts of it, is not at all the peaceful place that its Victorian or Edwardian predecessor was. Mechanisation, in any field, brings an increase, often a very marked increase, in the decibels in the working environment, a fact which is strangely absent from published business histories but which is often mentioned in conversations with office workers who have had to adapt themselves to the new machine world.

Three such conversations will illustrate the ways in which what one might call the provoked, encouraged or guided reminiscences of industrial veterans can be of immense help to the archaeologist, partly in providing previously unsuspected information and in suggesting new lines of enquiry, and partly in adding a different kind of significance to facts of which the archaeologist is already aware. Personal contact of this kind can not only lead us to the archaeology, but help us to make sense of it when we see it.

Roneo, one of the two longest established British companies in the office-equipment business — the other is Gestetner — was founded in 1899 as the Neostyle Manufacturing Co., by A.D. Klaber, a naturalised British subject whose parents had come from Prague. Klaber invented a rotary duplicating machine, the first on the British market, and he registered its trademark as Neoro. This name was discovered to have little appeal so the components were reversed to form Roneo, which had an immediate success.

The earliest machines were very un-sophisticated. The operator had to feed through the paper sheet by sheet and carry out the linking by hand. The price of the machine varied, according to its size, between £5 and £10. Roneo had a service department from the beginning, with mechanics based in London, Birmingham and Liverpool. But this was at a time when everyone travelled by train, pony and trap, and bicycle, and if a customer in, say Norwich, had major troubles with his duplicator, it had to be put in the guard's van at Norwich to be taken back to the workshop in London. Having arrived at Liverpool Street Station it then had to be moved with the help of a porter and a barrow to a cab. The process had to be repeated when the problem had been solved and the duplicator returned to the customer.

This interesting piece of information comes from Mr J. Dorlay who joined Roneo in 1931 and has always taken a keen interest in the history of the Company.[5] He, in turn, has taken every opportunity to talk to people who have longer memories of Roneo than he has himself, including a lady who was first employed by the Company as a duplicator operator in 1905. Among other interesting things she told Mr Dorlay how she once demonstrated one of the firm's machines to the infamous murderer Dr Crippen, who bought one, and she taught one of his victims how to use it.

Roneo's first headquarters was in Petticoat Lane, Middlesex Street, London, and then in Greenfield Street. Their first 'prestige office' was a corner building on Holborn Viaduct. Moving upwards as their market grew, the next Roneo centre was further along Holborn, next to the Tudor buildings facing Gray's Inn Road and the Prudential. They stayed there from 1912 until 1934 when they took a long lease of a large block in South-ampton Row, on the corner of Kings-way and Holborn. They gave this up in 1964 for a new building in Croy-don. Each of these premises marked a stage in the progress of the Company, and all but one is still standing.

Mr Dorlay first went to work in none of these buildings. When he joined Roneo in 1931 he was employed by one of their subsidiaries called Neopost, which made postal franking machines and was housed 50 yards down the road from the Head Office. Any preconception that 'Roneo was duplicators' would need radical overhaul after a conversation with Mr Dorlay. He points out that:

The business was split into two main groups. The one which was known as Machines covered duplicators, addressing machines, letter copiers — which no longer exist, but which were very profitable at the time — and an office printing machine, using type. The other side of the business was Steel Furniture, including filing systems and record systems; furniture, that's to say, filing cabinets, desks, tables, and cup-boards, and, in what was known as the Contracts Department, special equipment on a very large scale for banks, libraries, post offices. We specialised in bookstacks. Roneo would handle the whole contract from the bare inside walls, including the inside structural steel-work to support the multi-stacks: Cambridge University Library, the Bodleian Library, that sort of scale. But that was all separate from our run-of-the-mill standard lines. It was all made at the works at Romford.[6] Both sides of the business were important. They both contributed to the Company's reputation and its coffers, but nevertheless Roneo was founded on the basis of the duplicator and therefore for a long time furniture was wrongly regarded by many people inside and outside the Company as something of an adjunct to duplicators.

Roneo was always at the top end of the market. In the 1920s the firm had to face competition on the furniture side from a number of newly-establish-ed concerns which were not interested in real quality. The well-established firm 'had a pride in their product — the finish, the paintwork, no sharp edges underneath to cut your hands off, that sort of thing. After the War, you began to see the emergence of a number of firms who took the line that so long as it worked all right on the outside, no matter how tinny it was, it would sell.'

The Company went public in 1908. It did very well during the First World War, not least because wars are always a great stimulus to the growth of bureaucracy, and the bureaucracy of 1914-18 had an insatiable appetite for duplicated instructions of all kinds, and hence duplicators. There was also an enormous demand for shelves and filing cabinets to store the papers produced.[7] Financially, however, it suffered from its Victorian traditions of good workmanship and good service: 'What happened in the late Twenties and early Thirties was that the company fell on bad times as a result of poor management. It wasn't noticed by the outside world; the products were good, the service to the customers excellent. The problem was financial.' The bank stepped in, outside directors were appointed, and by the time war broke out in 1939 Roneo was on a sound footing again. In 1962 the Romford factory was given up after a deal had been arranged with Vickers, which placed the whole production of Roneo steel furniture at the Vickers factory at Dartford. In 1966, when the Americans were trying to buy Roneo, Vickers decided to take it over com-pletely, in the well-founded belief that, our society being what it is, offices and the handling of paper must have a fine future.

IBM has shared this belief. The historical model for IBM in Britain features electric typewriters and computers, playing down or ignoring the fact that IBM's first foothold in Britain was gained with its subsidiary, International Time Recorders (ITR). This company, with its headquarters at Hammersmith, made time-record-ing clocks, and, from the mid-1930s, also acted as agents for IBM's

<hr/>

[5] Successively, Managing Director of the steel furniture division; Export-Manager and Export Director; Managing Director of Roneo Neopost; and Marketing Director of Roneo Ltd., the parent company.
Conversation with the author, 19 March 1977.

[6] The Romford factory has a story of its own. It began as the Ormond Cycles' factory and formed part of the industrial empire of Terence Hooley, a spectacular figure, who eventually went bankrupt. His properties also included Bovril and Dunlop Tyres. After the demise of Ormond Cycles, the factory was operated for a short time by the Ranice Fibre Co. which made gas mantles.

[7] A vast paper-generating bureaucracy appears to be an essential part of the Second Industrial Revolution and, if only for this reason, Roneo is indisputably a Second Industrial Revolution firm.

110

American-built electric typewriters. After the Second World War it established an administrative headquarters at 41 Moorgate, a building which has since been demolished. IBM United Kingdom was formed in 1951, comprising three divisions — Electric Typewriters[8], ITR and Data Processing. ITR failed to grow, despite every effort to find it new and more saleable products, and was eventually sold off to the American Simplex Clock Co. Manufacturing was started in a temporary factory at Greenock and a London headquarters office was established in Wigmore Street, in a building now occupied by Ardente Hearing Aids. Nothing could illustrate the growth of IBM better than the difference in size between the tiny Wigmore Street premises and the Company's huge new headquarters at Cosham, Hampshire.

Norman Hearson joined IBM from the Army in 1951 as a typewriter salesman and rose to become Resident Director for Hampshire. When he first went to IBM there was great resistance to buying electric typewriters, at least in Britain. At that time only one per cent of office typewriters offices was electric; today the figure is near to 80 per cent. The reason for this remarkable change is almost a parable of our time. In Mr Hearson's view, 'the reason we became so successful, exactly as in the States, was that the cost of the secretary became disproportionate to the cost of the machine, so that the employer was looking much more towards retaining a good secretary and paying her well and much less towards the cost of buying an electric typewriter.' In other words, as secretarial salaries went up so did the sales of electric typewriters, helped, no doubt, by the fact that an electric typewriter soon became a status symbol and by the well publicised piece of information that with a manual typewriter a girl used 2.5 lbs of energy each time she touched it and with an electric typewriter only 2.5 ozs.

People moved fast in IBM in the 1950s. Mr Hearson was a salesman for only eight months. He then became Assistant Sales Manager, a job he held for a week, after which he found himself to be Sales Manager. Three months later he was General Manager and he stayed in that job for 19 years, watching the London headquarters always bursting at the seams and

always having to take on auxiliary premises.[9] In 1965, when there were very tight restrictions on building offices in London, and when the Company was growing very fast, IBM worked out its need for office space and discovered that there were only two available buildings which were big enough. One was over Gunnersbury Station and the other in the Euston Road. IBM took the Gunnersbury site and another major British growth company, Rank Xerox, took the other. Ten years later the very large new building at Cosham was added to the one at Gunnersbury.

At Cosham, a long way ahead of most of its contemporaries, IBM has finally come to grips with the fact that, under modern urban conditions, driving and parking a car is an exhausting business, absorbing energy which should be available for company matters. Being at Cosham has taught IBM a lot of lessons about ways of relieving pressure, and the buildings the Company has occupied during the past 25 years should certainly be seen by the industrial archaeologist with considerations of environment, tension and pressure in mind, as well as scale. It is not simply a question of asking 'when was the firm in this building and what did it do there?', but 'what effects did this building and its location have on the people who worked in it?' One can also usefully ask 'what kind of people work here and how do they interact with the building?' At any period and in any industry, people have certain expectations of the kind of environment which should be provided for them to work in. It is obvious that these expectations are a good deal higher for everyone in Britain now than they were 50 or 100 years ago, partly because legislation demands it, and also because the general standard of living has improved. One is bound, even so, to observe that the expectations of one industry are not necessarily those of another. Railway employees, like railway passengers, put up with conditions which would not be tolerated for a moment by the staff at airports. Workers at a motor factory may do better in the way of amenities than workers at a quarry, but they do several times worse than working at Marks and Spencer, IBM, or a nuclear power station. If conditions at IBM, Cosham, are to be regarded as tomorrow's norm, it is obvious that most industrial concerns

have a long way to go before they reach it.

The computer past is, curiously, badly documented. There are, for example, many old cars in museums (and indeed on the road) but only bits and pieces of old computers. The technical history of computers has an abundant literature; their human history, the story of the kind of people who have worked with them, improved them and kept them in order has hardly been investigated at all. There is even no reliable information above computer owners in the 1950s and early 1960s, so that the Rolls-Royce claim to have been the first industrial owner of a computer, in 1955, goes largely unchallenged. One might, therefore, usefully end this chapter with the outline of the method which the author used to build up the history of the computer installations at the University of Southampton. The very co-operative University authorities admitted that they had no records which might be helpful, but suggested that a meeting with Miss Margaret Davis, a member of the staff of the Department of Mathematics, might be fruitful; and so indeed it proved to be. Miss Davis, who had been appointed to the new post of Graduate Programmar/Computer Operator in 1961, had an interesting file of documents and photographs and a rich store of personal memories. Her revelations made proper sense of the history of the University's original computer building, a major piece of computer archaeology.[10]

The University's first computer was a Ferranti 'Pegasus', which was installed in January 1958, at a cost of £40,000. By 1961, when Miss Davis arrived, the staff consisted of a Computer Operator, who was paid £280 a year, and two Maintenance Engineers, who received £850. Miss Davis herself had an initial salary of £700. Miss Davis recalled that when she was appointed there was no question of her receiving any training. She had a degree in mathematics and she was simply told to pick up the

[8] Renamed the Office Products Division in 1964.

[9] Conversation with the author, 4 April 1977.

[10] Conversation with the author, 4 August 1976.

158 Former computer centre,
University of Southampton: now
used as the Student Health
Centre.

159 Computer centre, University of
Southampton: technician with
replacement units. The hundreds
of valves were largely
responsible for both the size and
the heat generation of the
installations.

160 Operator working in the
computer centre, University of
Southampton. No examples of
the equipment shown here are
known to survive; the photograph
is the only record.

When the University installed its
first computer in the late 1950s,
neither it nor the manufacturers can
have had any idea of what
subsequent developments in the
computer field were likely to be. The
building erected in 1958 was
designed for the equipment available
at that time. Once the second and
much more compact generation of
computers was on the market, the
building became redundant. The first
computer no longer survives, but its
archaeology, in the form of what is
now the Student Health Centre,
serves to remind one of the
difference of size and heat-generating
capacity of the earlier and later
computer installations.

It is pure chance that the computer
building has survived, and good
fortune that it was ever
photographed. With the University
expanding rapidly, on a far from
adequate site, it might well have been
expected that this pleasant but far
from solid structure would have been
demolished and something larger and
more massive put up in its place. The
photographs are a good illustration of
the chance which characterises
documentation of the Second
Industrial Revolution.

necessary techniques as she went along. There was a handbook, produced by the manufacturers, and she worked her way steadily through it. Before her appointment the work was done *ad hoc,* and on a more or less amateur basis, by the academic staff. At that time, the Computation Laboratory, as it was called, was a sub-department of the Department, with a Lecturer in charge of it.

Between 1958 and 1966, when it was sold to the Road Research Laboratory, 'Pegasus' was adapted to magnetic tape storage — it originally had drum storage — and speeded up. It did not like this and, towards the end of its time with the University, it gave a good deal of trouble: 'I lost faith in it', Miss Davis recalls. The Road Research Laboratory already had a 'Pegasus' computer at Datchet. It was, however, due to move to Crowthorne, where the Southamptom 'Pegasus' was installed to obviate any possible break in computing service during the move. The Road Research Laboratory reported in a letter dated 8 September 1976 that:

the ex-Southampton University Computer behaved fairly well and did useful work. We had no regrets in making the decision to purchase it and it was finally sold in 1969 for a very nominal sum to the Geodetic Survey Office in Feltham, who, I believe, used it for spares. The 'Pegasus' was installed in a room about 12 feet high with windows down one side, and the only air conditioning was provided by two window-mounted, temperature controlling units. The warmer weather was dealt with by opening all the doors to create a draught through the room.

The University's second computer was an ICT 1909, modified and converted in 1967 into an ICT 1907. It had transistors, not valves, and was therefore very much smaller and cooler-running than 'Pegasus'. It went straight into a corner of the Mathematics building, and the original purpose-built computer building was given to the Student Health Service. The maintenance engineers became

redundant because maintenance of the new computer was carried out by the manufacturers under contract, and because, in any case, the second computer needed less maintenance than the first. One engineer left the University; the other took an M.Sc. degree in electronics and is now a member of the University's academic staff.

'The 1907', said Miss Davis in 1976, 'is now on its last legs. Politics is causing it to die.' In this case 'Politics' meant computer politics, not University politics. The University had recently taken possession of a new ICL 2970, which had been financed by the Computer Board. Since the Board refused to pay or help to pay for running two computers at the same place, the 1907 had to be allowed to collapse into senility.

If we had this kind of information about every computer installed in Britain we should have the raw material for something which at present is badly needed, a social history of the computer.

Further Reading

The list has been confined to books which can be obtained without too much difficulty through a good library in Britain.

Chapter 1

Allen, G.C., *The Industrial Development of Birmingham and the Black Country, 1860-1927* (Cass, 1966)

Ballin, H.H., *The Organisation of Electricity Supply in Great Britain* (Maidenhead: Electrical Press Ltd., 1946)

Burstall, A.F., *A History of Mechanical Engineering* (Faber, 1967)

Campbell, W.A., *The Chemical Industry* (Longman, 1971)

Clow, N.L. and A., *The Chemical Revolution: a contribution to social technology* (Batchworth, 1952)

Dunsheath, P., *A History of Electrical Engineering* (Faber, 1962)

Hardie, D.W.F., and Pratt, J.D., *History of the Modern British Chemical Industry* (Pergamon Press, 1966)

Hennessey, R.A.S., *The Electrical Revolution* (Oriel Press, 1972)

Mathias, P., *The First Industrial Nation: an Economic History of Britain, 1700-1914* (Methuen, 1969)

Miall, S., *A History of the British Chemical Industry, 1634-1928* (Benn, 1931)

Parsons, R.H., *The Early Days of the Power Station Industry* (Macmillan, 1940)

Plummer, A., *New British Industries in the Twentieth Century* (Pitman, 1937)

Pollard, S., *The Development of the British Economy, 1914-67,* 2nd edn.

(St. Martin's Press, 1969)

Reader, W.J., *Imperial Chemical Industries: a History,* Vol. 1: *The Forerunners, 1870-1926;* Vol. 2: *The First Quarter Century, 1926-1952* (Oxford University Press, 1975)

Chapter 2

Alford, B.W.E., *W.D. and H.O. Wills and the Development of the UK Tobacco Industry* (Methuen, 1973)

Burnett, R.G., *Through the Mill: the life of Joseph Rank* (The Epworth Press, 1973)

Corley, T.A.B., *Quaker Enterprise in Biscuits: Huntley and Palmers of Reading, 1822-1972* (Hutchinson, 1972)

Curtis-Bennett, N., *The Food of the People* (Faber, 1949)

Pyke, M., *Food, Science and Technology* (Murray, 1970)

Reader, W.J., *Birds Eye — the Early Year* (privately printed, 1963)

Wilson, C., *The History of Unilever* (Cassell, 1954)

Chapter 3

Chapman, S., *Jesse Boot of Boots the Chemists* (Hodder & Stoughton, 1974)

Corina, M., *Pile it High, Sell it Cheap,* the authorised biography of Sir John Cohen, founder of Tesco, (Weidenfeld & Nicolson, 1971)

Davis, A., *Package and Print: the development of container and label design* (Faber, 1967)

Davis, D., *A History of Shopping* (Routledge, 1966)

Havenhand, G., *Nation of Shopkeepers* (Eyre & Spottiswood, 1970)

Jefferys, J.B., *Retail Trading in Britain, 1850-1950* (Cambridge University Press, 1954)

Mathias, P., *Retailing Revolution: a History of Multiple Trading in the Food Trades* (Longman, 1967)

Minchinton, W.E., *The British Tinplate Industry* (Oxford University Press, 1957)

Pasdermadjian, H., *Management Research in Retailing: the international association of department stores* (Heinemann, 1950)

Pound, R., *Selfridge: a biography* (Heinemann, 1960)

Reader, W.J., *Metal Box: a history* (Heinemann, 1976)

Rees, G., *St. Michael: a history of Marks and Spencer* (Weidenfeld & Nicolson, 1969)

Waugh, A., *The Lipton Story: a centennial biography* (Cassell, 1951)

Chapter 4

British Aluminium Company, *The History of the British Aluminium Company Limited, 1894-1955* (privately printed, 1956)

Bowley, M., *Innovations in Building Materials* (Duckworth, 1960)

Brockman, H.A.N., *The British Architect in Industry, 1841-1940* (Allen & Unwin, 1974)

Cherry, G.E., *The Evolution of British Town Planning* (Leonard Hill, 1974)

Collins, P., *Concrete: the Vision of a New Architecture* (Faber, 1959)

114

Hudson, K., *Building Materials* (Longman, 1972)

Lewis, W., *The Light Metals Industry* (Temple Press, 1949)

Madge, J.H., *Tomorrow's Houses: new building methods, structures and materials* (Pilot Press, 1946)

Reboul, P., and Mitchell, R.G.B., *Plastics in the Building Industry* (Newnes-Butterworth, 1968)

Sennett, A.R., *Garden Cities in Theory and Practice* (Bemrose, 1905)

Sutcliffe, A., (ed.) *Multi-Storey Living: the British Working-Class Experience* (Croom Helm, 1974)

White, R.B., *Prefabrication: a History of its Development in Great Britain* (HMSO, 1965)

Chapter 5

Corley, T.A.B., *Domestic Electrical Appliances* (Cape, 1966)

O'Dea, W.T., *The Social History of Lighting* (Macmillan, 1958)

Political and Economic Planning, *The Market for Household Appliances,* (PEP, 1945)

Whyte, A.G., *The All-Electric Age* (Constable, 1922)

Wright, L., *Clean and Decent* (Routledge, 1960)

Chapter 6

Beer, E.J., *The Beginning of Rayon* (privately printed, Pheobe Beer, 1962)

Coleman, D.C., *Courtaulds: an economic and social history* (Oxford: Clarendon Press, 1969)

Dobbs, S.P., *The Clothing Workers of Great Britain* (Routledge, 1928)

Hague, D.C., *The Economics of Man-Made Fibres* (Duckworth, 1957)

Hard, A., *The Story of Rayon and other Synethetic Textiles* (Union Trade Press, 1939)

Steward, M., and Hunter, L., *The Needle is Threaded: the History of an Industry* (Heinemann/Newman Neame, 1964)

Wray, M., *The Women's Outerwear Industry* (Duckworth, 1958)

Chapter 7

Andrews, P.W., and Brunner, E., *The Life of Lord Nuffield: a study in enterprise and benevolence* (Blackwell, 1955)

Beynon, H., *Working for Ford,* (E.P. Publishing, 1975)

Castle, H.G., *Britain's Motor Industry* (Clerke, 1950)

Oliver, G.A., *Early Motor Cars: the vintage years, 1919-61* (Evelyn, 1961)

Overy, R.J., *William Morris, Viscount Nuffield* (The Europa Library of Business Biography, 1976)

Rolt, L.T.C., *Horseless Carriage: The Motor Car in England* (Macmillan, 1951)

Chapter 8

Andrews, C.F., *Vickers Aircraft Since 1908* (Funk, 1969)

Duval, G.R., *British Flying Boats and Amphibians, 1902-52* (Barton, 1966)

Gibbs-Smith, C.H., *Aviation: an historical survey from its origins to the end of World War II* (HMSO, 1960)

Hudson, K. and Pettifer, J. *Diamonds in the Sky: A Social History of Air Travel* (The Bodley Head/BBC, 1979)

Jackson, A.J., *British Civil Aircraft, 1919-59,* 2 vols. (Putnam, 1959, 1960)

Jackson, A.J., *De Havilland Aircraft* (Putnam, 1962)

James, D.N., *Gloster Aircraft Since 1917* (Putnam, 1971)

Chapter 9

Briggs, A., *The History of Broadcasting in the United Kingdom,* 4 vols. (Oxford University Press, 1961-79)

Eckersley, P.P., *The Power Behind the Microphone* (Cape, 1941)

Geddes, K., *Broadcasting in Britain, 1922-1972: a brief account of its engineering aspects* (HMSO, 1972)

Gorham, M., *Sound and Fury: 21 Years in the BBC* (Percival Marshall, 1948)

Hibberd, S., *This — is London ...* (MacDonald & Evans, 1950)

Low, R., and Manvell, R., *The History of the British Film,* Vol. 1, *1896-1906;* Vol. 2, *1906-14;* Vol. 3, *1914-18;* Vol. 4, *1918-29* (Allen & Unwin, 1951-74)

Moore, J.N., *A Voice to Remember: the Sounds of 75 Years on EMI Records* (EMI, 1973)

Oakley, C., *Where We Came In: the story of the British cinematography industry* (Allen, 1964)

Chapter 10

Bernstein, J., *The analytical Engine: Computers Past and Present* (New York: Random House, 1964)

Gestetner, *Gestetner, 1881-1951: a guide to the first fifty years* (1951)

IBM, *IBM, 1951-1976* (1976)

Millington, R., *The Birth of the Computer* (privately published by the 3M Company, 1974)

Appendix

Key Dates in the Development of the Second Industrial Revolution

What follows is not intended to be a comprehensive list of the most important inventions and innovations. It does, however, illustrate the wide front over which nineteenth and twentieth-century technology has advanced. The aim has been to include those inventions and developments which arguably have had the greatest impact on the lives of successive generations living through the Second Industrial Revolution.

1830-39

1830   Bench micrometer (GB)
1832   Babbage's calculating machine (GB)
1834   Refrigeration compressor (GB)
1835   Electric telegraph (USA)
1835   Commutator for dynamo (GB)
1839   Daguerrotype (France)

1840-49

1840   Steel-cable suspension bridge (USA)
1841   Vulcanisation of rubber (USA)
1841   Standard screw-threads (GB)
1841   Photographic paper-positive (GB)
1842   Manufacture of superphosphate (GB)
1844   Wood-pulp paper (USA)
1845   Reliable Portland cement (GB)
1846   Sewing machine (USA)
1846   Nitro-cellulose (Germany)
1846   Rotary printing press (USA)
1846   Nitro-glycerine (Italy)
1848   Safety match (Germany)

1850-59

c.1850   Still pictures transmitted by wire (GB)
1850   First underwater telegraph cable, from England to France (GB)
1850   Petroleum refinery (USA)
1850   Concrete road (Austria)
1851   High-tension induction coil (Germany)
1852   Morse's telegraph code (USA)
1854   Reinforced concrete beam (GB)
1855   Celluloid (GB)
1855   Tungsten steel (Austria)
1856   First commercially successful synthetic dye (GB)
1856   Bessemer process for steel making (GB)
1856   Siemens' open-hearth process for steelmaking (Germany)
1857   Concrete mixer (France)
1858   Continuous kiln (Germany)
1858   Overhead travelling crane (GB)
1859   Lead accumulator (France)

1860-69

1860   Gas engine (France)
1860   Twist drill (USA)
1860-3   First underground passenger railway (GB)
1861   Solvay ammonia-soda process (Belgium)
1862   Universal milling machine (USA)
1862   Machine gun (USA)
1863   Margarine (France)
1865   Yale lock (USA)
1866   First commercial dry-cleaning service (GB)
1866   Dynamo (Germany)
1867   Dynamite (Sweden)

1868   First successful typewriter (USA)

1870-79

1873   Barbed wire (USA)
1873   Refrigeration using ammonia compressor (Germany)
1876   Universal grinding machine (USA)
1876   Telephone (Canada)
1876   Four-cycle gas-engine (Germany)
1877   Edison's microphone (USA)
1877   Phonograph (USA)
1877   Electric welding (USA)
1877   Production of liquid oxygen (France, Switzerland)
1878   Air-compressor (GB)
1879   Incandescent electric lamp (GB, USA)

1880-89

1880   Thermostat (GB)
1880   Electric lift (Germany)
1882   First central power station (USA)
1882   First electric train service (GB, Germany)
1883   High-speed petrol engine (Germany)
1884   Forced lubrication (GB)
1884   Steam turbine (GB)
1884   Rayon (France)
1885   Electric transformer (USA)
1885   Seamless steel tube (Germany)
1885   First commercially-used adding machine (USA)
1886   Linotype (USA)
1887   Rotary cement kiln (GB)
1887   Celluloid film (USA)
1888   Commercial production of aluminium by the electrolytic process (France, USA)

1888 First successful pneumatic tyre (GB)
1888 A.C. electric generator (USA)
1888 Cordite (GB)
1888 Roll-film (USA)
1889 Hand-camera, using roll-film (USA)
1889 Lilienthal's glider (Germany)
1889 Modern type of moving-picture camera (USA)

1890-99

c.1890 Knife-cutting machines, allowing production of large plywood sheets (USA)
1890 Punched-card system used for US Census (USA)
1890 First steel-framed building (USA)
1890 Milk pasteurisation (France)
1891 Zip fastener (USA)
1891 Carborundum (USA)
1892 Nitro-cellulose process for making rayon (France)
1893 Asbestos-cement sheet (Austria)
1893 Aspirin (Germany)
1893 Diesel's engine (Germany)
1893 Maybach's carburettor (Germany)
1894 Cinematograph (France)
1894 Plasterboard (USA)
1895 X-rays (Germany)
1895 First public showing of a motion picture (France)
1897 Monotype (USA)
1897 Aluminium sheet (Italy)
1897 Gear-shaping machine (USA)
1899 Turbo-alternator (GB)

1900-09

c.1900 First effective vacuum-cleaner (GB)
1900 Glass-fibre (Germany)
1900 Zeppelin's first airship (Germany)
1900 Cellophane (Switzerland)
1900 Escalator (USA)
1900 Caterpillar tractor (USA)
1901 Razor-blades produced commercially (USA)
1902 First rotary duplicator marketed (GB)
1902 Wireless waves first used to carry the human voice (USA)
1903 Wrights' first flight (USA)
1904 Thermionic valve (GB)
1904 Silicones (GB)
1904 Photo-electric cell (Germany)

c.1905 Pumpless refrigeration (Sweden)
1905 Artificial silk (rayon) first made by viscose process (GB)
1906 Ready-to-eat breakfast cereals first produced commercially (USA)
1906 Triode valve (USA)
1906 Thermionic diode valve (GB)
1907 Bakelite (USA)
1907 Electric washing machine (USA)
1908 Synthesis of ammonia (Germany)
1908 'Model T' Ford (USA)
1908 Block and slip gauge system (Sweden)

1910-19

1911 Neon tube-light (France)
1911 Electric self-starter (USA)
1913 Stainless steel (GB)
1913 Kaplan turbine (Sweden)

1920-29

c.1920 Tungsten carbide cutting tools (USA)
1920 Autogyro (Spain)
1920 First electric recording (USA)
1920 Radio broadcasts (GB)
1923 Sound-films (USA)
1924 Loudspeaker (USA)
1926 First public showing of sound film (USA)
1926 Transit concrete-mixer (USA)
1928 Transatlantic flights by Zeppelin (Germany)
1928 Latex foam (GB)
1928 Penicillin (GB)
1928 Pre-stressed concrete (Germany)
1928 Quick-freezing of foodstuffs (USA)
1929 Experimental television transmissions (GB)

1930-39

1931 Electric shaver (USA)
1932 First operational Telex (GB)
1933 Polythene (GB)
1935 Radar (GB)
1935 Parking meter (USA)
1936 First successful electric typewriter (USA)
1937 Jet engine (GB)
1938 Nylon (USA)

1940-49

1940 Plutonium (USA)
1940 Boeing 307 Stratoliner, first

pressurised commercial aircraft (USA)
1941 Terylene (GB)
1942 Nuclear reactor (USA)
1946 Electric blanket (USA)
1946 Lockheed Constellation, first pressurised transatlantic airliner (USA)
1946 Flight of first jet-propelled aircraft (GB)
1946 First successful electronic computer (USA)
1948 Transistor (USA)

1950-59

1950 First commercial xerox copier (USA)
1952 First pure-jet flight with paying passengers (GB)
1957 First nuclear power station (GB)
1959 Hovercraft (GB)

Index